# Protest in Belgrade

# Protest in Belgrade

## Winter of Discontent

Edited by
Mladen Lazić

Central European University Press
Budapest

First published in Serbian as *'Ajmo, 'ajde, svi u šetnju!* by
Medija centar & ISI FF, Belgrade 1997

English edition published by
Central European University Press

Október 6. utca 12
H-1051 Budapest
Hungary

400 West 59th Street
New York, NY 10019
USA

Translated by Liljana Nikolić

© 1999 by Central European University Press
English translation © by Liljana Nikolić 1999

Distributed in the United Kingdom and Western Europe by
Plymbridge Distributors Ltd., Estover Road, Plymouth PL6 7PZ,
United Kingdom

ISBN 963-9116-45-9  Paperback
ISBN 963-9116-72-6 Cloth

Library of Congress Cataloging in Publication Data
A CIP catalog record for this book is available upon request

Typeset by PP Editors Ltd., Budapest
Cover design by Picture Elements
Printed in Hungary by Akadémiai Nyomda

# Contents

List of Contributors                                                    VII

Introduction: The Emergence of a Democratic Order in Serbia        1
  *Mladen Lazić*

## Part I

Potential for an Active Society                                     33
  *Marija Babović*
General Character of the Protest and Prospects
  for Democratization in Serbia                           60
  *Slobodan Cvejić*
Citizens in Protest                                                78
  *Vladimir Vuletić*
Social and Political Consciousness of Protest Participants          100
  *Vladimir Ilić*
The Walks in a Gender Perspective                                   113
  *Marina Blagojević*

## Part II

Value Orientations and Political Attitudes of Participants
  in the 1996-97 Student Protest                          131
  *Bora Kuzmanović*
Student Protests: Comparative Analysis of the 1992 and
  1996–97 Protests                                        151
  *Dragan Popadić*
A Generation in Protest                                            168
  *Andjelka Milić, Ljiljana Čičkarić and Mihajlo Jojić*

VI

## Part III
Protest as an Urban Phenomenon      193
    *Sreten Vujović*

## Appendix
Chronology of the Protest      211
    *Milica Bogdanović, Ljiljana Milovanović and*
    *Miodrag Shrestha*
Sample Design      231
    *Slobodan Cvejić*
Questionnaire      233

# List of Contributors

**Marija Babović,** assistant professor, Faculty of Philosophy, University of Belgrade

**Marina Blagojević,** associate professor, Faculty of Philosophy, University of Belgrade

**Milica Bogdanović,** student of sociology, University of Belgrade

**Slobodan Cvejić,** assistant professor, Faculty of Philosophy, University of Belgrade

**Ljiljana Čičkarić,** associate of the Institute of Sociology, Faculty of Philosophy, University of Belgrade

**Vladimir Ilić,** associate professor, Faculty of Philosophy, University of Belgrade

**Mihajlo Jojić,** associate of the Institute of Sociology, Faculty of Philosophy, University of Belgrade

**Bora Kuzmanović,** professor, Faculty of Philosophy, University of Belgrade

**Mladen Lazić,** professor, Faculty of Philosophy, University of Belgrade

**Andjelka Milić,** professor, Faculty of Philosophy, University of Belgrade

**Ljiljana Milovanović,** student of sociology, University of Belgrade

**Dragan Popadić,** associate professor, Faculty of Philosophy, University of Belgrade

**Miodrag Shrestha,** student of sociology, University of Belgrade

**Sreten Vujović,** professor, Faculty of Philosophy, University of Belgrade

**Vladimir Vuletić,** assistant professor, Faculty of Philosophy, University of Belgrade

# Introduction: The Emergence of a Democratic Order in Serbia

*Mladen Lazić*

The articles in this collection present great challenge for the authors. They seek to investigate social processes that started to unfold suddenly and were still in full swing while this analysis was being developed. These papers examine two ongoing events and their participants: the protest that developed in Serbia in late 1996 and early 1997 organized by the opposition coalition *Zajedno,* and the student protest. The two events appeared almost simultaneously, prompted by the same motive, with basically the same demands, and continued to intertwine in many aspects (in terms of their participants, some organizational forms, etc.). There are, however, several important factors which have led us to study the two movements separately. The students are a specific social group; they, from the very beginning, insisted on the nonparty nature of their movement; the forms of their protest were, as a rule, strictly separated from civil ones; their demands included certain specific elements; and so on. This division had practical consequences for the researchers: the civil protest (linked with the *Zajedno* coalition) was explored by a group of associates of the Institute for Sociological Research of the Faculty of Philosophy, Belgrade, while the student protest was studied by the associates of the Institute of Psychology of this same faculty (although here again there was some intertwining, as will be revealed later).

The civil protest that emerged as a result of the electoral fraud by the ruling Socialist Party of Serbia (SPS) in the second round of local elections in a number of large towns in Serbia allowed the researchers no time for preparations. They plunged into a huge wave of demonstrations which started in the last week of November 1996, without knowing whether it would subside before developing characteristics that would enable it to be at least provisionally studied. The authors did not hesitate to begin collecting the data and did not wish to wait for these data to be processed in detail before they were published. During the work on this study, the authors had two objectives. First, they wanted to provide at least a partly systematized documentation of the stormy events whose appearance and course surprised everyone: the perpetrators of the electoral fraud, those who provided unexpectedly strong and persistent resistance to it, and domestic and foreign observers and analysts. Second, they wanted to ensure that the data they had collected and tentatively analyzed could serve as a basis for self-awareness of the current mass protest. In this sense the study was conditionally conceived as a part of growing, branched-out and diffuse social movement.

The research was undertaken without any preparation, since events unfolded quickly and the data had to be collected by participants in the demonstrations while they were underway. This accounts for the many unavoidable weaknesses of this study. Three young assistant professors at the Faculty of Philosophy (M. Babović, V. Vuletić and S. Cvejić) decided to try to study the participants only a few days after the civil demonstrations in Belgrade had started. Their senior colleagues decided to help them by offering their advice rather than joining them in the research (I will presently explain my personal reasons for this decision). The questionnaire had to be adjusted to a "moveable" survey since the respondents answered while walking in a column of demonstrators. This meant that the questionnaire had to be brief and the questions clearly and simply formulated. On the other hand, it was necessary to cover as many relevant topics as was practical in order to obtain as complete a picture of the participants as possible (their socio-demographic characteristics, some social-psychological features, political orientations, etc.). Thus certain areas were treated only on the basis of one or two indicators, particularly in cases where it was possible to rely on previous experience that the indicators concerned may provide a relatively dependable insight into more general trends. Naturally, in these cases the conclusion of the analysts is a hypothesis rather than a confirmed view.

The sample for this research gave rise to important problems. The authors were aware that they could not work out a firm structure. The interviewers (students who were themselves participants in "parallel" demonstrations—a fact which definitely should not be lost sight of) were given instructions to choose respondents at random, but it was not always possible to strictly observe these instructions. Finally, the speed with which this study was written and published (the Serbian-language edition was printed in February 1997) did not establish firmer grounds in other similar undertakings or make wider references to relevant literature and more comprehensive comparisons. In that sense, this analysis should be understood primarily as a research report.

While preparing this book for publication in English a few months later, we did not wish to substantially change its nature, even in instances where this was possible, for example, by situating individual insights into the existing theories of social movements and drawing parallels with other post-socialist countries, thus correcting some hasty conclusions. In other words, we believed that subsequently incorporated theoretical "wisdom" would have added less than what it would have taken away from this study: its documentary value. It was this feature, after all, for which the study itself had been conceived as a modest contribution to the emerging social movement. Subsequent editing is, therefore, generally reduced to additional clarifications a foreign reader may require; major changes only occur in the epilogue in the introductory article and in an addition to the chronology (which, in the Serbian text, ends with December 31, 1996).

By contrast with the sociologists, the researchers of the Institute of Psychology at the Faculty of Philosophy who studied the student protests were in a somewhat different position. They had some experience in carrying out this type of research, having monitored the 1992 student protest in the same way. Their methodology, developed in 1992, enabled them to observe the current movement from the very beginning and from a number of angles. Thus their study focused on the following elements: the course and organization of the protest; the public activities of the protests; the participants' production (official releases, leaflets, drawings, slogans on banners, etc.); media presentation of the protest (papers, radio, television, Internet); and the attitudes, values and expectations of participants in both the student and civil protests, as well as of individuals who failed to participate in the protest and did not support it. The research work was coordinated by D. Popadić, while the data were collected and processed mostly by psychology students. D. Popadić and B. Kuzmanović's chapters in this collection rely primarily on the survey findings of attitudes, values and expectations of participants in the student protest (at the time this study was published, the integral research had not been completed yet, and only parts of it were incorporated). We should also note that L. Čičkarić, M. Jojić and I. Petković, postgraduate students of the Institute for Sociology of the Faculty of Philosophy, also carried out independent research on the participants of the student protest. Some of the findings of this research have also been included in the article written by A. Milić and the first two authors of the research.

Finally, I would like to mention a problem of principle which led to my decision not to take part in the research itself but, nevertheless, to edit the book and write an article for it. The events to which this book testifies confront an intellectual with a dilemma: whether to be involved in their unfolding primarily as a participant or a researcher (the former and the latter could be conditionally referred to as demands of civil and professional self-consciousness, respectively). It is quite clear that serious engagement either way leaves no room for the other. This division is merely a consequence of the development of modern science, which, due to its unavoidable, fast-increasing specialization, does not allow for complete coverage of a whole even within a single scientific area. To that extent it is even less possible to achieve the former ethical ideal of unity of thought and action, especially if the specific ("professional") procedures of study resulting from modern scientific achievements (in this case, those of social sciences) are also understood as a form of thinking. I believe that either of these two choices is legitimate as long as sufficient numbers of intellectuals opt for either of these. In this particular case we may be grateful to our younger colleagues for choosing the professional approach and thus providing us with systematically collected evidence of the stormy events in Serbia in the winter of 1996–1997.

## Historical background: Escalating crisis as a factor limiting social transformation

The mass protests that broke out in Serbia in November 1996 were undoubtedly a delayed echo of the movement that brought about the collapse of the socialist system in Central and Eastern Europe (CEE) in the late 1980s. The causes of this collapse are addressed in greater detail elsewhere (Lazić, 1994) and will not be discussed here. Furthermore, the scope of this book does not allow for an extensive explanation of the factors which have put off social transformation in Serbia, and I will, therefore, only mention them in the briefest terms (for more details, see

Lazić in: Bolčić, ed., 1995). First of all, the specific features of the socialist order in Serbia and the former Republic of Yugoslavia (SFRY) had a major role in delaying the onset of social transformation in this territory. This order was relatively autochthonously reproduced in the SFRY and this accounts for the absence of an important mobilizing incentive characteristic of most other CEE countries, namely, of linking the system with foreign—Soviet—domination (and even occupation). This autochthonousness, in order to be maintained, also implied a relative openness of the country toward the West and, consequently, a generally more flexible nature of the system.

Small-scale private ownership was sustained in agriculture, crafts and services. The regular inflow of credits from the West enabled household consumption well beyond the country's production potential (cf. Madžar, 1990). Open borders made it possible to "cushion" the economic crisis by simply exporting the unemployed. The foreign-exchange remittances of Yugoslavs abroad, in turn, improved the living standard of their kinsfolk and offset the country's adverse foreign trade balance. Self-management, although basically an ideological construct, imposed and controlled from the "top," granted a number of rights to the employees (job protection and a certain increase in wages). The political monopoly of the ruling party was sustained with a relatively low degree of open repression: the "liberal" variant of Yugoslav socialism, only occasionally present in some CEE countries (such as Czechoslovakia and Hungary), gave intellectuals, since the late 1950s, sufficient latitude for critical opinion inevitably formed in permanent contacts with the West, which was not a transient phenomenon. Thus the economic, political and value safety valves of the Yugoslav socialist system reduced the dissatisfaction of the population.

Yugoslavia's lasting exposure to the West limited the efficiency of the "demonstration effect," strongly manifested in CEE countries after the introduction of the policy of *glasnost*. The lifting of the Iron Curtain has, namely, enabled the populations of these countries to compare their conditions of life realistically with those in developed countries and draw conclusions about the need for systemic change. These specifics help us understand what accounts for the success of ruling circles in the SFRY republics in shifting the growing demands of the population, spurred by the fast and radical changes in other CEE countries, toward the resolution of ethnic and statehood problems.

Naturally, this redirection would not be possible but for the persistence of the problems in the former Yugoslavia, and the fact that, by a historical coincidence, they were triggered precisely at the time when the socialist order started to collapse. There is no need to go into the historical background of conflicts among the nations on the territory of the former Yugoslavia: their origins in the end of the last century, the conditions for their escalation in the Kingdom of Yugoslavia or their tragic culmination during World War II. It is just as unnecessary to make wider references to the smoldering and occasionally erupting nationalist movements (the Albanians on several occasions in the 1960s, 1970s and 1980s and the Croats in the late 1960s, etc.) during the rule of Josip Broz (who skillfully used them to reinforce his own position, mediating between the rival republican/national factions of the ruling class; for mechanisms producing conflicts within this class in socialism (cf. Lazić, 1987: 37–52). Of key importance for us is the fact that in the late 1980s, the highest ranks of power stimulated a mass national movement of the Serbs. Its long-term basis consisted of enduring latent and occasionally manifest ethnic conflicts between the Serbs and Albanians (for the historical dimension of the conflicts, see Janjić, 1994). The "fuse" to ignite the movement was the constitutionally unsettled relationing among Serbia "proper" and its autonomous provinces, which made the provinces—although formally part of the republic—legally independent and even gave them the right to veto decisions relating to Serbia "proper". This movement elicited immediate reaction from other republican leaderships, which just as easily (using this "background") mobilized the national movements of their own ethnic groups. Incited and manipulated by the ruling circles, all these national movements channeled the accumulated dissatisfaction of the population—caused by the long, drawn-out economic crisis of the 1980s—in a direction that could only sharpen the social and state crises instead of resolving it. They once again legitimized the authoritarian regime, provided it with an excuse for the tragic military adventure and, primarily in Serbia and Croatia, ensured its survival even at a time when, under the pressure of the breakdown of the socialist regimes in the East, it had to agree to introduce some forms of a pluralist political system.

The coincidence of national mobilization in Serbia (and most of the former Yugoslavia) with the major social transformation in the East produced disastrous consequences. The old regime could present itself as radically reformist while at the same time introducing only superficial changes in the social order. In the political sphere a pluralist system was established. However, the newly formed political parties, deafened by the sound of national trumpets and fearing they might end up without mass support, essentially accepted the new legitimacy pattern of the existing authorities. Paradoxically, their "opposition" activity only reinforced the position of the ruling group. By condemning themselves *a priori* to a marginal position, they guaranteed their failure: conflicts among the leaders, party splits (the Democratic Party alone gave rise to three current parliamentary parties) and mutual confrontations came as a logical consequence of the fact that they supported the current regime where it was the strongest and challenged it where they themselves appeared undefined (for example, for years none of the opposition parties has made an effort to develop a more comprehensive program of privatization).

The crisis of the state and the breakup of the country in a civil war enabled the ruling group in Serbia to retain economic as well as political domination. After the initial momentum provided by the federal government of Ante Marković in the late 1980s, privatization was practically halted in the early 1990s. On the basis of a liberal federal law, Serbia privatized about a quarter of its enterprises in 1991. The Ownership Transformation Re-evaluation Act of 1994, however, cancelled most of this process, while major firms, primarily in infrastructure, were nationalized (cf. Lazić and Sekelj, 1997). Thus the highest ranks of power, using their political power and various forms of state and quasi-state ownership (the remaining "socially owned" property, joint stock companies with state firms as majority shareholders, etc.), managed to preserve their monopoly over the overwhelming majority of the country's economic resources (cf. Zec *et al.*, 1994). The escalation of the war in Bosnia and Herzegovina, and particularly the imposition of international sanctions, gave a specific group of people the opportunity to plunder the economy directly (the spoils of war, for example) or indirectly (state-generated hyperinflation, which amounted to 116 trillion percent in 1993, cf. Dinkić, 1995) to gain control of enormous wealth. This stratum largely originated from the circles of the ruling hierarchy (according to the findings of my research in 1993, as many as two-thirds of elite entrepreneurs belonged to the previous nomenklatura or were members of their families) or had close connections with it—offering their services in the war, violating the international trade embargo, etc. (cf. Lazić, in Lazić, ed., 1995: 127–159). A resultant combination of political and economic factors created a specific coalition of the then ruling class and the *nouveau riche* with a shared interest in blocking the process of post-socialist transformation of Yugoslav society for as long as possible. Naturally, the blockade enabled them to retain power and thereby continue the transfer of social wealth into private ownership unimpeded.

In contrast, the sudden sharpening of the economic crisis resulted in a drastic pauperization of the overwhelming majority of the population. However, this indisputable fact must be approached with some qualifications if subsequent events are to be understood. Not all social strata experienced impoverishment equally, nor was their position—primarily in relation to the state—equal. The most endangered category was the retired. For the vast majority of them, the only source of income was the state budget, and when this was drained, they were the group that was easiest to marginalize. Although at first sight, it may appear that the unemployed must have been an even more endangered group, being deprived of any regular source of income, it turned out that they had somewhat more room to maneuver. Since, as a rule, they were substantially younger, many of them managed to join the rapidly swelling gray economy. Thus, the relative position of this group was better than expected (for the material position of social groups in the period of the deepest crisis—1993—and the gray economy, see: Lazić, ed., 1995).

The position of workers was quite specific. Their jobs were mostly, at least formally, protected: the state, as the main employer, guaranteed them "paid idleness" at a time when most enterprises had hardly any operation at all. Since this made them also dependent on the (almost empty) budget, their wages were minimal and irregular, but they also had time to engage in the gray economy. This meant that their position toward the state was ambivalent. They depended on the state (in 1993 more important than wages was what they received from the state in kind), but they simultaneously ensured their existence outside their firms, where everyone was for himself. These conditions for survival led to a complete atomization of the working class. By the same token, the uncertain prospects of "individualist" strategies channeled their long-term expectations once again toward the state (under the circumstances of overall economic collapse, their request to the state to guarantee their jobs in case of a market transformation of the economy is only understandable; naturally, this is also what their decades of experience in socialism advised).

The peasants were also in a rather peculiar position. They were able to meet a large part of their needs, generally reduced to the barest necessities, by themselves. In addition, however deep the crisis may have been, the demand for their products could decrease but not entirely disappear. On the other hand, the technological level of production they have reached was in some ways irreversible, which means that they also needed state intervention to secure some supplies (such as oil, seeds, fertilizer and herbicides) that were scarce even on the black market. These conditions have produced a number of important consequences. The material position of the peasants declined drastically but less so than that of other groups (excepting the ruling one). In addition, their relationship with the state, as mentioned above, placed them in a relatively dependent position, regardless of their status as private owners.

At the height of the crisis, one of the most widespread claims was that of the "disappearance of the middle class" as a result of the drastic pauperization (the thesis was naturally articulated by the members of this group, who predominantly formed public opinion). This claim implied that society would be unable to democratize since its main protagonists were disappearing. While the material position of this group has indeed taken a nosedive, it has nevertheless remained in the "middle," i.e. higher than the position of the workers (cf. Lazić, ed., 1995). This was due to a number of factors. Middle-class incomes, however, low they may have been, were still above those of the workers. Furthermore, this group was even more intensively engaged in the gray economy, once again with earnings higher than those of the workers. And finally, the material reserves of this group were larger. Of course, the dissatisfaction of most members of this group with the drastically worsened conditions of life was largely aimed abroad; this was also the case with other social strata (state propaganda blamed the economic disaster on international sanctions, just as it explained the causes and the course of the disintegration of the SFRY by the influence of "foreign factors"). The energy deriving from this dissatisfaction was spent in devastating military adventures—by accepting that these were inevitable, this stratum and the entire population also accepted the necessary consequences: economic collapse, overall impoverishment, international isolation, etc. Caught in the struggle for mere survival, members of all strata discovered that the only support they could hope for would be from the state (meaning those who rule). This existential limitation was well-matched with the traditional inertia of the local population—extremely patriarchal and authoritarian, it is not prone to changes and, if forced to make them, would prefer a sudden and radical switch over gradual and continuing transformation.

## Stabilization as a precondition for demands for change

Based on these observations, it should already be clear why the ruling party (and with it the dominant social group), which obviously led the country from a bad situation into a worse situation, consistently obtained the majority electoral support of the population. Anyway, what could have been expected at the height of the crisis in 1993? The sheer struggle to provide the bare necessities was inevitably conducive to social atomization: people were all forced to concentrate exclusively on their own problems. The next year brought the first change: monetary stabilization. That was when the problems of the regime started. Its representatives thought it logical that they should be politically rewarded for curbing hyperinflation (despite the fact that they themselves had produced it). But the technical job of stabilization was carried out by a man who had thus far been outside the power structure, and a good part of the success was spent to build up the personal charisma of the then-governor of the central bank, Avramović.

In the sphere of the economy, things continued to develop in this manner. The year 1994 was used to strengthen the security of the regime, which was to be based on the satisfaction of the population with a "strong dinar." This satisfaction, however, could only be temporary. The following year, popular expectations were already higher due to a greater increase in production, a substantially improved standard of living, etc. Very few of these expectations came true, especially on a subjective level: people compared their living conditions not only with the period of deep crisis but also with the times preceding it. (In 1993 the real wages dropped to less than a fifth of their 1989 level; after the initial growth in 1994, they started to oscillate and in January 1996 amounted to about 90 percent of average real wages in July 1994—cf. Arandarenko,

1997.) One expectation was betrayed and joined by another, still more powerful one. The suspension, and then the lifting, of the UN-imposed economic sanctions was accompanied by unreasonable promises of impending prosperity. The effect of this propaganda on the authorities themselves, positive in the short term, proved counterproductive in the long term, since the regime wasted another year (1996) without achieving much of anything and without even starting the structural adjustment of the economy. (The reasons for this are obvious. This reform would have deprived it of economic domination. Moreover, the reform was bound to exact new painful sacrifices, and the regime was aware that the foundations of its support were too weak to sustain any additional burden.) Thus the year ended not only with huge economic difficulties (continuously experienced by most inhabitants in daily life) but also without offering any prospects and without an external "culprit" to which the regime could shift responsibility. (The monetary collapse cut industrial production to a third of its capacities; compared with that, the growth of the GDP of 6.5 percent in 1994 and 6 percent in 1995, with a similar modest increase in 1996, indicated that the crisis was not being overcome but was deepening; cf. Grupa ekonomskih eksperata, 1997.)

As for the political sphere, developments for those in power were just as unfavorable. The authorities dealt with the first powerful challenge of the March 1991 demonstrations relatively easily, since the main demand of the opposition, as already mentioned, was the implementation of the national program, a battleground where the regime had already acquired a decisive advantage. A new attempt at mass mobilization by the opposition parties the following year, along with the student protests of that time, also failed to seriously shake the regime for a number of reasons. The parties managed to bring mostly their own supporters out into the streets. Their objectives could not obtain wider support, both on account of the social/political/economic conditions and on account of their nature. Namely, their main slogan—the abolishment of the communist order and the democratization of society—appeared vague and even improper to the majority of the population amidst an all-out war. Official propaganda succeeded in proving: that the communist paraphernalia had already been discarded (hadn't the party in power already changed its name from a communist to a socialist one?); that democracy had already been introduced (wasn't the legal existence of opposition parties, along with multi-party parliamentary elections, proof of that?);

and that the Serbian people needed unity rather than internal dissent (didn't the civil war prove that the very survival of the people was in jeopardy?). Widespread acceptance of this propaganda, in other words, meant that the ruling group still enjoyed legitimacy, which was actually reinforced by the war. The student protest of the time, which initially had a somewhat wider basis, soon succumbed to the dominant social dynamics. Its leadership placed itself under the wing of opposition parties, which sought only to control it (competing for supremacy between themselves) instead of trying to turn it into a catalyst for wider civic resistance. They thereby destroyed the weak organization generated during the protests and helped lose the wider mass support the students initially enjoyed.

However, the regime encountered serious political trouble as a consequence of its behavior toward the Serbs in Bosnia and Herzegovina and Croatia. That was where its bestial indifference and cynicism were manifested. When the leadership of the Bosnian Serbs started to deny Milošević unquestioning obedience, he imposed economic sanctions on Republika Srpska. Naturally, as in the case of Yugoslavia, the sanctions affected primarily the population, rather than the "disobedient" leadership (while, analogously, they failed to delegitimize Radovan Karadžić). All previous propaganda against the unjust UN sanctions imposed on Serbia blatantly contradicted Milošević's move. The nationalist supporters of the Serbian regime were angry. An even more drastic act followed. The astonishingly rapid fall of Krajina in Croatia clearly could not have happened without Milošević's complicity. This complicity is indirectly evidenced by the fact that the state-controlled Serbian media marginalized the events as much as possible.

True, the regime was already working to increase its legitimacy. The sanctions were depleting its resources at a fast rate: the economy was facing collapse, the crisis was starting to jeopardize even the payments for members of the repressive apparatus and the endangered population started to find the fact of their unbearable economic circumstances more important than the (allegedly external) culprit. The turnaround was inevitable: peacemaking replaced the defense of national interests on the regime's banner. But this additionally restricted its sphere of influence. Many people felt betrayed: those who remained dedicated to the initial objective, the Serbs coming from Croatia and Bosnia and Herzegovina, and numerous members of their families who gave them shelter, etc.

Others who had supported the peace option before could not accept this about-face. The regime actually retained a strong footing among the indifferent, the "silent majority" focused on its private life (awaiting the outcome in the economy).

The regime entered November 1996 with shaken economic as well as political and also legitimacy foundations. The claim that it was rattled but not defeated is evidenced by the seemingly contradictory results of the federal versus local elections: the ruling Left coalition scored a convincing victory in the former but was heavily defeated in the latter. A number of factors account for this discrepancy. The technical elements are perhaps the most important. The government has carefully set the number and boundaries of electoral units for the federal parliamentary elections (by legally identifying 29 such units). Its rural supporters managed to outvote the city opposition (almost half of Serbia's population is still rural). The abstention of the Albanians secured the ruling coalition in Serbia all the seats in Parliament belonging to Kosovo (Serbs there still believe that Milošević's state is the only guarantor of their survival). Moreover, the opposition had no control of the electoral process in numerous smaller places, which provided sufficient opportunity for electoral fraud (the scope of which was revealed by the local elections). None of these factors applied to local elections in urban centers. In addition, coming to cast their votes in local elections, the people saw on the ballot the names of representatives of the regime who had been infamous for their plundering, violence and abuse of power. Thus the second round of these elections uncovered the narrow basis of the ruling party's success at the federal level. Namely, the ruling party remained firmly entrenched only in its main strongholds: the villages and the suburbs. Although there is no reliable empirical evidence to this effect, one may—on the basis of the ensuing events and even the data provided by this research—approximately form the new social and political configuration of the electorate in Serbia.

To all appearances, the peasants were the most homogenous stratum in terms of their support for the "Left coalition." It turned out that among the many losers, they were still the ones who best managed to offset the shocks of the economic catastrophe. On the other hand, the program of change supported by opposition parties has the least to offer them directly. As private owners, they are not influenced by ownership transformation, and they cannot even glimpse any tangible benefits from democratization. With their short-term orientation, they probably look upon the promises of prosperity offered by the rival parties with equal skepticism and, therefore, prefer the safety of the current government. In any case, their perception of the opposition has largely been created by the government-controlled media (primarily the state television, which is the only one covering the whole territory of the republic). Although the peasants may have their doubts as to these media presentations, they can hardly obtain any "positive" information on the "other Serbia."

The workers here, today, cannot be referred to as a single group. Moreover, it would be very difficult to distinguish even homogenous subgroups among them. It is said that, due to the conditions of operation of the Yugoslav economy, the workers have been atomized and made remarkably dependent on the state. This is best evidenced by their strikes which, despite the multiple reductions of real wages, retained the characteristics of socialist times (which were relatively prosperous for them). In other words, the strikes have never gone beyond the limits of a single enterprise and, as a rule, covered only some of the employees of a firm; their demands were remarkably narrow, usually payment of (minimum) wages in arrears; and they ended if only some of these modest requests were fulfilled. In addition, the economic reform programs offered by the opposition (privatization and market restructuring), even if the workers had access to their contents, could only alienate them: the experience of other CEE countries shows that workers would be the ones to pay the largest price for the restoration of capitalism. Democracy, for its part, may also seem a luxury to people who are continuously struggling for survival. Accordingly, the opposition cannot count on wider influence among the workers, even if it could win the battle for "media liberation." This has been clearly demonstrated by the Belgrade protests we are analyzing here. In addition to alternative (non-government) media, which systematically reported on the course and nature of demonstrations, especially in Belgrade, the scope and duration of mass actions themselves ensured the visibility of the participants and their demands. Yet the workers generally remained outside the protest, and a few attempts by the "Nezavisnost" (Independence) trade unions (which is, unlike the majority Autonomous Trade Unions, outside state control) to mobilize them ended in a pitiful failure.

We may only assume that most of the pensioners once again voted for the ruling party (excluding a segment of the urban, highly educated members of the older generation). Their choice can hardly be explained by objective reasons based on their interests: the regime deprived them of practically everything that could be taken away. In the case of this group, social-psychological factors prevailed—especially its firm conservatism and its powerful identification with the previous socialist regime—which has been carried over to the existing order and rejects the very existence of opposition parties. This aversion was certainly encouraged by a part of the opposition. The insistence of the Serbian Renewal Movement (SPO), the strongest populist opposition party in Serbia,[1] on the rehabilitation of Draža Mihajlović (at the cost of falsifying the fact of his collaboration with the Germans during World War II), despite the party's stated intention to "reconcile" the descendents of former enemies, certainly antagonizes those who once defined their former social position and value orientation on the idea of the unpardonable treason of Mihajlović and his movement. These people far outnumber those with opposing views, particularly among the older generation. (The research findings, for example, reveal that the population only rarely accepted the monarchist option, the second blustering slogan of the SPO.)

In contrast with these strata, the majority of the middle-class urban population (including a substantial number of small enterprise owners) opposed both the domination and the manner of rule of the Socialist Party. This was already indicated by the results of the local elections showing opposition victories in almost all large towns in Serbia (the middle class is, naturally, concentrated in the towns). The same thing has subsequently become clear from their direct participation in the mass protests, since the distribution of the demonstrators clearly indicated their predominant affiliation to middle strata. Finally, this research finds, as we will later see, that the middle strata account for the majority of the population which defended the vote it manifested in the local elections of November 17 by demonstrating.

This became a case of opposing rather than merely denying support to the ruling party, because the opposition had already won a substantial number of votes at the previous elections (the votes of those who, we may reasonably assume, essentially belonged to the same group which today backs these parties).[2] The latest events revealed new elements: the partial expansion of the electorate of the opposition, and, in particular, the surprisingly active resistance of the voters whose electoral options were eliminated by the regime's machinations. The birth of this activism can, ostensibly, be attributed to a series of factors, only a few of which will be mentioned here.

These are, in the first place, the erosion of the legitimacy of the regime as a result of its refusal to at least start the structural adjustment of the economy—in the wake of the monetary stabilization, termination of the war in Bosnia and Herzegovina, suspension of sanctions, etc. It is small wonder that it was precisely the educated city population that grew increasingly dissatisfied (albeit with a delay) over the ruling circle's unwillingness to initiate the kind of transformation that was already underway in almost all CEE countries. This population's lack of economic prospects was reflected in a relatively mild political form in the local elections, where the vote in favor of the opposition should have warned the ruling party of the possible consequences of blocking reform. The arrogant and obvious forgery of electoral results, however, abruptly released the brunt of frustrations the middle classes had been accumulating for years; this one act revealed to them how deep the problem of Serbian society was. The conduct of those in power demonstrated the irrelevance of the existing pluralist system and revealed their attempts to preserve political monopoly as an integral element of the blocked transformation in Serbia and the FR of Yugoslavia. Economic and political problems, aggravated by the behavior of the state-controlled media, combined to create a wall dividing modern from pre-modern civilization. The members of the middle classes collided with this wall, taking them off their path of lethargy and bringing them into the streets and squares.

At this point the conduct of the ruling circles became decisive. Surprised by the citizens' reaction, the regime itself appeared hesitant to use violent means. The citizens rightly interpreted this as a sign of weakness: prolonged demonstrations dispelled fear, one of the main instruments for maintaining the previous and existing order, and thereby acted as a force of their own to enlarge and spread the protest throughout the towns of Serbia. The media's smear campaign against the opposition, which was not backed by force, proved counterproductive when confronted with actual events so broad-based that they ensured all citizens direct experience in the protest. Thus the middle strata, prompted by their position and the initiated delegitimation of the regime, through their own action, simultaneously completed this delegitimation and their own homogenization, becoming the main proponents of a movement against the ruling group.

Naturally, these statements are even more applicable to students as the emerging members of the middle classes. Their social prospects in an untransformed Serbia/FRY appeared even gloomier and their sensitivity to manipulation still more pronounced. Furthermore, they had no obligations toward the previous social and political order. Consequently, the student protest was able to remain genuinely principled: its demands invoked universal principles of freedom, justice and the legal order, and it distanced itself from the civil protest. The regime exploited this principled stand, presenting it as a conflict between student and civil protests while showing a certain "benevolence" toward the students. This tactic was, again, counterproductive, because in terms of its intentions the civil protest also goes beyond party affiliation. In other words, acknowledgement of the right to protest for reasons of principle could only encourage a large number of party-unaffiliated citizens to join the columns which insisted on respect for the right to vote, establishment of the truth concerning electoral results and elimination of the electoral fraud. As a result, not only were the student and civil protests mutually supportive, but they were indirectly assisted in that effort by the tactics of the party in power.

## The framework for crisis resolution

Having gone through the destruction of the socialist order, a civil war, the breakup of the state, a war, and economic and political isolation, the regime in Serbia has, unexpectedly and seemingly without proper reasons, found itself in a profound crisis. On November 11 it self-assuredly announced its unchallengeable rule, invoking the forces which had provided it stable support in the previous period. These forces supported the regime once again in the federal elections and in large measure did not fail it at the local elections either. This regime, once again, obtained the votes of the uneducated, uninformed, pre-modern Serbia. That is the Serbia dominated by authoritarianism and, which therefore needs a leader but cannot manage to find a replacement for the existing one. Conservative Serbia fears change and finds an inferior present more desirable than an uncertain future. Finally, it is a Serbia which has lost a lot, but not as much as the other, urban Serbia, and which, therefore, dreads the possibility of becoming the main loser under the changed rules of the game. That Serbia won the federal elections and local elections in sub-urban and rural areas.

Along with the social and social-psychological characteristics of ru-ral and suburban voters, the key element in the electoral failure of the opposition in the federal elections was, once again, the opposition itself. Its insufficient organization, shortage of resources, absence in remote places and lack of access to the main media as well as the fact that elec-toral units had been structured for the regime's benefit—were important but not decisive elements for the opposition's defeat. Until the very last moment the opposition vacillated between a joint and a separate ap-proach, and just who would join the coalition in case the former ap-proach was adopted remained unclear until the submission of electoral lists. And there was more! Frictions and even fierce conflicts among the potential members of the coalition were quite obvious both before the elections and even in between the two electoral rounds (when the leader of the Democrats, Djindjić, admittedly made a remarkable political move: by sacrificing direct party interests for long-term ones—ceding some of his party's mandates to the Democratic Party of Serbia so that it would join the coalition—he started a rapid political maturation). The opposi-tion coalition—as reflected in its name *Zajedno* ("Together")—put for-ward as the guiding idea of its approach precisely what appeared to be one of its weakest points (the other weak point was the emptiness of its program as an inevitable result of the basic conceptual disagreements).

The success of the opposition coalition on local elections in urban centers was not the result of its force but primarily the weaknesses—or rather the wear—of the ruling party. Some of the urban population voted primarily against the entire bankrupt policy of the Socialists, while there were also those who voted (only) against their thuggish local representa-tives. At this point a whole series of problems arose that was insur-mountable for the ruling group. It could no longer change either the policy or the people who implemented it. Thus from that moment on, the social basis the ruling party relied upon could not grow but only crumble. The loss of control in the cities meant less control over the most significant economic resources and the media. Most importantly, a symbolic turning point was reached. The socialists had lost in local elections before, but the defeat in Belgrade, Niš and Novi Sad marked the collapse of the myth of the authorities' invincibility, which represented one of the most important factors of their superiority thus far. The blatant, brutal and even stupid falsification of electoral results was a clear indicator of the panic that overwhelmed the party's leadership.

That fraud was a fatal mistake. This move gave the citizens who voted against the party in power irrefutable proof that they had been right. This was no longer merely a question of a violation of their will but a savage attack on their honor. It was too much not only for the "modernized" Serbia but also for part of the patriarchal one. The regime has thus consolidated against itself the devoted members and voters of opposition parties, their less committed sympathizers and also those who voted for the coalition as the least inadequate solution, and even those who probably did not vote at all. When the students joined the civil protests, a movement was formed whose breadth apparently surprised even the opposition parties. This time they reacted in the right way, organizing the walks as an extremely well-suited form of protest. Peaceful, with mass attendance, developing in plain view and not particularly exhausting, the demonstrations, by the very fact that they were taking place, attracted an ever-larger circle of participants, and this centripetal force fused the initially loose coalition of parties.

The regime found itself at an impasse. The discipline of protest participants excluded the possibility of crude provocations, so that a reason to use force, the most efficient response the regime had left, could hardly be found. Although the demonstrations failed to elicit strong support abroad for quite a long time, at least the publicity they were given solidly protected them against mass reprisals. Then the external understanding of the crisis changed. The West, proverbially disoriented concerning the Yugoslav tragedy, finally understood that Milošević's destabilization was the consequence not only of opposition activity but primarily of the inherent nature of the regime and that a regime of this kind was incapable of securing the stability of the region. In addition, the process of learning politics imposed on the opposition by the rebelling population clearly provided a potential alternative partner on the Serbian scene. By supporting the *Zajedno* coalition, the West definitely limited the regime's maneuvering space. In this context the economic aspect is apparently more important than the political one. Namely, one may assume that xenophobic isolationism could once again ensure the acceptance, if not approval, of the pre-modern Serbia. But the economic potential for cutting off the country from the world again no longer existed. Without foreign capital the economy would not only rapidly collapse, but the resources for maintaining the repressive apparatuses—the last defense on which the regime could rely—would disappear. This would simultaneously divest the regime of both legitimacy and protection. (Unofficial as well as official information from military circles saying that the army declared itself a defender of the constitutional order, rather than the protector of the existing power structure, hint at this outcome.)

In summary, the following conclusions may be drawn. The extremely long continuance of civil mass protests has had a remarkably delegitimating effect on the regime. The first step in that direction was made by the ruling party itself, when it annulled the results of the elections (thus alienating some of its own cadres and supporters). The number and persistence of the participants, as already indicated, increased this delegitimation. The frustration of the regime, faced with processions of demonstrators extending for kilometers, relieved the citizens of fear, the penultimate guardian of the regime. Naturally, it seemed that brutal repression as the last defense of the regime was still available (hopelessly anachronous means such as counter-demonstrations of regime supporters during December 1996, or cables of support to the then-president signed by directors of firms, had the opposite effect, if any). But this possibility should not be excluded, because the stakes go beyond power itself (this plunder is incomplete, and previous ones are still too fresh and have left too many traces). Still, the use of force could not obtain support in the current situation: the picture of the "butcher of the Balkans" in Western public opinion, though it may have improved over the past year, has not faded completely and has started to reemerge. Without this support, with a ruined economy and irreparably damaged legitimacy, a regime based on bayonets would have no chance of long-term survival. In one way or other, on the basis of the electoral procedure or collapse of the repressive apparatuses, the regime is condemned to a relatively fast breakdown. The speed of this breakdown depends on a number of factors, primarily on the opposition itself. If the opposition manages to retain its hard-won credibility and continues resolutely, it will ensure the end of the regime. But regardless of its success in achieving its direct objectives, if it becomes engaged primarily in its internal relationships (primarily the struggle for supremacy), the dirge to the current regime will resound amidst a whirlwind of chaos.

Serbia has awakened from years of lethargy, but it has not yet faced reality with its eyes wide open. Casting off the weight of the regime's corpse seems to have been a difficult task, but cleaning up the traces of its long decomposition will be an even grimmer job. The first step is, however, the most important one, because once it is made we will not be able to turn back, even if we want.

## Epilogue: Prolonged agony

It took only a few months after the previous text was written for events in Serbia to resume their course of hopelessness. The inertia of institutionalized political actors overcame the energy of citizens: the pessimistic alternative stated above has for the most part already been realized.

Toward the end of February 1998, only the most insistent skeptics anticipated the negative turn of events! The persistence of the rebelling citizens from within and the mounting pressures from without forced the thus far unchallengeable ruler of Serbia, Milošević, to make a concession: an OSCE commission was invited to judge the fairness of local elections. Naturally, there could not have been any doubt as to the commission's findings. What, then, was the purpose of the whole show? The finale laid it bare. After some stalling, which further tested the persistence of protest participants, Milošević went along with the demand of the Gonzalez Commission and passed a special act acknowledging the results of November 17 elections. This maneuver achieved a few results. First, it showed that decisions in Serbia are not taken by citizens or courts, or even Parliament, but by Milošević himself: the decision he took could only be understood as an act of grace by the ruler (this message was sent to the pro-authoritarian Serbia). Then he underlined that the bestowal of this grace was a consequence not of internal, but of external demands. Thereby he underscored the hierarchy of power: a concession was made to those who were more powerful outside the country, meaning that he was still stronger than his domestic opponents (the message was primarily intended for the traditional Serbia, which judges power by itself, but also as a warning to the opponents). Next, the fact that the opposition's demands were mediated by the institutions from the West served as "proof" that the opposition parties were in the service of foreign powers (a message to the xenophobic Serbia). Finally, by relinquishing the administration of urban centers to the *Zajedno* coalition, he gave it an opportunity to demonstrate its immaturity (a message to all, both at home and abroad: once you see how miserable their work is, you will realize that I am your only hope).

Milošević's move obviously demonstrated the strengths and weaknesses of his political skill. Under the circumstances he did the best he could for himself. But why did he bring himself into that situation? The fatal weaknesses of the opposition coalition were visible already in November 1996 and, had he acted in line with the last of the reasons above, it is almost certain that the opposition would have been swiftly discredited. But by provoking a widespread civil rebellion (an element he failed to anticipate), he, at least temporarily, reinforced the opposition parties.

True, the decomposition of this force started almost at once. After securing the right to govern the towns, the *Zajedno* coalition called on the citizens to stop the protests and immediately set out to divide the spoils. In doing that it left the student protest—the driving force of the demonstrations—in the lurch. The students had to continue for a whole month (supported only by their professors), fighting for the fulfillment of their specific request—the replacement of the rector of the University of Belgrade. The fact that one of their requests was finally observed for the first time in the long history of student protests in Belgrade indicates that the regime was aware that the burning fuse of the student street demonstrations was the only binding force of the opposition coalition. Once the students withdrew from the streets, the conflicts among the coalition partners burst out with full force.

When speaking of the relations within the Serbian opposition, it is necessary to distinguish between two levels: the local level and the party-leadership level (which can most often be reduced to the personalities of party leaders). Conflicts on the local level mostly related to the distribution of offices in municipalities where the opposition parties had won power. In line with the socialist heritage, whereby political positions ensured control over the whole of social reproduction, the local power enabled direct conversion of political into economic capital (the blocked transformation in the FR of Yugoslavia has kept this legacy alive even to this day). In other words, these positions bring substantial economic benefits. (The local power, for example, controls the use of expensive business premises, which may be leased for a fee or given to one's relatives and friends; directors of public enterprises are appointed at the local level, as well as salaried members of managing boards of state or quasi-state firms; etc.) Conflicts among the parties concerning this distribution often intertwine with those inside the parties. That is why it is hardly surprising that, in addition to mutual conflicts, the parties started to show internal divisions and form interest groups which developed beyond party limits, including transfers to competitors and ousting of prominent local leaders from their respective parties.

However, corruption on the local level not only has disintegrating effect on the opposition; to a certain extent, it also has an integrating one. Divisions between coalition partners deprive them all of local power and, therefore, of profitable positions. Thus it is not surprising that the official disintegration of the *Zajedno* coalition in the early summer of 1997 did not immediately result in the termination of cooperation in the cities where the coalition had been victorious the previous November. Even the expulsion of Zoran Djindjić, president of the Democratic Party, as the mayor of Belgrade (the fact which transferred this party with the largest number of seats in the town hall into the opposition benches) did not directly cause division among coalition partners in other Serbian towns. Naturally, maintaining a working coalition here involves the direct pressure of party membership, sympathizers and voters, in view of the—probably justified—fear of punishment by the electorate of the coalition partner who publicly causes the breakup of the alliance.

It would be too simplistic to say that the sources of conflicts on the party-leadership level lay exclusively in the leaders' vanities and ambitions (although those are, no doubt, extremely powerful antagonizing factors). What sharpens the conflicts is the knowledge, confirmed time and again by experience, that given the present inter-party relations the opposition parties supporting structural social change cannot win a parliamentary majority either individually or jointly. This frustrating situation has led the most powerful party—the Serbian Renewal Movement (SPO)—to adopt a specific strategy: it devoted itself to the elimination of all other opposition parties from the political scene. Therefore, over time, its attacks on coalition partners grew fiercer until they surpassed the criticism of the ruling regime. The reduction of the number of parties in Serbia—the objective which the SPO occasionally proposes to explain its behavior—may, to some, appear rational: there are over 100 parties registered in Serbia, but most of them are ghost organizations backed by the Socialist Party of Serbia and established for the sole purpose of fragmenting the electorate to increase the possibilities for manipulating the public. The problem, however, is that the SPO cannot rally the anti-regime forces, since its traditionalist and populist nature repels the urban middle strata who are the main opponents to the regime (while, as already noted, the strata which might be attracted by such an approach are already attached to the regime coalition).

The political scene for republic and presidential elections in Serbia in September 1997 was, in brief, set as follows: The international community, which, since January, had started to give clear support to the *Zajedno* coalition, withdrew to a safe distance of neutrality after *Zajedno*'s internal conflicts and disintegration. Milošević moved to the office of the president of Yugoslavia and from there continued his destructive policy of generating conflicts to facilitate his domination of the weakened opponents, potential competitors or insufficiently obedient supporters. (The focus of the conflict was shifted to Montenegro and Republika Srpska; later on—naturally, independently of his will—it became fixed in Kosovo and Metohija.)

Encouraged by the self-destructive dissent in the opposition, the Socialist Party of Serbia calmly waited to confirm the continuation of its unchallengeable rule. This calm was, in the economic sphere, backed by $1 billion obtained from the sale of a part of the telecommunications system to foreign firms and aimed at purchasing the support of a substantial number of voters (through the payment of a part of wages and pensions in default). In addition, the adoption of the Privatization Act (in the summer of 1997) was to simulate the regime's readiness for radical economic reforms. (However, the managerial right to opt for privatization or otherwise, as the basic element of the law, still gives the ruling circles a possibility to choose the manner, time and speed of privatization, in other words, to themselves define the proportion of their control of the economy via the state or their own private ownership.) In the political sphere, the ruling party, once again certain of itself, changed the electoral law at the last moment, thus ensuring for itself an additional advantage through the increased number of electoral units. The number of deputies was reduced in the districts where the Socialists expected defeat and increased where they counted on certain success (in

Kosovo, e.g., due to the expected continuation of the Albanian population's boycott of the elections). But to be on the safe side, the entire administrative, control and judicial mechanisms which performed the fraud in the November 1996 elections were left in their respective positions.[3]

Rightly convinced of a defeat under the circumstances, part of the opposition decided to boycott the elections. The trouble with this decision was that it was doomed to fail: its delegitimating effect was rendered senseless by the refusal of certain parties (primarily the SPO) to join it. The other part of the opposition rejoiced at the withdrawal of its former allies and counted its losers' gains: the local parties (the *Vojvodina* coalition) and parties of certain ethnic minorities (Hungarians, Muslims) sought confirmation of their particular legitimacy, while the SPO sought proof that it was the largest among the defeated. By contrast, the Albanian parties, with their ongoing boycott of the elections, as well as the entire legal political process, wanted to ensure legitimacy exclusively within their own ethnic group, since this also "proved" that they did not belong to the state system of Serbia/Yugoslavia. The fascistoid Serbian Radical Party was taken seriously only in verbal statements by oppositionists of all categories, who considered it a pawn of the Socialist Party. Particularly ambivalent in this sense were the messages of the SPO leader, Drašković, who attacked the SRS program but praised the personal qualities of its demagogic leader, Šešelj.

The results of the September elections, however, confirmed the previous analysis in all important points, betraying the expectations of most of the players on the political scene. The SPS's reckoning that the short-term maneuvering would restore its power proved miscalculated. The long, drawn-out process of this party's decomposition continued: it won the smallest number of votes ever and was once again (after 1992) left without a majority in Parliament. Its lost votes were picked up by the Serbian Radical Party, but this time—in contrast with 1992—the Radicals could take a more independent attitude toward their weakened mentor. This was dramatically indicated by the fact that in the second round of the first presidential elections, the SRS candidate, Šešelj, obtained more votes than the SPS candidate. The failure of these presidential elections (due to the fact that voter turnout fell short of 50 percent) revealed that these two parties combined enjoyed the support of less than half the electorate in Serbia. However, in view of the indomitable ethno-political divisions in the country (especially where the Albanians are concerned), it turns out that the parties that pretend to shape the democratic order cannot count on the support of more than a quarter of the electorate either.

When it seemed that the previous text could be completed with only a few more sentences, events accelerated ahead of the publishing schedule, creating the need to write an epilogue to the epilogue. Naturally, we are not talking about the repeated presidential elections in Serbia, because at the formal level they kept the political course in its previous vicious circle. After the first round of the elections, the competitors in the electoral race were once again the candidates of the Socialists and the Radicals. In the second round the ruling party resolutely used its control over the state apparatuses to make the victory of its candidate formal. Phantom votes, especially from Kosovo, accounted for the required voter turnout of over 50 percent. It hardly needs explaining why, this time, the Radicals relatively calmly accepted the fixed electoral defeat: this party has actually achieved its short-term objectives. It implicitly confirmed loyalty to its mentor, Milošević, by playing the role of an apparent contender in a political contest, thus marginalizing other competitors who could have presented a real threat to the domination of the Socialists. On the other hand, by maintaining its position as the second strongest party, it could secretly await the possible collapse of the SPS and subsequently emerge as the ruling political group in Serbia. (Šešelj's Radicals realized a part of their two-faced calculation in March 1998 when they formed a republic-wide national coalition government as junior partners to the SPS.)

Then, once again, the Kosovo problem exploded. It has already been mentioned that the fundamental change in the constitutional position of the provinces in Serbia in the late 1980s represented the beginning of the disintegration of the Yugoslav state but also that the "loss of autonomy" cannot be the cause for the current rebellion of the Albanians (as is generally claimed in the West). Mass, long-term protests by the Albanian population occurred periodically after World War II, not only while a remarkably high formal-legal autonomy of the province, including numerous elements of statehood, existed, but also while the Albanian political elite had a *de facto* political monopoly (from the early 1960s until Milošević). The current demand for independence is merely an adjustment—meaning explication in terms of its final consequences—

of the previous request to give Kosovo the status of republic and the Albanians the status of a nation (instead of a national minority). In this context, we should bear in mind that under the previous circumstances there was a formal legal link between the status of the republic, i.e., the nation (since the republics were defined as national states with the exception of Bosnia and Herzegovina) and the right to secession (which belonged to the nations). Thus the Albanians fought for the legal framework that would, at an opportune moment, enable them to form their independent national state—like other nations in Yugoslavia.

The whole course of events over the past 10 years or so unambiguously evidences that what is happening in the Balkans is a completion of a (belated) process of the formation of national states. The current outcome of the breakup of the former Yugoslavia means that this process has been discontinued before it logically ended, since the Serbs (primarily in Bosnia and Herzegovina, and partly also in Croatia) and Albanians (in Serbia and Macedonia) are denied the right given to other ethnic groups—to separate from the existing state structures and form relatively homogenous national states (a denial the members of both groups rightly consider unjust, since it means that the Slovenes, Croats, etc., were granted not a right—which ought to be equal for all—but a privilege). This also means that an almost insurmountable obstacle has been placed for the development of democracy in this territory. The formation of states on the territories where pronounced conflicts exist is a process that bears a high risk of a war. In addition, under the present conflict-ridden circumstances, mobilization of the population on an ethnic basis is far more successful than that based on an abstract principle of political equality (especially in environments that are economically underdeveloped, traditionalist, without democratic experience, etc.; cf., e.g., Dahl, 1979). Serbia continues on a downward spiral: ethnic homogenization prevents structural—interest-based—differentiation and also the development of democratic processes; the absence of democratic mechanisms increases the potential for an attempt at a violent resolution of conflicts; and this leads to further ethnic homogenization. Milošević and Rugova symbolize the first ring of the spiral; Albanian terrorism and the brutal response of the Serbian regime symbolize the second; and the entry of Šešelj's Radicals into the Serbian government and the political ascent of the "Kosovo Liberation Army" mark the descent to the third ring.

In the latter case, a part of the current process brings us back to the main subject of our study. On the eve of the first anniversary of the end of their protest, the students of Belgrade organized street demonstrations to show solidarity with Priština students of Serbian nationality. This event symbolically indicates some of the potential of the downward spiral. The students supported the nationalist demands of their Priština colleagues not to allow the Albanian students to use the university buildings. (Naturally, the "educational" demands of the latter were only part of the mosaic of their overall ethno-political instrumentalization.) True, the number of participants in the demonstrations was remarkably small, which indirectly confirms the finding of our study that this political option lacks significant support among the student population. Democratically oriented students remained passive at that moment, and with good reason: the set of circumstances makes a sustainable and just democratic solution of the problem impossible. Within a pre-democratic social framework, the national challenge easily elicits a response even from a group with the largest potential to take over the role of (one of) the actors of democratization, thus simultaneously undercutting the mobilization of alternative options. Under the present conditions in Serbia, this may result in putting off the birth of democracy indefinitely. Meanwhile, no rational solution exists to the numerous intertwined hotbeds of crisis—economic, political and ethnic. On the surface of current events, sometimes dimly, sometimes clearly, the outlines of the threatened outcome appear: the unraveling of the tangle in a whirl of uncontrolled conflicts.

## Notes

1. The Serbian Radical Party—SRS—cannot be considered oppositional for a number of reasons. In terms of organization, it was established and introduced into Parliament by the ruling party, in order to obstruct the opposition from the inside, as testified by the Socialist Party's "apostates" who, at that time, occupied high offices. Supported by the state media, this party, already in 1992, attracted over 20 percent of voters and gave the minority Socialist government security in Parliament. In ideological terms, it supports the program of

the Socialist Party of Serbia's extreme wing and attracts the same circles of the population, whose support, from one election to the next, fluctuates from one of these parties to the other. If given the opportunity, however, there is no indication that the SRS, this illegitimate child, would not be ready to commit fratricide.

2. In the federal elections in May 1992, the SPS obtained 1,665,458 votes (43.48 percent of those who took part in the elections; in the repeated elections in December 1992 it won 1,473,913 votes (31.50 percent), while in November 1996 it had 1,847,610 votes (42.41 percent) within the Left coalition. Corresponding figures for the SPO are 794,786 (15.78 percent); 809,731 (17.20 percent—within the DEPOS coalition); 969,198 (22.25 percent—the *Zajedno* coalition). The Democratic Party (DS) won 280,183 votes (6 percent) on December 1992 elections—cf. ToD, 1997.

3. Bickering over the crumbs of local authority, the opposition "forgot" to use its wide domestic and foreign support in the spring of 1997 to dismantle the mechanism. Thereby it wasted an opportunity not only to secure itself against similar acts in the future but also to further delegitimize the regime.

## *Bibliography*

Arandarenko, M. (1997): "Tržište rada u tranziciji—Nastajanje industrijskih odnosa u Srbiji" (Labor market in transition—The emergence of industrial relations in Serbia) (unpublished doctoral thesis), Ekonomski fakultet, Belgrade.

Bolčić, S., ed. (1995): *Društvene promene i svakodnevni život: Srbija početkom devedesetih* (Social change and everyday life: Serbia in the early '90s), ISI FF, Belgrade.

Dahl, R. (1979): *Poliarhia,* Yale University Press.

Dinkić, M. (1995): *Ekonomija destrukcije* (Economy of destruction), VIN, Belgrade.

Grupa ekonomskih eksperata (Group of economic experts) (1997): *Pismo javnosti o merama za izlazak iz ekonomske krize* (A letter to the public concerning the measures to overcome the economic crisis), Belgrade.

Janjić, D. (1994): "National Identity, Movement and Nationalism of Serbs and Albanians," in: D. Janjić and Shkelzen Maliqi, eds., *Conflict or Dialogue,* Open University, Subotica.

Lazić, M. (1987): *U susret zatvorenom društvu* (Toward a closed society), Naprijed, Zagreb.

Lazić, M. (1994): *Sistem i slom* (System and breakdown), Filip Višnjić, Belgrade.

Lazić, M., ed. (1995): *Society in Crisis,* Filip Višnjić, Belgrade.

Lazić, M. and L. Sekelj (1997): "Privatization in Yugoslavia," *Europe-Asia Studies*, Vol. 49, No. 6.

Madžar, Lj. (1990): *Suton socijalističkih privreda* (The twilight of socialist economies), Ekonomika, Belgrade.

ToD (1997): Center for Transitions to Democracy, *Newsletter*, special issue, January.

Zec, M., ed. (1994): *Privatizacija: nužnost ili sloboda izbora* (Privatization: a necessity or freedom of choice), Jugoslovenska knjiga, Belgrade.

# PART I

PART 1

# Potential for an Active Society

*Marija Babović*

The 1996–97 civil protest was not the first demonstration against the regime in Serbia, but it displays a series of specific features compared with earlier ones. One of these specifics is certainly its long duration, that is, the persistence of its participants until their basic demands were met. This very characteristic has enabled a group of researchers from the Faculty of Philosophy in Belgrade to carry out an empirical survey that, in terms of its subject, marks a pioneering endeavor in Yugoslav sociology. This is due to the fact that civil protests are a new phenomenon in Serbian society, appearing with the onset of the transition.

The mass character and long duration of the 1996–97 protest gave the researchers the opportunity to use a survey technique to ensure a solid empirical basis to respond to numerous questions posed by civil demonstrations. At this point, in view of the simultaneous evolution of the civil and student protests, we must note that this research covered only the former of the two events, led by the *Zajedno* coalition of opposition parties (for the student protest cf. articles by Kuzmanović, Popadić, Milić and others in this volume). The data were collected from December 8 to 14, 1996, on a sample of 483 respondents.

A group of authors from the Institute for Sociological Research of the Faculty of Philosophy at the University of Belgrade embarked upon this research project with limited objectives, aware that the phenomenon of the protest was merely one aspect of events in Serbia, which could not yet be defined as a radical change toward democratization. The research team was motivated primarily by the need to secure systematized evidence on various aspects of the protest and to come up with professional answers to some of the basic questions and dilemmas raised by the protest, such as:

—Who are the protest participants in terms of their socio-demographic characteristics and political profile?

—What are the basic objectives and demands of the participants and, hence, does the protest have a primarily political or wider social nature?

—What are the behavioral characteristics of the protest?

The present article seeks to answer the first set of questions, namely to assess whether this has been a widespread popular revolt or a revolt of a select population. In the second part of the article, the analysis turns from the empirical toward the theoretical level in an attempt to assess to what extent the protest participants are actually actors seeking change conducive to a modern, "active society," starting from Etzioni's analytical concept of an active society (cf. Etzioni, 1968).

## Socio-demographic characteristics of 1996–97 protest participants

### *Sex and age distribution*

Since the sex distribution is addressed in a separate article in this collection (see article by M. Blagojević), we will, at this point, only note that protest participants included almost equal shares of men and women (55 : 45 percent). This proportional representation of both sexes reveals a significant participation of women in the struggle for civil rights.

Protest participants are, in our analysis, divided into seven age groups. The first includes the youngest participants (up to 19 years of age) and is followed by a number of ten-year age brackets, ending with the group of participants over 70 years of age. This distribution of age groups indicates the largest participation of the young from 20 to 29 years (29.9 percent) and the "middle-aged" from 40 to 49 years (22.9 percent).

Compared with the data on the socio-demographic characteristics of the population of Belgrade,[1] we note that the age group from 21 to 30 had an above-average participation in the protest, compared with their respective share in the total population of the capital.

Middle-aged groups (from 31 to 40 and 41 to 50 years) were represented in the protest almost proportionately to their shares in the total population of the capital, while older categories register a smaller number of participants compared with their share in the total population (Figures 1 and 2).[2]

Men are more numerous in age groups of 20 to 39, while women outnumber men in 40-69 age groups. In the last age group men again take over the lead with an overwhelming share of 91.7 percent.

The above-average participation of the young (20–29 years old) indicates a remarkable political activism of these generations and their greater

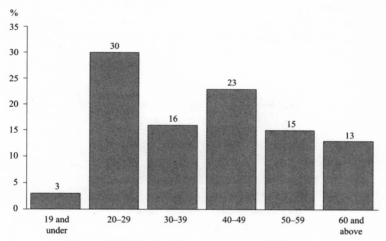

*Figure 1.* Distribution by age—protest participants

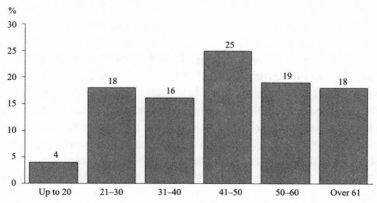

*Figure 2.* Distribution by age—population of Belgrade

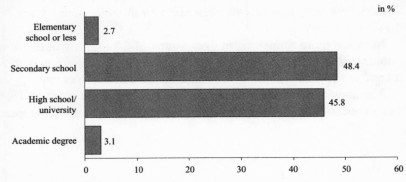

*Figure 3.* Distribution by education—protest participants

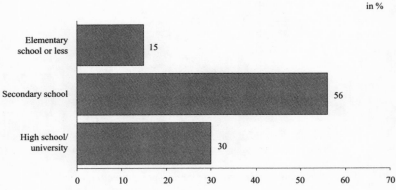

*Figure 4.* Distribution by education—population of Belgrade

orientation toward change. The high share of this age group is partly attributable to the rather large participation of students in the civil protest, which is also indicative of their extremely developed social consciousness, political activism and orientation toward democracy (cf. articles by B. Kuzmanović and D. Popadić in this volume). Older categories of the population (51 and over) are less represented in the protest compared with their share in the total population of Belgrade. This confirms the thesis that these parts of the population largely represent the mainstays of the current regime and are much less likely to develop civil consciousness.

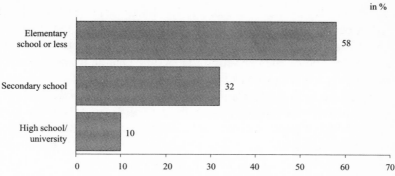

in %

*Figure 5.* Distribution by education—population of central Serbia

## Educational and professional distribution

Protest participants display the largest differences compared with the total population of Belgrade and Serbia precisely with respect to these two socio-demographic indicators (Figures 3 to 5). Demonstrations were attended by very few citizens with elementary or lower education. The protest was actually carried by citizens with secondary, higher or university education. It is interesting that the participants included more people with master's degrees and doctorates than citizens in the lowest educational category.

In order to arrive at a more precise educational distribution of participants, we have excluded all secondary-school students from the lowest educational category and students from the medium-educated category. This has left us with 1.7 percent of participants in the lowest educational category and 27.5 percent in the medium educational one. That is why we may conditionally conclude that the secondary-school and college students, whose education is still under way, "lower" the already above-average education of protest participants.

Since the educational distribution of protest participants compared with that of the population of Belgrade (cf. Vujović, 1990) and beyond, in central Serbia (cf. Bolčić, 1995), reveals that the population in the lowest educational category accounts for over half the population of central Serbia (58 percent), it is clear that the protesters had a distinctly above-average education.

The trend of explicit political (civil) activism of the population with a higher education, as manifested in the demonstrations, shows that education is a precondition for the development of consciousness on basic civil rights and on the need for a democratic change in the underdeveloped post-socialist society of Serbia.

Distribution by profession largely echoes that of the educational distribution and reveals the dominant share of professionals in the protest. They are followed by college and secondary-school students, pensioners, clerks and technicians. Highly indicative is the remarkably low share of industrial workers (2.3 percent), as well as employees in the service sector (3.8 percent), who together have a share of 6.1 percent. The unemployed account for 8.2 percent of protest participants.

A comparative analysis of the professional distribution of the total population in Belgrade and its share in the protest is, again, indicative of the selective composition of demonstrators. Only clerks, technicians and the unemployed are proportionately represented. While students and, especially, professionals show an above-average participation in the protest, pensioners, managers, peasants and, in particular, industrial workers, are under-represented (see Figures 6 and 7).

There are several reasons for the conspicuous absence of the workers' social strata among protest participants. On the one hand, the workers probably fear a radical social change, since it implies the major restructuring of the economic system and is expected to result in greater unemployment. However, the results of the November 1996 federal elections indicate that the workers are not exclusively oriented toward the existing regime, because the *Zajedno* coalition came out victorious in some traditionally working-class municipalities in Belgrade (e.g., Rakovica). However, these strata display an obvious discrepancy between a passively manifested electoral option and direct political activism in demonstrations. As we often hear, this part of the population, faced with the drudgery of mere existence, may find the struggle for democratization a luxury.

Almost 70 percent of employed protest participants work in the public sector, while 24 percent have jobs in the private one. Of the total number of participants, 28 percent are employed in education, science, culture and arts, 13 percent in trade, 10 percent each in health care and industry, while employees of other branches of economy register a share below 10 percent.

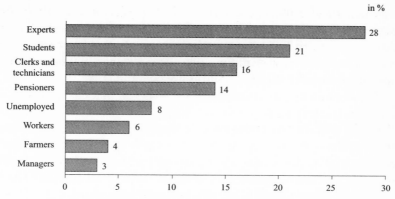

*Figure 6.* Distribution by profession—protest participants

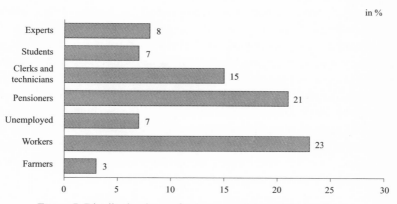

*Figure 7.* Distribution by profession—population of Belgrade

If these data are compared with those for central Serbia, which indicate that in 1994 the public and private sectors employ 85 and 15 percent of all employees respectively, we may note that the private-sector employees were represented in the protest above the average for the republic, as opposed to those working in the public sector, who are under-represented.

The educational and professional distributions point to a phenomenon of key importance: we may claim, although with a degree of professional caution, that the 1996–97 protest was primarily a protest of the

middle strata. This caution is due to the fact that the class-strata structure is defined by a combination of a number of dimensions while, in
this case, we only had two at our disposal. Given that the research could
not cover all the relevant dimensions, the thesis that this was a protest of
the middle strata may be accepted only conditionally.

## Marital and ethnic distribution

It is interesting to note that among protest participants, the largest group
consists of married people (47.5 percent); somewhat fewer are unmarried (41.4 percent), while the divorced/widowed account for 11.1 percent. A quarter of protest participants have underage children. Among
these participants, most have only one child (57.6 percent), followed by
those with two children (39.2 percent) and 3.2 percent of parents with
three or more children.

As expected, most participants in demonstrations are Serbs (83.5 percent), while members of other nationalities total 4.2 percent. In addition, 12.3 percent do not identify their national affiliation or are nationally unaffiliated. The ethnic homogeneity of protest participants differs
markedly from the ethnic heterogeneity of the Serbian population (according to the 1991 population census, Serbs account for two-thirds of
the population of the republic, while the remaining third consists of
members of other ethnicities), but certainly much less than from the
ethnic distribution of the population in Belgrade.

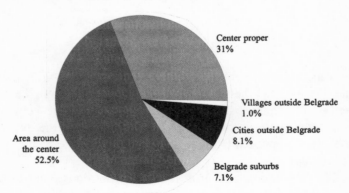

*Figure 8.* Place of residence—protest participants

## Urban protest

The distribution of protesters by their place of residence shows the obviously urban nature of the demonstrations. As many as 91.5 percent of protest participants live in urban environments: 31.3 percent in the center of Belgrade, 52.5 percent in the outskirts of the city proper and 7.7 percent in other towns in Serbia. The population of rural settlements on territories of Belgrade municipalities accounts for 7.3 percent of participants, compared with 1.3 percent of the rural population from inland Serbia (see Figure 8).

Protest participants from rural areas include more men (73.2 percent) than women (26.8 percent). Men are slightly more numerous among protest participants from the outskirts of the city proper (54.4 percent) than women (45.6 percent), while women from the city center are a little more numerous (53.3 percent) than men (46.7 percent).

The data on this aspect of the socio-demographic profile of protest participants also corroborates the thesis that this is a protest of middle strata. Once we exclude the rural population, whether from border areas of Belgrade municipalities or from inland Serbia, the educational and professional characteristics of this population show the prevalence of people with intermediate and high education.

The research findings lead to the conclusion that the population that participated in the protest may be classified with a high degree of reliability as middle urban strata. The heterogeneity in the basic socio-demographic characteristics indicates an almost equal representation of both sexes and all age groups (with the prevalence of the young, from 20 to 29 years of age, and the middle-aged, from 40 to 49 years). The data, furthermore, reveal an above-average educational distribution of participants, a fact that becomes obvious compared with the educational distribution of the population of Belgrade and, in particular, with the educational distribution of central Serbia. The professional distribution also indicates selective participation due to the almost complete absence of industrial workers among the protesters, despite the fact that they account for almost a quarter of Belgraders. On the other hand, professionals and students are over-represented. Finally, the distribution by place of residence testifies to the clearly urban character of the protest, since most participants come from the city center or the outskirts of the city. Therefore, we may conclude that, despite the heterogeneity in basic

*Marija Babović*

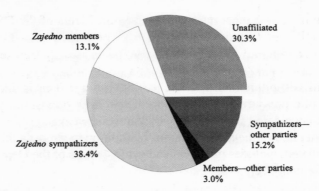

*Figure 9.* Party affiliation

socio-demographic specifics, protest participants manifest remarkable structural homogeneity in terms of belonging to the middle urban strata and that the heterogeneity of groups within the protest derives from the otherwise heterogeneous nature of the new middle strata.

## Political profile of 1996–97 protest participants

The findings of this research show that according to the party affiliation and political orientations of its participants, the protest represents a wider civil revolt which cannot be reduced to the formulation commonly used by the state media: "protest of *Zajedno* coalition supporters." Members and supporters of the *Zajedno* coalition definitely account for over half the protest participants (51.5 percent), but 30.3 percent of respondents claimed they were not members or sympathizers of any political party. In addition, 18 percent of protest participants are members and supporters of other opposition parties outside the *Zajedno* coalition (Figure 9).

Members of *Zajedno* coalition parties account for 13 percent of protesters. Most numerous among them are members of the Serbian Renewal Movement (SPO) (9.5 percent), followed by members of the Democratic Party (DS) (3.1 percent), while the smallest representation is that of members of the Civic Alliance of Serbia (GSS) (0.4 percent), which is proportionate to these parties' balance of power in the electorate. As for the sympathizers of the *Zajedno* coalition, this distribution is somewhat different: most numerous are sympathizers of the DS (11.8 percent), followed by those of the SPO (10.8 percent) and the GSS (1.2 percent). In addition, 14.7 percent of participants identify themselves as sympathizers of the *Zajedno* coalition as a single political organization, rather than as supporters of specific parties within it. This is due to the strong public pressure for unification of the three opposition parties, otherwise considered fragmented and, therefore, weaker.

The other half of the demonstrators, in addition to almost a third who are unaffiliated, includes members and sympathizers of the Democratic Party of Serbia (DSS)[3] (10.4 percent), members and sympathizers of the Serbian Radical Party (SRS) (2.9 percent), members of other parties (1.0 percent), people who generally identified themselves as sympathizers of the opposition (2.9 percent) as well as participants who identify themselves as sympathizers of other parties and movements (0.8 percent).

The political profile of protest participants reveals a much more heterogeneous composition of the demonstrating population than was expected at the outset of this research. Since the demonstrations were triggered by fraud at the local elections, which denied the *Zajedno* coalition its mandates, the researchers expected that most protest participants would be members and sympathizers of this coalition. However, it turned out that a wider circle of citizens who are not politically oriented toward the parties from the *Zajedno* coalition are ready to defend the principle of regular elections and the right to vote as a fundamental civil right.

Protest participants are highly critical of the Serbian president and the current regime. Only 6.7 percent of respondents do not object to anything in particular about Milošević, while 93.3 percent object to various aspects of his policy. The most important criticism of the Serbian president, stated by over a quarter of participants, relates to his undemocratic and authoritarian rule. Almost a quarter of demonstrators object to the statesmanship and the entire political activity of the president. Milošević is considered responsible for the war and the disintegration of the former Yugoslavia by 14.8 percent of participants, while 13.7 percent disapprove of his personal characteristics, such as, arrogance and stubbornness. The outstanding national question was noted as a basic objection to Milošević by 10.3 percent of protesters.

A critical attitude toward the president and the ruling regime is also reflected in the high number of demands for Milošević's resignation or the removal of the regime. A third of protesters rank these among the basic demands of the protest, immediately after the most important demand for the recognition of local-election results.

The data obtained by this research also reveal fairly intensive previous political activity by the 1996–97 protest participants. Most of them (70 percent) took part in some of the earlier protests against the authorities. In addition, 63.3 percent of them took part only in opposition protests (March 9, 1991; St. Vitus' Day Convention in 1992; student protests in 1991 and 1992; peace protests), while 6.7 percent attended pro-Milošević rallies organized in the late 1980s, then joined the opposition's protests as early as 1991. A small number of protesters (1.7 percent) previously participated only in regime-organized rallies. Protest participants also comprise 19 percent of people without any previous "hands-on" experience in demonstrations, that is, people who are now taking part in a mass protest for the first time. Most numerous among them are students, but there are also managers and pensioners. It is interesting that not one "new" worker appears in the 1996–97 protest, i.e., a worker who has not already participated in protests against the authorities.

We have also tried to judge the political preferences of the participants on the basis of their rating of political leaders. On a scale from 1 to 5, the highest average mark was given to Zoran Djindjić (president of the DS). He was followed by Vuk Drašković (president of the SPO), Vesna Pešić (president of the Civic Alliance of Serbia), Vojislav Koštunica (president of the DSS) and Danica Drašković (member of the SPO Main Board and Vuk Drašković's wife). A barely passing mark was given to Vojislav Šešelj (president of the SRS), while negative marks were given to Serbian President Slobodan Milošević and his wife and leader of the Yugoslav Left, Mirjana Marković (Figure 10).

These data indicate an interesting change. Judging by numerous research findings and electoral results, Vuk Drašković was considered the most influential opposition leader until the protest, while it turned out that the protest brought Zoran Djindjić to the fore. This remark may be substantiated by the rating of the leaders' political activity by protest participants. Those without party affiliation ranked Djindjić the highest of all leaders. However, supporters of specific parties gave the highest marks to their respective leaders but ranked the leader of the Democratic Party the second, with only a slight difference.

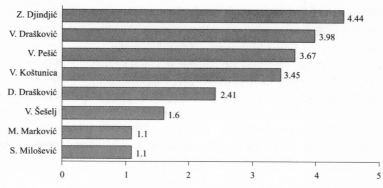

*Figure 10.* Rating of political leaders' activities

Since the demonstrations in the winter of 1996–1997 have been the largest against the authorities in Serbia so far, the researchers tried to establish whether protest participants include former supporters of President Milošević and if so, how many of his former followers transferred to this political bloc. This was a very tall order given the circumstances under which this research was carried out. In the midst of demonstrations against the president's regime, one could hardly expect respondents to "confess" to having supported him and thus acknowledge some degree of "responsibility" for the outcome the protesters fought against. With a fair amount of caution, we may conclude that the then president of Serbia was supported by 17 percent of 1996–97 protest participants, at least during the events in Kosovo (1989) and the disintegration of the League of Communists of Yugoslavia at its 14th Congress (1990).

We have classified into this sub-group of "Milošević's ex-supporters" those respondents who, when asked about the positive contributions of President Milošević, mentioned "the awakening of national consciousness" (6.7 percent of the total number of participants) and the "anti-bureaucratic revolution" (3.1 percent). We also included those who responded to the question concerning their previous participation in demonstrations and rallies, either that they participated in rallies in support of Milošević in 1989, but that they joined the opposition's protests in 1991 (5.8 percent), or that until the most recent protest they only took part in regime-organized rallies (1.9 percent).

Milošević's "ex-supporters" in the protest display some different characteristics compared with other participants. They include a much larger number of men (72.7 percent) than women (27.3 percent), almost half of them have intermediate education (50.9 percent) and they generally come from the outskirts of the city (70.4 percent).

Objections which this sub-group expresses against Milošević are not particularly different from those voiced by other participants (mostly his undemocratic style of rule), but they criticize his inappropriate handling of the national question somewhat more and, unlike all other participants, do not accuse Milošević of contributing to the disintegration of the former Yugoslavia.

Most people in this sub-group are now supporters of opposition parties. Only a quarter of them identify themselves as unaffiliated, but, in contrast with other participants, they give slightly lower marks to opposition leaders and somewhat higher to Milošević and Mira Marković (although still negative).

The relationship of protest participants toward international factors represents yet another element of the demonstrators' profile we have tried to examine. Our findings indicate that they are not primarily oriented toward international factors. Only 4 percent of respondents believe that the protest owed its long duration to international support. About 15 percent are glad for the support from abroad. Their relationship toward the foreign factor may, perhaps, be best perceived in their attitudes toward the means that could force the authorities to honor the protest's demands. A third of participants consider external pressure one of the most important measures to make the authorities fulfill their requests. However, a much larger importance is attached to internal factors. As many as 57 percent of participants believe that a general workers' strike would generate the crucial pressure, while 34.4 percent of respondents see the best means in a long-lasting peaceful protest.

Orientation toward the international community derives from a number of factors. After a long international isolation during UN sanctions, protest participants have visibly demonstrated their wish to reestablish links with the world (by carrying the flags of many foreign countries). However, the domestic public was, for a long time, convinced that the international community tacitly, as well as openly, supported the regime in power and that it would, therefore, fail to support the civil protest. International support, which followed after the protest persisted for some time, raised the hopes that the regime would have to give in to pressure from the outside.

On the basis of findings on the political profile of the demonstrators as given above, we may note that the 1996–97 protest was no doubt articulated by the *Zajedno* coalition, which at that time represented the strongest opposition political force and was hurt most by the annulment of local-election results. Most demonstrators support this coalition. However, almost a third of the demonstrators have no party affiliation, and other demonstrators are members and sympathizers of other political parties and movements. This reveals that the protest has incorporated wider opposition groups and that it can be referred to only conditionally as the protest of *Zajedno* coalition supporters. This thesis is sustained by the fact that only 6.2 percent of respondents believe that opposition leaders should be given the credit for the long duration of the protest. One may conclude that protest participants place their trust in the *Zajedno* coalition, although they do not protest exclusively to support the coalition's leaders, but rather to fight for their own demands including, most importantly (as indicated by the research findings), the acknowledgement of local-election results.

## Is there a core for an active society in Serbia?

In this part of the article, we will leave the empirical level and try to perceive the research findings in the light of a theoretical concept. Starting from the analytical model of an "active society" construed in the late 1960s by one of the leading American theoreticians of modernization, Amitai Etzioni, we will seek to determine whether the actors of the 1996–97 protest have the potential to "change the code" of current Serbian society as a necessary precondition for modernization. We will try to respond to the following questions:

— Does the activism of protest participants include the basic components of a movement for an active society?
— Does it lack some characteristics of this type of movement?
— Which internal and external limitations are imposed on this movement?

Finally, we will discuss the conditions a movement for an active society should seek to attain in order to arrive at a change of the basic forms of social relations.

The concept of an active society in Etzioni's approach represents an ideal-type or an analytical model, which allows specific societies to be defined as more or less active compared with the model. While the societies of Western democracies approach Etzioni's ideal type, totalitarian and authoritarian societies run counter to this concept in terms of their structural and systemic characteristics.

An active society is capable of continuously changing its systemic code and thereby enables sustained transformation in line with the values and needs of its (also changeable) membership. This society is founded on a specific mutual relationship of control and consensus. Societies that are closer to Etzioni's ideal type have a larger number of active individuals, groups and collectivities; they also have multiple social control, i.e., control of social controllers; and they continuously build and renew the consensus among autonomous social actors (individuals and groups).

Serbian society today is of an authoritarian type; its populations are subjects rather than citizens, estranged from the process of managing the society and deprived of the possibility to control the authorities. In this context, we are primarily interested in seeing whether the participants of the 1996–97 protest have an active orientation aimed at changing the code of this kind of society.

## Elements of active orientation

An active orientation consists of three main components: a conscious or self-conscious actor, one or more objectives this actor is committed to attaining and the social power that enables the change of the social code. All three components have to be in place in order for the active orientation to be successful.

The research into the 1996–97 civil protest did not start from this theoretical framework, so the data it obtained do not create a complete empirical basis for all elements of the analysis. Still, they enable fairly reliable conclusions to be drawn on specific elements, while other aspects of the analysis must rely on either indirect indicators or events in the protest's environment.

The social consciousness of protest participants is a dimension on which we can draw only tentative conclusions on the basis of available data. The contents of this dimension comprise the consciousness an actor has about his social environment, its structure and relationships within it. This consciousness also includes the perception of other actors and is based on the specific social position of the actor and his interests. In addition to a developed social consciousness, the self-consciousness of an active collectivity is highly important, since it implies the perception of one's own interests, possibilities and limitations.

The development of consciousness in the social environment is a part of transforming a passive unit into an active unit. However, the highly complex conditions of Serbian society over the past 10 years or so have constricted that development in various ways. I am thinking primarily of the national question, war and existential problems in a thoroughly unfavorable hyperinflationary environment.

On the basis of the research results, one may conclude that the consciousness of protest participants still includes a mixture of different, occasionally even mutually exclusive, value orientations. There is a fairly clear orientation toward liberalism and democracy, yet a degree of authoritarianism and egalitarianism still persists (cf. article by V. Ilić in this collection). Within the framework of the political dimension, this consciousness is characterized by an explicitly critical attitude toward the existing political system and the regime. Objections to President Milošević reveal the elements in the environment which the protest participants consider the most problematic for further development. The most frequently voiced objection is the lack of democracy of his rule, while a substantial number of participants object to the president's entire political activity. These objections indirectly indicate the consciousness of an excessive concentration of power in Milošević's hands, which demonstrates that the dissatisfaction was generated not only by the president's manner of rule but also by the absence of the principle of division of power characteristic of democratic societies.

In addition, the nature of the consciousness of protest participants may also be perceived from the responses to the question on the types of change they expected after a possible replacement of the current regime. The most important change, for 43 percent of respondents, would be reflected in greater civil freedoms, which indicates their liberal orientation.

A much higher degree of "homogeneity" of consciousness among protest participants is revealed in their vision of a future society which should be built after the change of the current regime. As many as 92 percent of participants believe that the future society should be built according to the model of modern Western democratic societies. Although this concept implies societies which are in many ways differently arranged, protest participants have obviously selected some of the common foundations characteristic of the developed democratic societies.

There are two more factors of importance for the development of consciousness which may expand or focus its horizon: the level of education and the process of communication. We have already shown that the educational distribution of protest participants is substantially higher than the average educational distribution of the total population. As for communications, the existence of the free media is particularly important, since information is necessary to build consciousness on various aspects of society in which an actor lives and works. It is thus significant that after 1990, certain independent media have continued operating in Belgrade, albeit with exceptional difficulties. The protest participants are aware of the need for independent media, as evidenced by the demand for freedom of the press listed among the most important rights.

The onset of the protest, i.e., the activation of a part of the population, has reinforced and sharpened certain aspects of consciousness and started the development of self-consciousness. This could not happen before the collectivity took a compact form. With the protest, various groups of citizens sharing joint objectives have, for the first time, begun to perceive themselves as a distinct collectivity. The previous atomization of society, isolation inside the most intimate circles and a focus on daily problems of survival did not allow their linking into a relatively "delimited" collectivity. The annulment of the second round of local elections triggered an explosion of energy pent up in the private spheres of individuals. Their going out into the streets enabled mutual "recognition". It showed citizens that they are not alone in their orientations and efforts but that there are numerous like-minded people and that common objectives link them with others. The collectivity of the "active" first acquired a degree of identity and then self-awareness. Protest participants have managed to develop the main elements of self-consciousness—recognition of their own identity, assessment of their possibilities, self-control. This identification has been reinforced by different symbols which make the collectivity visible: badges, slogans, whistles and other audible and visible paraphernalia. Joint participation in the project, commitment to the same objectives and participation in a social movement are effective ways to increase collective self-consciousness.

However, there is yet another factor which contributes to its strengthening—confrontation. The research into the civil-rights movement in the United States in the late 1960s and early 1970s has already demonstrated that confrontation, e.g., with police forces, adds to the cohesion and self-consciousness of a movement more than peaceful negotiations, even though the latter may result in concessions (Etzioni, 1968: 232). This is also confirmed by the experience of the 1996–97 protest, since the presence of police forces and the beating of demonstrators failed to cause the crumbling of the movement but, on the contrary, increased its activism manifested in still more intensive, imaginative and witty protest actions, such as, creating gridlocks, blocking police cordons, generating noise during the broadcasting of state TV daily news, tying up the phone lines of state institutions and officials, etc.

The other component of active orientation—commitment to objectives—may be more completely perceived on the basis of the research data. They reveal a clear orientation of protest participants toward relatively precisely formulated objectives. The acknowledgement of results of the second round of local elections was considered the most important objective by 44 percent of respondents. Second in importance was the replacement of the existing political regime, which was also the most important demand of a third of participants. Media freedom was also one of the protest's objectives in 17 percent of the cases. Only the demands for democratization appear as more generally formulated objectives (put forward by 28 percent of respondents).

The degree of commitment to objectives may be judged on the basis of the intention of protest participants to pursue their demands until the end. An overwhelming 98 percent of respondents declared their wish to continue with the protest until the fulfillment of their demands, no matter how long it might take.

In addition, the degree of commitment may only be assessed indirectly and in line with the persistence of the protest despite various pressures applied by the regime. Aggressive attacks of the state media, physical threats with police cordons, arrests of protest participants and even counter-demonstrations with the assistance of the president's supporters failed to stop the protest, which indicates a powerful commitment to objectives and a high degree of activism.

The third component of active orientation is the social power of actors. Etzioni defines power as the ability to overcome resistance, whether in part or in full, and to implement the change despite the opposition (including maintaining the course of action or the status quo which would otherwise be stopped or changed) (Etzioni, 1968: 314). This definition largely restricts the concept of power, but since it represents an element of approach which precedes the analysis, we will use it in its original meaning. In addition, power is also understood as energy deriving from the resources of a social actor. The quantity of power created by a social unit is defined by its resource basis and the proportionate conversion of this basis into power as well as by the quality of the conversion process.

The sources of power may be different, and often the power of one actor comes from a few sources. The power of 1996–97 protest participants also comes from different sources. One of the most important bases of political power is legitimacy. Legitimacy obtained in local elections represented an important source of power for the protesting collective. However, the problem was that, precisely because the authorities refused to share the "power pie," the *Zajedno* coalition and the citizens who elected its members as their representatives in the government bodies could not institutionalize their power based on legitimacy. Additional power was required. And it came from other sources.

One of the most important sources of power is international support. That is where the balance of power becomes even more complicated. Power finds a point of reliance in dependence. The regime in Serbia has only just raised its head above the wall of international isolation, and its further survival is largely dependent on assistance (primarily economic) from abroad. It is dependent on international institutions, which gives these institutions power over it. Therefore, the power which the international factor has over the regime in Serbia, due to its support to demonstrators, increases the power of the protest.

The power of protest participants partly derived from a source which is highly important in developed societies—knowledge. The above-average education of the demonstrators, as well as the high share of professionals of different profiles, and even students as potential professionals, represented another "reservoir" of power. Finally, the power of the protest also derives from the large number of its participants and its duration.

Still, despite the diverse sources of power, it appears that the participants do not perceive it as sufficient to reverse the balance on the scales. This consciousness is manifested primarily in the choice of means which may force the regime to fulfill the protesters' requirements: only 26 percent of participants are convinced that a peaceful protest is in itself sufficient. In most cases the participants seek additional mainstays of power, finding them primarily in a general strike of workers (43 percent) or international pressure (25 percent).

Transformation of sources of power into active energy develops with the help of the mobilization process. In order to start mobilization, it is usually necessary to have a concrete project or a motive. The motive of the 1996–97 protest, for instance, was to fight the annulment of electoral results. The motive sets the process of mobilization in motion, which transforms the resources into energy and brings the active collectivity to the "take-off" stage when activism begins. The resources which the mobilizing force of the civil protest should transform into energy are limited in some ways. Namely, the economic resources are modest, while the political power as a resource does not suffice to force the authorities to fulfill the demonstrators' demands. The largest resource of the protest is the human one, which proved capable of producing a fairly large quantity of energy.

Every mobilization has its limits beyond which it cannot transform resources into energy, either because the resources have been depleted or because the cost of any further conversion would exceed the gains. Experience shows that stormy, abrupt mobilizations are usually short-lived; that soon after the take-off they decline and that the active unit returns to passivity. Experience also suggests that a more comprehensive, lasting mobilization always follows the model of a slow chain reaction. Usually, the elites are activated first, followed by sub-elites and different other sub-collectivities.

The mobilization of 1996–97 protest participants seems to mark a departure from these rules. From the first day of the demonstrations, 80 percent of participants were activated, including 40 percent of party-unaffiliated protesters. Therefore, one definitely cannot say that members of the political elite were the first to be activated (among whom we might include the leaders and members of the highest leadership of parties within the *Zajedno* coalition), since the first wave of mobilization already covered the largest number of participants. On the other hand, the participants themselves, due to their remarkably high average level of education, may be considered an "educational elite". In addition, despite the sudden "take-off" made possible by an almost explosive mobilization, the protest has shown an exceptional ability to endure.

It is important to note that real activism conducive to an active society cannot exist unless all three components are there. A developed consciousness is a precondition of activism, but activism, in turn, also reinforces the development of consciousness. Without consciousness one cannot formulate the objectives. On the other hand, without commitment to objectives, there can be no activation, no matter how developed the consciousness.

## Limitations of action and counter-action

Every active orientation has its internal and external limitations. The relationship of limitations and the potential of the active collectivity decide the success of activism. Previous attempts to activate the population (March 9, 1991; St. Vitus' Day Convention, 1992; student protests; peace protests; demonstrations in front of the Federal Parliament, 1993; etc.) were not successful precisely because the internal and external limitations overpowered the active potential. Internal limitations derive from the absence, or insufficient development, of one of the components of active orientation.

The center of resistance to the protest is the ruling forces of the Left coalition, which holds all the levers of social control in its hands. A remarkable concentration and centralization of power develops with a semblance of a multi-party system which formally possesses the basic elements of democracy. The distribution of power among institutions of power evidences the authoritarian nature of the political system, in which the ruling Socialist Party of Serbia, recently "reinforced" by the United Yugoslav Left, holds all the reins of power. Since the Left coalition has had control not only over legislative and executive bodies but also over the judiciary, there is no doubt that its rule over society is unlimited. In addition, bearing in mind the distribution of power among the forces of the Left coalition, it would be no exaggeration to claim that it has an expressly authoritarian nature, i.e., that the decisions are taken by a narrow party elite or the party leaders almost exclusively.

Activism encourages counter-activism in the form of the confrontation of other social units and collectivities with objectives contrary to those of the active movement. Counter-activism came from the part of the population which supported President Milošević, but it did not have an authentic character or elements necessary for active orientation. Instead of consciousness it had an ideology, its objectives were not authentically formulated and the degree of commitment was obviously insufficient for internal mobilization, while the power it wielded did not derive so much from internal resources as from the outside. Therefore, the mobilization of counter-activists ("counter-ralliers") was not spontaneous but rather induced by the political elite, which is why it lacked the power and ability to maintain the level of the action after the take-off. That is precisely why the counter-action lasted for only a few days.

There are always more than two actors in a system. In addition to two confronted parties, most often, there is also a third party which is not directly included in the conflict between the activists and the resisters. This third party consists of passive groups which are acted upon with influence rather than power. In contrast with power, the objective of which is to overcome resistance to action, influence seeks to change views and thereby also the behavior of subjects. This third party, in the 1996–97 protest in Serbia, was highly heterogeneous, and the active movement tried to exercise its influence in different ways on different collectivities which were outside the direct line of conflict of the proponents of action and resistance. There were some actors the active movement did not try to win on its side or mobilize in its favor. Instead, it was rationally satisfied with the kind of influence that maintained their passivity (primarily the army). There were also other actors the movement did not seek to mobilize in terms of their joining the protest, but tried to activate them in their specific domains, so that their action supported that of the movement (the international community, the church,

Montenegrin representatives in the federation). The third group of factors were units which were not dedicated to the objectives of the protest movement and were potential allies of the mobilized parties: other political parties uninvolved in the conflict, parts of the population which were either unaffiliated or lacked activation.

The research has revealed a remarkable absence of workers in the protest, but there are no data from which one can conclude that the workers were involved in the counter-active collectivity. Some other indicators do not favor such a thesis. For example, the opposition won a landslide victory in some workers' suburbs of the Belgrade municipality of Rakovica. This shows that a part of the workers is, at least passively, on the side of the active movement but lacks other preconditions for activation.

## Change in the social system's code

The main precondition for radical change is the recoding of the system. In the ideal-type sense, this means erasing the existing system's code and building a completely new one which will be capable of continuing transformation in line with the interests and values of numerous social actors. However, in reality, this means that the "recoding" first applies to the key elements of the system which represent the largest sources of opposition to change and then follows with the gradual change of code of other sub-systems.

Research findings have indicated that the protest action is primarily focused on the political system, which is thus revealed as the current center of resistance. However, the change of code does not imply a simple change of the proponents of power but also the restructuring of the system to establish a different one with a different logic of functioning.

In order to change the code of the political and social systems, it is necessary to provide the new bases for the two key elements of managing the society: consensus and control. On the basis of the different nature and mutual relationship of these elements, Etzioni distinguishes between different types of society (this is again the case of ideal types that real societies approach to a greater or lesser degree):

Low levels of control and consensus are mainly found in underdeveloped societies;

A high degree of control with a lower level of consensus is characteristic of authoritarian and totalitarian societies;

Greater lack of capacities for control than consensus is observed in societies which are close to modern developed societies;

Active societies have both elements developed, but they, for now, represent only an alternative or an open option in the development of real societies.

We will deal with the first element—the consensus—first. The "interwoven consensus" is characteristic of authoritarian societies in which the common values spread across the social structure, but this type lacks an essential dimension—attainment of different interests of parts of the social structure. It contains normative and even cognitive dimensions which are, true, more imposed than freely accepted, but it definitely does not succeed in articulating the different interests of special groups and social units.

The second form of consensus is of a "segregational" nature. It befits more democratic societies. Since these are societies with relatively autonomous units and collectivities, the process of building a consensus becomes much more complex. It starts developing within groups and collectivities formed primarily on the basis of joint interests, then between groups and collectivities, thus gradually leading to a wider agreement on the most fundamental values and principles on the basis of which a given society should be founded and ruled. Its character is changing since, due to the changeability of groups and collectivities as well as their interests and objectives, it has to be continuously rebuilt.

Of course, one of the main deficiencies of Serbian society is precisely the lack of consensus on the fundamental principles of the social order. The type of consensus reflects the manner of distribution of power in a society, but in a situation where the balance of power has already been disrupted, it is necessary to rebuild a consensus of a new quality and on substantially different principles suitable for a segregated type. Unfortunately, the current proponents of power do not wish to acknowledge the need to build a consensus, and the balance of power will decide whether this need will be temporarily suppressed (which will only make it deeper, since unsatisfied interests are always conducive to reactivation with the same demand), or cause a more radical decoding of the system so as to start building a new consensus, in which the current proponents of power will probably have incomparably weaker positions than they do now. There can be no development of democracy until a consensus is built with an ever-wider basis, mobilizing the thus far excluded collectivities and incorporating them in political processes. With all that the consensus must be more authentic, i.e., it must be based on the awareness of general and special interests rather than on persuasion.

Control is often in inverse proportion to consensus: the stronger it is, the weaker the consensus becomes. The task of an active movement must be the establishment of a balance between these two elements of governing society. In modern societies control is narrowed down in one aspect, while in the other it is multiplied. Control "from the top"—that carried out by the authorities—focuses on the key segments of society, while control "from the bottom" multiplies, so that citizens, collectivities, groups and movements control the regime and inevitably force it to assume greater responsibility. Without control over controllers, there can be no responsible government.

At this point in time, Serbia is very far from modern societies, and the idea of an active society appears a total utopia. Neither the research we have relied upon in this paper nor the wider context of events allows us to conclude that the 1996–97 protest has been a movement which will surely lead to a modern, let alone active, society. Still, the protest indicates that at least part of the population has shaken off its passivity, and its active orientation holds promise that we are getting at least a few steps closer to what today appears an unattainable ideal.

## Notes

1. Data for the population of Belgrade have been taken from a study carried out by the Institute of Sociological Research of the Belgrade Faculty of Philosophy in April 1994 on a sample of 800 respondents. The research was part of a project entitled *Sociological Study of New Characteristics of the Serbian Society in the Early '90s*. The authors of the questionnaire were Andjelka Milić and Silvano Bolčić. This article includes original tables from the research.

2. Age distributions revealed by the two research efforts are not identical, but the differences are negligible.

3. The Democratic Party of Serbia, a party with a pro-traditional and pro-national orientation, split off from the Democratic Party. It appeared within the *Zajedno* coalition in the 1996 federal elections but ran independently at the local elections held that same year.

## Bibliography

Bolčić, S., ed. (1995): *Društvene promene i svakodnevni život—Srbija početkom devedesetih* (Social change and everyday life: Serbia in the early '90s), ISIFF, Belgrade.

Etzioni, A. (1968): *The Active Society*, The Free Press, New York.

Vujović, S. (1990): *Ljudi i gradovi* (People and cities), Mediteran, Budva.

# General Character of the Protest
# and Prospects for Democratization
# in Serbia

## *Slobodan Cvejić*

A few projects of sociological research into Yugoslav society carried out over the past few years resulted in an abundance of data on the characteristics of the local "transition" which could, in the briefest terms, be described as a "stopped transformation" (Lazić).[1] The troublesome course of change of Yugoslav society and a whole series of historical and social characteristics which make this path different from the transition models of other Central and Eastern European countries have been succinctly presented in the introduction to this collection written by Mladen Lazić.

I will only sporadically touch upon some elements of this general picture that are relevant for a possible answer to the following question: Has the 1996–97 civil protest in Belgrade been any different from similar protests that occurred in Belgrade from 1991 until 1996? Does this particular case allow us to recognize the collective action of a part of civic Serbia as carrying a potential for a lasting change of the social order? Previous protests (students—March 1991, students and opposition parties—June/July 1992, numerous strikes, traffic blockades, etc.) certainly accumulated a substantial quantity of social energy and helped preserve certain contents of collective consciousness diverging from the xenophobic-egalitarian picture which has for years been carefully and hypocritically created by the state mass media. However, until the local elections in 1996, the ruling regime managed to hold on with mild changes in course. The massive attendance and long duration of the latest protest left the impression that the regime had run into a reef and was stranded forever.

The civil protest against the rigging of elections for local authorities in November 1996 broke out at a time when a whole range of social and political circumstances in Serbia was changed. The ruling regime suffered a series of defeats in the economic, state and political spheres. Its legitimacy was suspended on a thin thread of votes of a third of Serbia's electorate. This third was inflated into a parliamentary majority by skillful manipulation of electoral law and procedure and recklessly aggressive propaganda. On the other hand, the ruling order was eroded by waves of advancing transformation in most CEE countries as well as the destructive force of international sanctions. Finally, on the domestic level, the regime's real-life problems (primarily economic) came to the fore, while a few opposition political parties, for the first time, made a distinct departure from nationalist rhetoric in their public appearances. The moment when the arrogant local thug was caught in his transparent swindle merely provided an opportunity for an angry eruption by part of society which was the most conscious of the danger threatening its interests in the given social and political circumstances.

Naturally, this part of society was the middle class. The socio-demographic distribution and political profile of protest participants (see the article by M. Babović in this collection) clearly reveal that lawbreaking and the theft of votes (and more importantly, the usurped victory of the democratic opposition) in the second round of local elections directly provoked the urban and educated segments of civil Belgrade. The available information indicates that the protest had the same character in other large towns in Serbia. In contrast with the previous protests which only partly included the middle strata[2] and mostly took part in Belgrade,[3] this time we have seen a social action of a substantially wider scope. If we concur that group action "indicates a genuine readiness/ability of a group to engage in collective attainment of its requests" (Lazić, 1996: 285) and that it is the "main instrument to achieve group identity" (Lazić, 1996: 281), we may assume that the characteristics of the 1996–97 protest testify to major changes in the social consciousness of an important part of Serbian society.

Before offering arguments for this statement, we should outline the situation with respect to value orientations in Serbia over the past few years. The more recent research into this problem reveals a noticeable process of retraditionalization, marked by the growth of nationalist, authoritarian and statist attitudes. Although coexistence of different types of social characters is evident, the authoritarian-traditional one prevails (Golubović et al., 1995: 350). S. Gredelj arrived at similar conclusions (Gredelj, 1995). He maintains that a situation marked by anomie in the sphere of values and accompanied by a "clash of opposed normative systems" results in "a great mixture and even confusion in the attitudes of respondents." The impression is that the holistic (meaning pro-socialist) and traditional values happened to form a coalition against the liberal ones whose "historical roots are shallow in this soil, while its social basis is very frail" (Gredelj, 1995: 210-218). This statement agrees with that of S. Vujović, who believes that the development of cities and citizenry in Serbia was accompanied by numerous disruptions and deadlocks and that the impotent citizenry of a few "did not manage to impose itself as an actor of important social change" (Vujović, 1995: 128).

The mass participation and wide scope of the 1996–97 protest suggest that the social basis of free and differentiated thought in Serbia has been expanded. How stable is this opinion? Are liberal values an integral part of the social consciousness of the demonstrators? Before I try to sum up the basic characteristics of the Belgrade protest, I will use the next few pages to address the demands and values this protest has expressed.

## Ascent of liberalism

In view of the cause of the outbreak of the protest (the annulment of regular electoral results), it is small wonder that the respondents predominantly considered the demand for acknowledgement of these results most important (Table 1).

*Table 1*

Most important protest demands
(freely chosen by respondents)

| Demand | % of respondents |
| --- | --- |
| Recognition of electoral results | 56.5 |
| Slobodan Milošević's resignation | 25.4 |
| Democratization of society | 21.8 |
| Change of regime | 18.0 |
| Media freedom | 17.2 |

The respondents were asked to freely select the three most important demands of the protest ("Which demands of the 1996 protest do you consider most important?"). Given that this was an open-ended question and that a high homogeneity of responses was achieved, we may note a remarkable general consensus concerning the protest demands. In addition to the request for the recognition of electoral results, there were also responses which could be reduced to the demand for the resignation of Slobodan Milošević and responses which boil down to the general request for the replacement of the regime. These, taken together, account for 43.4 percent.[4] On the basis of this choice, we may conclude that the event which directly provoked the protest has also awakened deeper dissatisfaction with the regime and with the president whom many consider to personify this rule.

The data on the motives which made the respondents join the protest are presented in Table 2. These data have been obtained in response to a closed-type question ("What prompted you to join the most?"), in which every respondent was given a multiple choice of predetermined answers.

*Table 2*

Motives for joining the protest

| Motive | % of respondents |
| --- | --- |
| Desire for justice and free elections | 59.6 |
| Overthrow of communism | 23.8 |
| Construction of a new society similar to those in Western Europe | 23.2 |
| Overthrow of personal rule of Slobodan Milošević | 17.8 |
| Support of opposition leaders | 3.9 |

The table shows that most respondents decided to "go out for a walk" based of their endangered basic individual values and rights. But, just as with the selection of the most important demands of the protests, we have again registered another important motive—the overthrow of the existing order. This element is presented in Table 2 through the "overthrow of communism" and "overthrow of the personal rule of Slobodan Milošević" with a total of 41.6 percent of respondents. The question is whether the motive of "overthrow of communism" together with the "construction of a Western-European-type society" denotes a trend toward changing the type of the social system or whether it combines with the "overthrow of personal rule of Slobodan Milošević" and reveals a trend toward the toppling of the existing regime. I have opted for the latter, since the "overthrow of communism" as a motive appeared in the second combination 4.5 times more often than in the first one. One may also assume that the demonstrators expected a change of the social system to ensue from the demise of the existing regime, but the concreteness of the second trend gave the protest greater internal strength.

On the basis of the data presented in the two tables above, we may conclude that, on the general descriptive level, the objectives and motives of the demonstrators concur. They primarily sought the protection of their basic democratic rights, but they also largely believed that this would be possible only by changing the ruling regime. They looked upon the replacement of the existing authorities as an opportunity to change the existing order (92.9 percent of respondents opted for the construction of a Western-European-style social system). Additional data show the internal consistency of this view, namely that the objectives and motives stated by most respondents coincided. Bearing in mind that the demand for the replacement of the regime is more general than the one for the recognition of electoral results, we assumed that respondents were inconsistent if they stated that their reasons to join the protest were "the overthrow of communism" or "the overthrow of the personal rule of Slobodan Milošević" but did not include either Milošević's resignation or the change of regime among the objectives they considered most important. These respondents total 77 in the whole sample (15.9 percent). Another piece of information may confirm the consistency of choice of the interviewed demonstrators. Namely, 181 respondents (37.5 percent) cited their support for the protection of the right to vote and the legal electoral procedure in both their motives and objectives. This number, in my view, represents a large share of rational value options in a situation marked by an extraordinary emotional charge, where a multitude of values, positions, objectives and demands are being stated. Moreover, 109 (60 percent) of these 181 respondents said that the most important change they expected from the downfall of the existing regime had to do with their feeling of dignity and freedom.

Since the demand for the replacement of the regime was quite marked among the participants in the protest, it would be interesting to take a look at what they expected from a possible change of authorities. These are revealed by the answers to the question: "What would change in Serbia after the downfall of the existing regime?" The respondents were given a choice of answers, as presented in Table 3.

*Table 3*
Changes expected after the replacement
of the current regime

| Expected change | % of respondents |
| --- | --- |
| I would feel greater dignity and freedom | 52.0 |
| I would be sure of the future for my children and myself | 32.1 |
| The overall social standard would be increased | 19.9 |
| The Serbian nation would win the right to live in a single state | 8.3 |
| Advancement in professional career or a new job | 7.5 |

The data show that the universal values (dignity, freedom, and security of one's future) have substantially surpassed the more tangible options such as increased social standing or advancement in one's business career. This completes the picture formed on the basis of Tables 1 and 2 and reveals a firm link between the objectives of the protest, the demonstrators' motives and their expectations from the change of regime, which, at the same time, accounts for the duration and persistence of the protest. This link has to do with the protection of justice, dignity and certain fundamental human rights. The fact that the demonstrators also considered the theft of their votes—which amounts to a violation of individual rights and democratic procedure—an attack on their dignity and freedom suggests more than a traditionalist resistance to legal offense and crime in view of the social composition of protest participants (well-educated and relatively young urban population). This confirms that the liberal and civil values have become deeply embedded in the consciousness of the demonstrators. That particular fact characterizes this protest as deeply moral. It indicates the direction of a moral catharsis which may be glimpsed after years of crisis of all positive social values. This direction points toward rational objectives and values and represents a move away from the decades-old traditionalist ethnic foundation.

"Anomic" confusion in the sphere of value orientations has continued for years, and it has, by no means, been fully resolved yet (see the article by V. Ilić in this collection). Nevertheless, it is quite clear that the demonstrators adopted basic liberal premises and emphasized them during the protest. The impression that the proclaimed objectives and values hinged on freedom as a fundamental value of liberal ideology, deriving from the value orientations of interviewed demonstrators, is substantiated by the fact that 79.9 percent of respondents partly or completely agreed with the view that "social progress can be based only on private ownership." These specific data give the protest a liberal character.

## Peaceful and democratic protest

The demand to recognize electoral results somewhat overshadowed, by 13.1 percentage points, a more far-reaching demand for the replacement of the regime (see Table 1), displaying another essential characteristic of this protest. This fact allows us to conclude that Belgrade demonstrators wanted to build trust in the institutions of parliamentary elections and administration of justice, which is largely indicative of the maturing democratic consciousness of this part of Serbian society and of the democratic nature of the protest. In an attempt to further substantiate this statement, I have checked the frequency of joint occurrence of the two types of demands. The relevant data are given in Table 4.

*Table 4*

Combinations of demands for the recognition
of electoral results and replacement
of the ruling regime

| Combinations of demands | % of respondents |
| --- | --- |
| Only demand for recognition of electoral results | 40.2 |
| Only demand for Milošević's resignation and change of regime | 25.9 |
| Neither | 18.0 |
| Both | 15.9 |

*Note:* The two groups of demands also appeared in combination with other demands listed in Table 1, but in the given context, I believed that only the relations between demands presented in this table were essential.

We may note that cases when none of these demands appeared were more frequent than those when they appeared together. In addition, those who made only moderate ("legalistic") demands were substantially more numerous (40.2 percent) than those who made only radical ("putschist") demands (25.9 percent). In order to establish how extensive this division was, I tried to evaluate some characteristics of the two groups. The difference between their demands corresponded to the difference between their options for certain value attitudes. The statement that "it is more important for the success of a group to have an energetic and just leader whom everyone would obey" met with the complete agreement of 26.8 percent of the "legalists," compared with 52.8 percent of the "putschists." This difference was also manifested with another attitude used to measure authoritarianism. Thus, 40.3 percent of those who exclusively demanded the recognition of electoral results agreed partly or completely with the statement that "without a leader every nation is like a man without a head," compared with 56.8 percent of those who demanded only the replacement of the regime and Milošević. The "legalists" were somewhat less xenophobic than the "putschists." The former included 39.3 percent of those who partly or completely supported the view that "a man should not trust foreigners too much," while their percentage in the latter group was 50.4. In addition, those who put forward more moderate requests supported egalitarianism much less than the proponents of radical requests. The statement that "justice cannot be achieved without material equality" obtained partial or complete support from 39.6 percent of the "legalists" and 56.5 percent of the "putschists."

The trend of differentiation into "legalists" and "putschists" was steadily manifested through the correlation of demands with the motives for joining the protest. The first group mentioned the desire for justice and free elections as one of the motives in 70.1 percent of cases, while the other did so in 46.4 percent of cases. On the other hand, the proponents of moderate demands mentioned the overthrow of communism as one of the motives for joining the protest in 17.5 percent of cases and the overthrow of Slobodan Milošević's personal rule in 14.9 percent of cases, while the proponents of radical demands registered 31.4 and 21.6 percent of such demands, respectively.

The division into the two groups is quite obvious, as is the prevalence of those who state moderate and real requests and seek reaffirmation of representative and judicial institutions. The presented argumentation confirms the picture of the democratic nature of the protest, but it also points out another of its specific characteristics. Only 25.9 percent of the demonstrators said their sole objective was to topple the regime and the current president, which indicates that the protest had a very peaceful nature. This fact indicates the political maturity of protest participants.

Additional evidence affirming the peaceful articulation and democratic nature of the protest can be obtained from the account of its organizational structure. Were the people who, due to their behavior and attitudes, formed the core of the protest simultaneously the group that transmitted the objectives, demands and ideas from the possible organizer toward the participants? Those who voiced radical demands were only slightly more represented in the protest's core than in the changeable part (30 percent and 22.1 percent, respectively). This reveals that the peaceful, tolerant and persistent nature of the protest was not due to internal organization and control of rallies but rather to the self-control of each individual participant based on his/her support of values affirming the democratic spirit.

The core group, according to our criteria, consisted of demonstrators who participated in the protest from the first day, were there on an almost daily basis (over 80 percent of the days) and remained from the beginning to the end. They accounted for 44.7 percent of participants. The core and the changeable part of the demonstrations did not differ merely with respect to these behavioral characteristics but also with respect to a series of other features. Members of the core group had the longest demonstrating experience. Only 12.5 percent of them stated that they had never participated in any of the previous demonstrations, compared with 23.8 percent in the changeable part. The core group made up 20.8 percent of those who were not sympathizers or members of any political party, or almost twice less than the changeable part (38.2 percent), while those who were party-affiliated were mostly members and sympathizers of the Serbian Renewal Movement (14.4 percent each). Members of the core group were more authoritarian than others. They partly or completely accepted the first statement listed in Table 6 (see the table below) in 49.5 percent of cases, while others did so in 38.8 percent of cases. Corresponding numbers for the second statement in Table 6 are 50.9 percent and 43.2 percent. The strata which appeared in the core group with somewhat greater frequency than in the changeable part are pensioners (18.0 percent compared with 11.0 percent), professionals in the social sciences and humanities (10.4 percent compared with 6.8 percent) and the unemployed (10.0 percent compared with 6.8 percent). The situation is reversed with students, who registered smaller participation in the core group (17.5 percent) than among others (23.2 percent). Accordingly, we also note a difference in the age distribution. People over 50 accounted for 33.8 percent of the core group and 23.7 percent of the changeable part.

The claim that the protest's powerful cohesion derived precisely from the individual devotion of participants is also supported by the fact that our respondents assigned the greatest credit for the duration of the protest to the "resoluteness of individuals" and the "popular will." This may be seen from answers to the question: "What has influenced the long duration of the current protest most?" Table 5 presents the respondents' choice of answers.

*Table 5*

Causes for the long duration of the protest

| Causes for the long duration of the protest | % of respondents |
| --- | --- |
| Popular will | 38.3 |
| Personal resoluteness to persist in demands | 36.0 |
| Student protest | 21.3 |
| Pressure of the authorities | 12.2 |
| Biased media | 8.3 |
| Opposition leaders | 6.2 |
| International support | 4.3 |

The claim that the duration of the protest was not due to internal organization is also supported by the fact that the demonstrators rarely attributed the endurance of the protest to opposition leaders. This confirms a conclusion, based on direct observation, that the nature of the Belgrade demonstrations was spontaneous, as evidenced by a large number of genuine improvisations in communication, both internal and external (see the article by S. Vujović in this collection). One cannot disregard the fact that by refusing to leave Parliament in protest, the opposition leaders did help initiate the demonstrations (see the Chronology of the Protest in this collection), and that with their daily speeches to the gatherings of citizens they influenced the articulation of the protest. Even so, I am inclined to say that what they did was provide guidance based on common objectives and interests rather than organization of the protest. Additional evidence supporting this statement is that those who formed the core group of the protest were no "closer" to opposition leaders than those from the changeable part. The core included 7.9 percent of people who believed that the opposition leaders deserved the greatest credit for the duration of the protest, compared with 4.9 percent in the changeable part. In addition, 3.7 percent of the former stated they had joined the protest to provide support for opposition leaders, while the latter group included 4.1 percent of such answers. Regardless of their more active conduct and more pronounced authoritarianism, members of the protest core did not voice substantially more radical requests than others, nor did they represent the basis for a potential "strike force" to provoke wider unrest. Owing to such circumstances, the protest, despite numerous provocations by authorities, did not exceed the boundaries of a peaceful and democratic manifestation.

## No ethnic nationalism this time

The initial hesitation of international political organizations and Western powers to support the protest in Serbia may largely be explained by the fact that events in the Balkans over the past six or seven years have made the international community doubt the possibilities for a democratic outcome to the crisis, as well as by the media-propagated prejudice that the entire Serb nation is obsessed by exclusive nationalism. The dilemma of whether the 1996–97 protest was civil or nationalist is a false one. This inclusion is not based only on the fact that, at the very outset of the demonstrations, the protesters, feeling the need to wrap themselves in cosmopolitan symbols, carried the flags of other European countries and the United States at the head of their column. We have seen that our respondents linked themselves to democratic objectives and civil society and that the number of those who expected the affirmation of liberal values after the departure of the current authorities was overwhelming. Let us still try to recognize the nationalists among the demonstrators. There were the 13.3 percent of respondents who directly objected to Milošević for inflicting damage on the Serbian nation or national interests or for neglecting the Serbian national issue. While 89.2 percent thought that the current president had failed to do anything useful for Serbia in his entire career, only 6.7 percent believed that he had done the right thing in awakening the national consciousness. Furthermore, only 8.3 percent of respondents said that one of the changes after the replacement of the existing regime would be that the Serbian nation would secure the right to live in a single state. A comparison with other questions gives the impression that the latter variable is the most consistent in distinguishing the nationalists from others. While, as already noted, 13.3 percent of respondents in the whole sample objected to Milošević for neglecting the nation, such objectors account for 25 percent of those who would like to see "all Serbs in a single state" and 12.2 percent of the "non-nationalists." The respondents who appreciated Milošević's awakening of the national consciousness represented 10 percent (6.3 percent in the rest of the sample). These respondents supported the traditional position that "a nation that does not cherish its tradition deserves to perish" to a much higher degree (95 percent partly or in full) than the rest of the sample (75.2 percent). In addition, they agreed far more often with the position that "one should not trust foreigners too much" (67.5 percent partly or completely), in contrast with the non-nationalists, who did so in 42 percent of cases.

Furthermore, these people showed greater-than-average support for opposition leaders who used nationalist rhetoric more often (V. Šešelj and V. Koštunica). The nationalists gave Šešelj and Koštunica an average mark of 2.39 and 4.15, respectively, which are the highest average marks they assigned to any of the leaders mentioned above. As for the rest of the sample, these two were given average marks of 1.60 and 3.39, respectively. In addition, the nationalists gave the most consistent representative of the civil line, V. Pešić, a mark of 2.73 compared with 3.76 by the rest of the sample. Furthermore, asked who they would like to see on the rostrum during the demonstrations, the nationalists thought of Koštunica in 35 percent of cases, compared with 15.1 percent of the non-nationalists. Finally, a much higher percentage of the nationalists identified themselves as Serbs (95 percent) than did non-nationalists (82.5 percent). The nationalists in the demonstrations included more men (62.5 percent men, compared with 37.5 percent women). Inhabitants of the city center contributed less to the nationalists (17.5 percent) than to the non-nationalists (32.4 percent). Therefore, we can recognize fairly consistent nationalists in this group and, let us repeat, they accounted for 8.3 percent of the sample, while a more consistent operationalization of the concept of a "nationalist" would probably reduce this percentage further. Moreover, nationalists did not share in the core of the protest more often than in the changeable part of the participants (5.9 percent : 9.4 percent). That fact leads to the conclusion that the protest was of a remarkably civil nature.

## Concluding remarks

The facts I have presented so far clearly indicate the serious changes of content in the collective consciousness of an important part of our society. An additional confirmation of this finding may be obtained through a comparison with the results of previous research projects. I myself drew on research into the social structure carried out in late 1993 and presented in Lazić, ed. (1995). On the basis of the sample for this research, I created a sub-sample of Belgraders which is, in terms of their social and demographic characteristics (profession, education, age, sex), very similar to the current sample. Table 6 presents comparative shares of partial and complete agreement with some attitudes in 1993 and 1996.

Statements given in Table 6 are the only comparable material on the subject addressed in this article, and they may be taken only conditionally as an indicator of change in the sphere of value orientations. Still, even this information completes the picture presented on previous pages. It reveals that liberal democratic values are still a part of a controversial combination of values, but that they are gradually coming to predominate among the middle strata of the Serbian population.

In view of the demands it has raised, the protest could be characterized as political. The demonstrators most often demanded the protection of the legal means of political struggle (the vote) and somewhat less often voiced a broader political demand for the replacement of the ruling regime. In addition, although a fairly large number of demonstrators denied being either a member or a sympathizer of a political party, their protest did support the demands and political program of the *Zajedno* coalition. In this sense one may say that the indicated value orientations

*Table 6*

Comparison of acceptance of some views
in 1993 and 1996 research

| Statements | 1993 | 1996 |
|---|---|---|
| Most important for the success of any group is to find an energetic and just leader whom everybody will respect and obey | 54.4% | 43.5% |
| Without a leader, every nation is like a man without a head | 47.8% | 46.6% |
| One should not trust foreigners too much | 52.2% | 44.1% |
| Progress of a nation may only rest on private ownership | 67.4% | 79.5% |
| Justice cannot be achieved without material equality | 54.3% | 45.3% |

of our respondents represented the ideological background for articulation of their political interests. However, I think that it was about more than that. The objectives and values could cause conflict among various social strata or groups if they link with their group interests. But when universal values go beyond specific social and economic objectives (living standard, new jobs, etc.—see Table 3) in a situation where the majority of the population lives on or below the poverty line, we may say that for these people universal ideals have a value equal to economic interests, which is not surprising in view of the stratal composition of the demonstrators. The social structure of protest participants tells us that democratic, liberal and civic values may be an ideological reflection of the interest of the middle strata in an overall modernization of society. These interests were no doubt indicated by the frequently expressed support for Western-European-type civic society, private ownership and parliamentarism (90.5 percent of respondents partly or completely agreed with the statement that "the president must be responsible to Parliament"). Given the homogeneity of the demonstrators' stratal composition (marked by a predominantly middle civil strata and an absence of workers and peasants), education (mostly intermediate and high) and place of residence (generally the urban zone of Belgrade), it would be most accurate to say that it was a social protest articulated through a political struggle and aimed at political objectives and channels which created the greatest obstacles to the modernization of society.

On the basis of these characteristics of the protest, one may conclude that the protest had a generally modernizing character and that its demands broke through the sphere of the political and manifested the deeper interests of the middle social strata. The intensity of the expressed liberal and democratic values points to the changes in collective consciousness. The fact that their positive nature has remained clearly visible in a conflicting situation created by street demonstrations shows that these values were firmly embedded in the individual consciousness of most citizens surveyed, granting solidity and steadiness to changes in the ideological sphere. In view of the compact social composition of the demonstrators, their realism in expectations of political change and their calmness and persistence, we may say that Serbian society has sprouted a germ of a social strata which, through political articulation of its interests and values, may represent the backbone in pursuing structural changes in society.

Finally, we may also say that the reef of the liberal and democratic efforts of the civil Serbia has, this time, inflicted irreparable damage on the ship of the regime. The economic, social and moral situation in Serbia and Yugoslavia has, as of the November 1996 elections, been aggravated by the onset of a profound political crisis. What will the outcome of this crisis be, and will this reef grow to become another island of democracy and economic stability in Eastern Europe? The response to this question depends on a series of specific features of the local social and economic situation. It is highly unlikely that we will have a delayed repetition of the "model" of the Czech Republic, Hungary or Poland. The chances are slim that a "great social coalition" of a few social groups can be formed in a situation of a clear "clash of structures and ideologies" (Bolčić, 1994). The sequence of historical events in Serbia was somewhat different than in the Central European countries mentioned. We did not have the characteristic interregnum where the political vacuum forced a few different social strata to jointly initiate the transformation of the social order (see Lazić, ed., 1995: 7–10). The old system (that of the SFRY) did not "collapse" as a whole but was sustained in a few newly formed states, enveloped in more or less exclusive nationalism, and crumbled in each of them separately and to a different extent. Before a sufficient portion of the Serbian population managed to recover from chauvinist madness, we already had a multi-party political system (though with a series of "inbred" deficiencies). At this point, when the general historical circumstances mentioned in the introduction to this article have sharpened the crisis of Serbian society the most, different social groups have the possibility to identify with the proclaimed objectives of different political parties.

Participants in the Belgrade protest understood the "lesson" of the Prague Spring. There, the protest reached the turning point when, after hesitating for a few days, workers joined the demonstrations. In the Belgrade protest, 57 percent of the participants interviewed thought that the easiest way to persuade the authorities to recognize their protest demands was by a general strike. Rated second in this respect was a long-lasting peaceful protest (34 percent), followed by pressure from abroad (33 percent). However, workers did not appear in the streets of Belgrade in substantial numbers, partly because they were burdened with daily survival on the gray economic market and partly because they did not have to identify with the values and objectives of the protest. They had an alternative in semi-programs of political parties that did not support the protest and had already emphasized that the burden of the initial steps toward transformation in Poland, Hungary, etc., had been borne precisely by the working class. Even if we agree that the social consciousness and self-identification of lower social strata are slower to mature and that in the current circumstances we have to wait longer for them to join the movement of transformation into a liberal social order, we still run the risk that these strata will simply "slip" from one system of traditionalist-populist attitudes (primarily pervaded by nationalism) into another, similar system (primarily marked by egalitarianism). "Transcendence of existence" (Mannheim) would remain outside their perceptive abilities, which would, *eo ipso*, deprive them of the possibility to mount an action toward a democratic transformation of the existing society, either alone or with another social group.

In view of the current marginalization of the main proponents of liberal and democratic ideas on the Serbian political scene, it is difficult to expect a relatively rapid denouement of the political situation in a favorable, democratic direction. The data presented here on the size and foundations of the democratic core in Serbian society reveal that some progress has been achieved compared with the previous civil protests. Still, given the overall social and economic situation in Serbia, a few more generations of students in Serbia will probably have to wear out their shoes protesting in city streets and squares so that their predecessors of 1991 may one day receive regular pensions enabling them a dignified life.

## Notes

1. For findings of these research efforts, see, e.g., Bolčić, 1994; Golubović et al., 1996; Lazić, ed., 1995.
2. The difference in the number of participants in this protest compared with the previous ones is quite pronounced, especially since the previous protests in Belgrade were also attended by citizens from "inland."
3. Only the student protest elicited a response at universities in Niš and Novi Sad.
4. The authors of the project classified these two types of answers separately so as to obtain another nuance in presenting the options of the demonstrators, i.e., to see to what extent the protest addressed Milošević directly or expressed a general demand for the change of rule.
5. The sum of percentages of the three answers is over 100 because the respondents could choose more than one answer.

## Bibliography

Bolčić, S. (1994): *Tegobe prelaza u preduzetnicko društvo* (Difficulties of transition to an entrepreneurial society), ISI FF, Belgrade.

Bolčić, S., ed. (1995): *Društvene promene i svakodnevni život: Srbija početkom devedesetih* (Social change and everyday life: Serbia in the early '90s), ISI FF, Belgrade.

Golubović, Z. *et al.* (1995): *Društveni karakter i društvene promene u svetlu nacionalnih sukoba* (Social character and social changes in the light of national conflicts), Filip Višnjić, Belgrade.

Gredelj, S. (1995): "Dominant Value Orientations" in: Lazić, M., ed., *Society in Crisis*, Filip Višnjić, Belgrade.

Lazić, M. (1994): *Sistem i slom* (System and breakdown), Filip Višnjić, Belgrade.

Lazić, M., ed. (1995): *Society in Crisis,* Filip Višnjić, Belgrade.

Lazić, M. (1995): "Osobenosti globalne društvene transformacije Srbije" (Specific features of the global social transformation of Serbia), in: Bolčić, S.

ed., *Društvene promene i svakodnevni život: Srbija početkom devedesetih* (Social change and everyday life: Serbia in the early '90s), ISI FF, Belgrade.

Lazić, M. (1996): "Delatni potencijal društvenih grupa" (Action potential of social groups), *Sociologija* XXXVIII.

Manhajm, K. (1978): *Ideologija i utopija* (Ideology and utopia), Nolit, Belgrade.

Vujović, S. (1995): "Urbana svakodnevica devedesetih godina" (Urban daily life in the '90s) in: Bolčić, S., ed., *Društvene promene i svakodnevni zivot: Srbija pocetkom devedesetih* (Social change and everyday life: Serbia in the early '90s), ISI FF, Belgrade.

Vujović, S. (1997): *Grad u senci rata* (City in the shadow of war), Prometej i ISS FF, Novi Sad and Belgrade.

# Citizens in Protest

*Vladimir Vuletić*

The first thing one notices about a phenomenon is what characterizes it on the outside. Moreover, just as it often turns out in everyday communication that more important than what you say is how you say it, in the same way the form of a social event is often decisive for its evaluation. I will not go into problematizing the relation between form and content. Anyway, quite a few theoreticians consider this division meaningful only as an analytical tool. Suffice it to say that, for numerous social phenomena or processes, the question of the form is inseparably linked with their content. Thus, for instance, a chain of social events may be qualified as a revolution or an evolution exclusively on the basis of seemingly formal elements such as their speed, density and degree of violence. All these elements are no doubt formal features, and yet they alone make it possible to define the nature of a process. But that is not all. Social activity is always oriented toward others. In communication with others, due to a large number of contacts and alienation, actors often resort to typifications based on external characteristics of the others' behavior. In this way they create images of others which become social facts. Specifically, if the behavior of another person reveals elements which allow this behavior to be defined (typified) as nationalistic, militaristic or otherwise, this typification itself becomes a social fact. That is the second important reason which makes it impossible to separate the social form from the social content.

## Behavioral characteristics of the protest

It is in that sense that we should understand the effort in this article to identify some elements of behavior of participants in the civil protest in

Belgrade in the winter of 1996–97. If it is possible at all to speak of the protest's form, then this was undoubtedly provided by the behavior of its participants. On the other hand, this formal characteristic of the protest has, in the domestic and international public, assumed features which are attributable to content. That is why the protest events have been referred to as peaceful, non-violent, imaginative or civic demonstrations more often than a middle-class revolt, anti-socialist demonstrations or the awakening of a modernizing or democratic movement in Serbia. Naturally, the reasons for bringing the formal characteristics of the protest to the fore do not have to be of an epistemological nature. Instead, they often derive from practical necessities of daily politics. Thus, for instance, although in terms of their contents there was practically no difference between the demands of the student protest and the civic one led by the *Zajedno* coalition, some representatives of the regime declared the students' demands to be justified while characterizing others as non-patriotic and opposed to the state's interest.

Bearing in mind all the above reservations, which will be alluded to in other parts of this book, the first part of this paper will analyze the formal characteristics of the 1996–97 civil protest, i.e., some elements of the protesters' behavior.

This analysis will primarily address the following: the frequency of the citizens' presence in street demonstrations, their behavior during the rallies and their views and evaluations of the events they themselves took part in. Finally, starting from the observation that perception of events may become a social fact, I will try to offer some thoughts on the prospect of further street demonstrations.

## Presence in the protest

The first question arising in this context concerns the length of time spent in demonstrations. Namely, over the past 10 years, since the beginnings of the political movement set in motion by Slobodan Milošević, hardly a year has passed without a mass manifestation of the people in the streets. In all these events only the speakers changed, while the people remained the same. Occasionally divided into opposing and even conflicting groups, the people asked for more justice, freedom and prosperity. Naturally, they also looked for an enemy responsible for the loss of these assets and identified the culprits as the leaders of the opposing group. In this research we seek to find out if the group who took part in the 1996–97 protest was the same one that has been looking for the lost Holy Grail for the last ten years.

Briefly, almost a fifth of the participants (18.7 percent) were taking part in a street protest for the first time. But most of them are less than 29 years old, and many of them, in view of their age, could hardly have manifested their revolt in the streets independently. All others—thus over 80 percent of participants—had already taken part in demonstrations. The overwhelming majority consisted of those who from 1991 onwards took part in only opposition rallies (70.4 percent). However, even they display certain differences. Of all the participants observed, 25.4 percent participated in all kinds of protest activities under the aegis of the opposition. Exactly as many (25.4 percent) participated only in meetings organized and called by the opposition, while a fifth of current participants (19.5 percent) joined the demonstrations only when they occurred spontaneously, i.e., were provoked by the conduct of the regime.

## Participants' behavior

We wanted to establish whether—in view of the diversity of the above categories—the participants displayed any differences in behavior during the demonstrations we are examining. We especially compared the cohorts of those with experience in demonstrations and first-time protesters, as well as those who only took part in spontaneous or opposition-organized rallies.

In both cases our initial assumption, that essential differences do exist, proved unfounded. True, some (statistically negligible) differences are revealed in the behavior of the "beginners" and the "experienced" demonstrators. Namely, the "experienced" attended the rallies somewhat more often (the difference is still about 5 percentage points). They also stayed longer and were more active in shouting slogans and in whistling. However, even this difference could be more easily ascribed to political affiliation, because the latter group included a larger number of members and sympathizers of one of the parties within the *Zajedno* coalition.

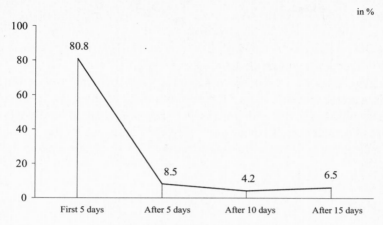

*Figure 1.* Time of joining the protest

Furthermore, statistically significant differences have not been noted even in the behavior of different categories of demonstrators, observed according to some socio-demographic characteristics. Generally speaking, most demonstrators participated in the protests from the beginning: the largest number of them joined in during the first five days of the protest (80.8 percent). In terms of their education, the vanguard include equal proportions of participants with elementary (76.9 percent), secondary (81.7 percent) and high (81.6 percent) education. A similar conclusion may be drawn by correlating the data on the age and sex of protesters and the time they joined the protest. Citizens over 55 years of age and women attended more often, but the differences still remain within a range of a few percentage points and may be considered statistically insignificant. More interesting is the fact that the inflow of new protesters did not subside even in the days that followed. In other words, the response of the citizens remained clear, so that even a fortnight after it started, the protest was joined by an additional 6.5 percent of demonstrators.

Naturally, this increase in numbers was not noticeable in the street due to the fluctuation of protest participants on two counts: first, the frequency of their presence and, second, the time spent in the protest.

Obviously, we could not interview those who might have taken part in the protests for fewer days and did not appear in the street during our

*Vladimir Vuletić*

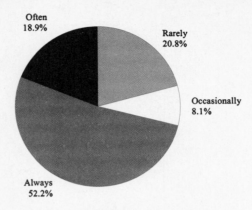

*Figure 2.* Frequency of attendance

survey. However, of those we did interview during a week—which is how long it took to collect the data in the field—only just over a half (52.2 percent) attended the rallies on a daily basis. The other half of intermittent participants may be subdivided into the following categories: occasionally present (one to three times)—8.1 percent, rarely present (four to ten times)—20.8 percent, and frequently present (eleven to seventeen times)—18.9 percent. Differences among adjacent groups with respect to education are small. As for attendance, citizens over 55 years of age took a particularly prominent role. Over two-thirds (67.9 percent) of members in this category attended the demonstrations every day. The smallest number of regular participants was registered among those under 30 (40 percent).[1] In addition, women were somewhat more devoted (55 percent) than men (49 percent). All these differences, however, could be interpreted primarily as resulting from the daily obligations of protest participants, since except for the university, all other institutions and enterprises continued operating normally (that is, for Serbian circumstances).

The fluctuation was, as already pointed out, also registered with respect to the time the citizens spent in the protest. Since at that time, the walks were unobstructed by the police,[2] the protest had a clearly defined program: assembling of protesters—walk—rally. The majority of citizens were present all the time (67.3 percent). The walks were preferred by 11.8 percent, 13.2 percent preferred the program, while 7.5 percent

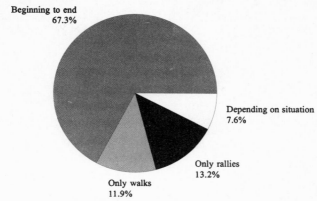

*Figure 3.* Participation in the protest

adjusted their behavior to their specific possibilities. In this respect, we may also note small differences with a similar distribution between different socio-demographic groups. Once again, the oldest citizens most often attended the entire gathering (75 percent), while the share of those in the most devoted group with the highest education was the smallest (57.1 percent). In addition, people with academic titles preferred walks to listening to the speakers. These data may also be best explained by the characteristics of daily life of individual categories of the population and psychological characteristics of individual groups. Mass and non-aggressive rallying undoubtedly enlivened the monotony and apathy of the daily, often lonely, life of the capital's senior citizens.

However, what makes the 1996–97 protest particularly impressive is its non-violent nature and, above all, the noise. Most participants (60 percent) stated that they either shouted slogans or whistled.[3] The remaining 40 percent merely attended the protests. It is interesting to look at the slogans the participants liked to shout most. The top-ranked slogan was the one from previous opposition rallies, "Red bandits!" which was the favorite of 15.0 percent of demonstrators. The slogan of the football fans, "Let's go, everyone attack!" which first appeared in opposition rallies, immediately gained popularity and was the first choice of 11.0 percent of citizens. But since this slogan may also be whistled to a tune, the number of its fans should include a part of those who merely whistled. Thus, one may say that this slogan marks the 1996–97 protest. In

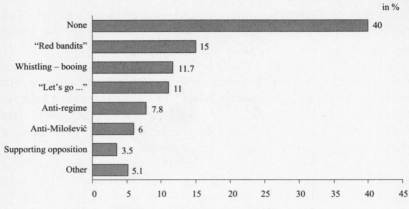

*Figure 4.* Slogans preferred by protest participants

addition to these two, the citizens listed a whole series of slogans aimed against the regime and Slobodan Milošević (13.7 percent), or in support of the opposition (3.5 percent). The most active in shouting slogans were party-affiliated citizens. Thus, over a half (54.1 percent) of politically unaffiliated citizens merely assisted the rallies, in contrast with the Serbian Renewal Movement (SPO) members, who were the noisiest and only a fifth of whom made no sound. Also fairly quiet were the most educated protest participants. Almost three-quarters of holders of doctorates and masters' degrees kept silent during the demonstrations, which could not be said of the participants with the lowest educational level, only a quarter of whom remained silent. In terms of the protesters' sex, women were more vociferous than men (57.8 percent : 42.2 percent). It is surprising, however, that the oldest participants were the noisiest. Only 17.3 percent of protesters over 66 years of age did not whistle or shout slogans.

We have already mentioned that the two most frequently shouted slogans owe their popularity to different groups of citizens. "Let's go, everybody attack!" was the most popular among the youngest participants of the protest (52.8 percent), while "Red bandits!" was cried most often by middle-aged people (55.6 percent). It is also interesting that slogans against Milošević were called out by the youngest participants the least frequently, which is no doubt the consequence of their focusing on the slogan "Let's go...."

In addition to the noise, an interested observer is probably most impressed with the non-violent nature of the demonstrations. It is almost inconceivable that in the Balkans tens of thousands of citizens—gathered in a mass which is, by definition, where individuals act the most irresponsibly—should demonstrate, day in, day out, for three months without causing a single major incident.[4] The reasons for such behavior are certainly diverse. Yet we should emphasize that the participants manifested strong civic self-consciousness. Namely, nearly all (93.1 percent) thought that the demonstrations should remain peaceful until the end. This, however, was not easy to ensure, not only due to frequent provocations of the regime (trying to cause unrest and thus justify the possible involvement of the police) but also due to the latent violence among the demonstrators. The fact that the need to keep the demonstrations peaceful is accepted on the cognitive level still does not ensure this outcome. The answers to the questions concerning the propriety of arresting the boys who hurled stones and broke window panes of the buildings of Radio Television Serbia (RTS) and daily *Politika* should be interpreted primarily as a gesture of solidarity with the arrested. However, there are grounds to assume that the 71.5 percent of respondents who considered the arrest unjustified simultaneously condoned manifestations of aggressiveness. This assumption, furthermore, suggests that violent behavior would not have been deprived of legitimacy, but that the demonstrators still believed that a peaceful protest was a more rational way to attain their objectives.

That is not all. Placing an emphasis on targeted rationality as an element determining the behavior of protest participants is justified if an irrational element—fear—is posed as its alternative. The most frequent reaction to the feeling of fear is either paralysis or manifest aggression. Neither could be seen on the faces of Belgraders who stood against a cordon of police armed to the teeth. Moreover, intimidation of citizens as a way to thwart the protest proved to be a poor choice of tactics by the regime. With every new provocation aimed at causing fear, a "reserve army of the protest" came to the aid of the hard core of the demonstrators—thus, the citizens who supported the protest and occasionally attended its rallies, went to the streets only if the regime or the police had caused an incident the previous day. In addition, our data suggest that most demonstrators left fear at home before going out into the street. This was shown by the answers to the question concerning the respond-

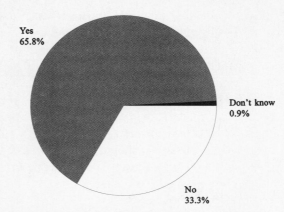

*Figure 5.* Readiness to hurl eggs in front of a police camera

ents' readiness to throw eggs (at one point a highly popular activity) even if they knew that they were being recorded by a police camera. A surprisingly high percentage of respondents (65.8 percent) answered in the affirmative. If there are no reasons to doubt the sincerity of their responses, this is certainly a good indicator to establish the limits of fear.

## Participants' perception of prospects

Finally, we should say that, while the protest was still going on, we tried to deal with the always problematic issue of the future prospects of the social phenomenon observed. To this end we selected some indicators to help us anticipate the outcome of the protest with some degree of reliability.

When asked whether they intended to support the protest actively until their demands were fulfilled, 98.2 percent of respondents said yes. However, we could not rely only on that information, since we assumed that it could tell us more about the respondents' subjective position and attachment to the protest than it could help evaluate their actual behavior. More indicative in judging the participants' behavior were the responses to a few other questions. Asked if they expected that the demands voiced

in %

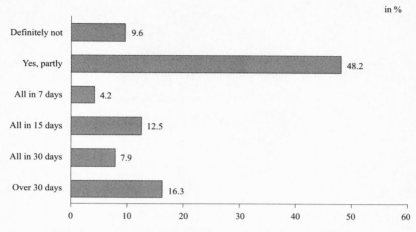

*Figure 6.* Fulfillment of demands — participants' expectations

in the protest would be fulfilled, a number of demonstrators responded negatively (9.6 percent). This percentage did not prove in itself that this subgroup might not be persistent. On the contrary, in a situation when people do not believe that their objectives will be attained but still persist in a certain activity, it should be assumed that they are guided by value-rational motives, which are often more powerful than instrumental ones. A much more important indicator suggesting potential vacillation over or abandonment of the protest is the high percentage of those who expected that their demands would be fulfilled only in part (48.2 percent). Again, this fact does not directly lead to the conclusion that these people would be content with the partial fulfillment of their demands, but it did start us thinking about the reasons for their disbelief.

We have already said that most participants crossed the limit of fear. However, a third of them were not ready to do anything that might seriously complicate their lives. Finally, the data on attendance of the rallies mentioned at the beginning show that only two-thirds of respondents belonged to a group which participated in the protest regularly or frequently. These data suggested, with a somewhat greater degree of reliability, that just over half of the respondents would persist in their demands until they were fulfilled.

*Vladimir Vuletić*

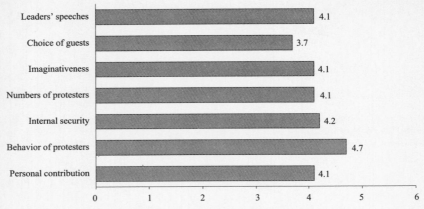

*Figure 7.* Participants' satisfaction with protest organization

On the other hand, a number of elements generated hopes that the protest would fulfill the expectations of its participants and actors. The first is the fact that the protest went on for another 50 days after this collection of articles was completed. In addition, the participants explained their persistence primarily by their own will to endure to the end. Finally, as emphasized at the beginning of this article, typification, i.e., perception of others' and even one's own behavior, also becomes a social fact. The protesters' high degree of satisfaction with various elements of protest organization reveals that the protesters felt safe, that they were not bored, that they trusted the speakers and, most importantly, that they were satisfied with themselves and the people around them. The epilogue of the events demonstrated that the persistence of the majority of participants overcame the wavering of the minority. In the end, the citizens left the streets of Belgrade at the moment when the city administration was taken over by the legally and legitimately elected authorities, i.e., when the newly established democratic political order was secured, if only for a while.

The establishment of this modern and democratic order (under the local circumstances) is the topic of the second part of this contribution.

## The modernizing nature of the 1996–97 protest

Though it seems obvious, it bears repeating that there are different levels of analysis and interpretation of phenomena depending on the angle and level of abstraction used in their observation. We must repeat this fact in order to justify the attempt to find a common denominator for a diverse phenomenon like a long-drawn-out protest of tens of thousands of people with different motives, intensity of aspirations, expectations and, ultimately, different objective interests. We seek to examine just how far down this diversity extends to cover the deeper levels where the phenomenon observed is manifested in a recognizable form.

Indeed, if a person travelling around the world who had passed through Belgrade on March 9, 1991, turned up in this same city in late November 1996, he would think, at first sight, that nothing had changed. Tens of thousands of people shouting and whistling, swearing at the president of their state and crying "Red bandits!" In front of them on the platform, the same people again—a clean-shaven Zoran Djindjić and a bearded Vuk Drašković, and next to them a diminutive woman, Vesna Pešić. However, even this observer would notice some changes: a completely different iconography, an absence of aggressiveness or violence, a much larger number of women and older people in the streets and their firm belief, which could be scented in the air, that what they fought for was right and deserved their persistence in the protest.

All these seemingly unimportant changes are still sufficient for us to ask whether something new was happening in Belgrade toward the end of 1996 and the beginning of 1997.

The response, actually the thesis I advocate in this paper, is that over the past six years, an essential change has occurred and that in the latter case it was a new protest which had a recognizable modernizing character, in contrast with the previous ones which aimed primarily at a political coup.

## Modernization theories

But before I try to explain this thesis, I have to make a few clarifications. These are related primarily to the very notion of modernization and its theory. First, the concept of modernization is understood differently in the context of modernization theory; second, the modernization theory has undergone a few changes itself. Finally, we can question the degree of adequacy of this theory, namely how applicable it is to the events we are discussing here.

I will deal with these theoretical problems in the briefest terms, only to the extent necessary for the purposes of this article, without going into a wider elaboration and problematization of the outlined issues.

The concept of modernization understood in its widest sense implies every change that can be measured on a scale of a consensually accepted understanding of social betterment. Taken this way, this concept obviously does not have a large analytical value and can therefore be considered almost impracticable. Classical theories of modernization have confined this concept to those processes which lead toward the transition of traditional societies into societies characterized by mechanical technologies, a rational and secular attitude toward life and a differentiated social structure. The subject of classical theories of modernization, and their golden age, was the modernization of Third World countries. Having sustained repeated criticism, these theories were revitalized in the late 1980s and early 1990s and reappeared in the form of new modernization theories focusing primarily on the issues of transformation of formerly socialist countries, or rather their joining of the developed world.

The concept of modernization in the new theories has not substantially changed. True, the historical content of the concept is less pronounced, since it led to an overemphasized ethnocentrism (in the form of Westernization). However, the parameters of modernization have remained, identifying it as a process which, at the structural level, leads toward increasing scientification, commercialization and mechanization (automation), urbanization, democratization, greater social mobility and rationalization; and, on the individual-psychological level, to an increased independence from the authorities, link with the public sphere, openness to new experience, orientation toward the future and faith in science and reason. In addition, the emphasis is still placed on the growing possibilities of choice as an essential determinant of modern society.

True, many of these characteristics of modernization have, in the view of most authors, lost some of their attractiveness to the Western world, but they may be considered worthy of pursuit by societies which have, until recently, been behind the Iron Curtain.

However, what is new in recent modernization theories compared with classical ones is reflected in a series of topics I will try to analyze below, on the basis of the available data.

1. In contrast with classical modernization theories based on observation of Third World countries and the conclusion derived therefrom that the enlightened governments of underdeveloped states have to modernize their countries from the top and make their tradition-oriented population embrace modern forms of life and work, the new modernization theories see the main protagonists of the process precisely in the masses[5] (the population, or parts thereof) who are working from the bottom up, from the margins of social life and, with the assistance of charismatic leaders, try to set the society on the road to modernization.

2. In this context, the impulse for the population to make the effort is its infatuation with the Western model of life—particularly its lifestyle, standard and freedoms—developed primarily under the influence of mass media, especially television.

3. While the classical theories brought the role of internal factors to the fore, the more recent theories increasingly emphasize the role of exogenous factors, namely the new world order and the geo-political balance—in other words, that of foreign assistance and influence on events in the transition countries.

4. Instead of the unilinear model of development, which is characteristic of the classical understanding of modernization, alternative models are now considered admissible.

5. Furthermore, contrary to the classical theories of modernization, the new ones do not assume an *a priori* negative attitude toward tradition. Far from it. Tradition is regarded as an element which may contribute to the modernization process, especially in countries which have a history of parliamentary life, democracy and capitalist economic system.

6. Significantly, the more recent modernization theories no longer insist on economic modernization as a precondition for overall modernization. On the contrary, they place the human factor in the foreground, i.e., emphasize the change of human consciousness as a prerequisite for economic growth.

7. Finally, new modernization theories do not radiate the optimism so characteristic of classical theories. Theoreticians of modernization

nowadays take a much more cautious view of the prospects of post-socialist societies and to a much larger extent emphasize the barriers to the modernization of these countries.

## What about Serbia?

Undoubtedly, one of the barriers to the process of modernization may be an untimely recognition of modernization potential and processes in post-socialist countries and, related to this, inadequate support from abroad. (This section is largely a reaction to offhanded assessments that the nature of the 1996–97 protest was nationalist.) In order to avoid that, it would be necessary to examine the modernizing potential of every specific social event in post-socialist countries much more comprehensively.

The discourse of the 1996–97 protest synonymously uses the phrase "the *Zajedno* coalition protest" with the greatest frequency. This description may be accepted to a certain extent, since the protest's purpose was to challenge the manipulation of the results of the second round of local elections in a dozen major towns in Serbia by the regime and primarily to the detriment of the political group—the *Zajedno* coalition. In addition, this coalition, or rather its leaders, were the ones to schedule the gatherings and generally run the protest. However, notwithstanding these conclusions and the agreement that on its manifest level the protest may also be referred to as the protest of the *Zajedno* coalition (or rather its members and sympathizers), the question of who the main proponents of the protest actually were remains open. The data obtained through the research clearly reveal that the members and sympathizers of parties within the *Zajedno* coalition accounted for only half the citizens gathered, while other protesters were politically undecided or members and supporters of other parties. Naturally, just as it is equally possible to say that a glass is half full or half empty, so these data may be interpreted in two ways, depending on the desired result.

It is indisputable that the specific tone of the protest has been provided precisely by sympathizers and members of the *Zajedno* coalition. (This may be concluded on the basis of the symbols and the behavior of different categories of demonstrators, i.e., the slogans and paraphernalia they used). It is also indisputable that they formed the core of the protest and were instrumental in resisting the diverse forms of manipulations and pressures the authorities employed to thwart it. (This may be judged on the basis of frequency of attending the demonstrations.) Yet politically unaffiliated citizens were also extremely active in the protest. This fact alone means that these events cannot be fully considered a protest organized by a single political group, but rather a phenomenon whose proponents are part of a population which—just as the first proposition of new modernization theories claims—are the prime movers of the protest.

The thesis that this was a mass protest may be substantiated by a few more indicators. Mass participation in the protests, in terms not only of numbers but also of quality, confirms the assumed lack of homogeneity of participants with respect to numerous socio-demographic and political characteristics[6] (see the article by M. Babović). In addition, the mass did not gather primarily to support the opposition or its leaders, as also revealed by the slogans heard at the rallies: slogans in support of opposition leaders were chanted by an exceptionally small number of protesters. Finally, the reasons for the endurance of the protests given by the participants themselves may also serve as a good indicator to judge its proponents. Most participants believe that the endurance of demonstrations can be attributed to the will of individuals and popular resistance.

All in all, we could say that this was primarily a mass and spontaneous protest led by the middle class. The role of political and cultural elites was small; moreover, the citizens obviously did not need this at all, as best shown by the fact that most of them were not particularly glad to have the support of any of the elite and did not expect it. (It is interesting that only 8 percent of respondents were pleased with the support of a certain member of a political or cultural elite, and only a slight fraction more—11 percent—stated that they would like to see a particular elite member at the rostrum.)

Another proposition of new modernization theories maintains that the population in socialist countries is infatuated with the West, or rather Western lifestyles and freedoms.[7] That is, according to the proposition, the key guiding motive of the proponents of change. To what extent does this proposition apply to the 1996–97 protest in Belgrade? This is a very interesting question in view of the specific position of Yugoslavia in the history of the world and the specific historical position of Serbia over the past two centuries. Its geographic position on the border of two civilizations, with a nation divided into areas which have long belonged to different worlds, accounts for the fact that the West is approached with ambivalent feelings. A similar conclusion may be drawn if we observe only the second half of the 20th century, marked by the Cold War division of the world, with Yugoslavia sitting on the fence. However, our survey—in view of its objectives and the conditions of its implementation—could not include the heterogeneous indicators on the basis of which we could reliably establish the actual degree of possible infatuation with the West among protest participants and the degree to which they really embrace Western values and standards of social life. Thus, I here rely on only one piece of information, one revealing the subjective attitude of the respondents. Asked if Serbia should build a social system similar to that in Western Europe, nearly all respondents (92.9 percent) answered affirmatively. It is, therefore, obvious that protest participants almost all prefer the Western model of organization of social life. In addition, an indirect indicator of this effect may also be found in the expected direction of change. The main change expected after a possible downfall of the existing regime has to do with the attainment of more freedoms, i.e., the emphasizing of freedoms as one of the main elements of the liberal ideology.

The influence of the foreign factor has been remarkably conspicuous throughout Eastern Europe. Therefore, it was only to be expected that it would also be felt in the protest in Serbia. Naturally, in this territory, foreign influence has, throughout history, been manifested in various ways, and one's allies outside the country's borders have always been taken into account, even in internal political struggles. This fact has, in a very specific way, been repeated in this particular case. Intensive contacts of both sides with foreign politicians, visits of different personalities and delegations to Belgrade on the occasion of the protest and the specific iconography of the protest itself (the waving of foreign flags), all indicate the importance of the foreign factor on processes unfolding in this country. This is also confirmed by the participants themselves, almost a quarter of whom (24.9 percent) believed that only external pressure could persuade the authorities to honor the victory of the opposition on the local elections. True, most participants did not attribute to the foreign factor decisive influence on the events in Serbia, but they did note its importance (just as suggested by the third proposition of new modernization theories). (In the end, it was precisely the influence of the international factor, i.e., the visit of the OSCE mission headed by Felipe Gonzalez, which prevailed upon the authorities to acknowledge electoral results.)

Since the empirical research did not seek to examine the hypotheses of any of the various theories of social change, but was more of a descriptive nature, we lack the complete data to identify the modernization model which comes closest to the movement embodied in the 1996–97 protest. Still, in view of a series of factors, one may assume that the Eastern European model was observed. Just as in Eastern Europe during the transformations, this protest displayed an aspiration to change both the political and economic systems; a wish for rapid change; the focus on political change as a precondition for economic transformation, which would mark a transition to the capitalist economic system; insistence on peaceful change; the particularly pronounced importance of the media (shown by the fact that the protest targeted the most important media houses in the country and that a storm of protest ensued after the regime attempted to terminate the few remaining independent media); and, finally, as already explained, the importance of international support, although we must also mention some concern that, due to their various interests, the international community will not resolutely take the side of protest proponents. All these characteristics may be illustrated using the data of our survey (Balcerowicz, 1995).

Furthermore, speaking of the role of tradition, the Yugoslav case largely corresponds to the above proposition on the positive role tradition may have in modernizing processes. This assumption is founded on the fact that, in the first half of this century, Serbia set out on the road to modernization following all the rules applicable in the leading Western European countries since the beginning of the 19th century (Zbornik, 94). In addition, references to the traditional friendship and alliance with America and the leading democracies of Europe in the previous wars also encourage a democratic transformation of Serbia. Generally, references to tradition in Eastern European countries, in view of the discontinuity caused by the rule of socialist regimes, do not have the meaning usually assigned to them, namely that of glorifying the pre-modern forms of social organization.

Finally, just like theoreticians of modernization, the protest participants are also aware of the barriers on the road to modernization which they support. This is most convincingly evidenced by different, often seemingly contradictory understandings of the scope and prospects of their efforts. The following are a few notable examples. While almost all participants (98.3 percent) declared their intention to continue in the protest until all their demands were fulfilled, many of them also believed that their demands would not be met in full (58.2 percent) or not at all (9.6 percent). In addition, although almost half the participants (43.5 percent) believed that the fulfillment of their requests required a general strike, it is quite clear that, in view of the distribution of participants, one could hardly expect the more substantial support of industrial and other workers necessary to make a general strike meaningful. But this is not all. Although swift and radical change was desired, most people (67.4 percent) simultaneously believed that, under the circumstances, the list of protest demands should not be expanded. All this leads to the conclusion that this was a protest of responsible people, aware of the limits and barriers in their way. It is clear, however, that faced with this discrepancy between aspirations and actual possibilities, most participants opted to persist peacefully in their demands until these were met. Precisely these people formed the nucleus of a population which is usually referred to as "the other Serbia."

## Conclusion

On the basis of these observations and, admittedly, incomplete data, the 1996–97 protest may be described as a part of a modernizing process (transition) according to a model which has already been used in Eastern European countries. In other words, in contrast with previous opposition protests, the protest of 1996–97 is an example of revolt similar to the protests in Eastern Europe that led to the overthrow of communism.[8] Its specifics derive from the fact that the degree of the political and general culture of the local population, namely the part which participated in the protest, is substantially higher, given its different experience during the era of socialism and a specific sort of catharsis after years of war in the territories of the former Yugoslavia. The main adversary to this kind of protest is the ruling authoritarian regime which, at least on a declarative level, pursues an alternative model of modernization, from the top down. This alternative model is characterized primarily by: an authoritarian political system (thus precisely what the protest participants object to about the current president most—his style of rule); an attempt to carry out modernization without actually changing the existing political system (which was the main motive for the protests— reaction to the refusal of the regime to relinquish power to the opposition in large towns and thus make real its nominal political pluralism), namely by limiting itself to changes in the economy, and even that only timidly; absolute control of the media; and, finally, substantial reliance on Western powers.

On the other hand, new questions are also being raised. First, does the modernizing process, whose proponents were the participants in the 1996–97 protest—in view of its relatively narrow class-stratal basis— have sufficient potential to incorporate, or at least win the support of, wider strata of the population and thereby prevail over the modernizing model supported by the narrow state-political elite?

Another important question—in view of the unstable geopolitical situation and the latent problem of Kosovo and Metohija—is this: is there a danger that, in a situation marked by ethnic conflicts, the initiated process may assume a different nature and give in to the possible challenges of nationalism? This question makes sense in view of the experience of less than seven years ago, when the top-down modernizing process initiated during the government of Ante Marković was suppressed by chauvinist hysteria in all republics of the former Yugoslavia.

The first question is difficult to answer definitively, since it depends on the interaction of a series of factors (behavior of the regime, foreign powers, the situation in the region, happenstance), but there is no doubt that the most important of these are the persistence and firmness of citizens.

The second question is also delicate, but the answer to it can be glimpsed on the basis of the collected empirical data. Namely, a remarkably small number of the 1996–97 protest participants were extremely nationally oriented (see the contribution by S. Cvejić), and we may therefore assume that the nationalist challenge would be resisted.

There are two more questions indirectly linked with the 1996–97 protest, more specifically, with the behavior of the regime in Serbia and of the world powers. In any case, regardless of the outcome of these events, there is no doubt that Serbia must take the course of modernization; it is a question of survival even for the existing regime. The dilemma—modernization or ruin—is central for the regime, too, because unless the overall conditions and standard of living are improved, it will soon be faced with protests by that part of the population whose support it currently counts on and passively enjoys. The only question that remains is the one of the price of alternative models of modernization—whether a repeat of the events in Tiananmen Square in 1989 would be too high a price.

On the other hand, the question is whether the international community will firmly stand by its proclaimed protection of democratic rights in all countries of the world, or whether the logic of capital and higher geostrategic interests will override political and moral principles, as in the case of China.

True, compared to China, whose modernization model is obviously emulated by the current regime, Serbia does not have power or international influence. More importantly, the Serbian regime has already made some compromises (changes in the political system, complete loss of control over a part of the media) which do not allow it to pursue its line as consistently as the Chinese leadership and which force it to play a double game which, in the long run, will invariably end in disaster.

## Notes

1. This is only understandable, since this category comprises the largest number of students, who could not participate in two protests at the same time.

2. The regime initially misjudged the prospects of the demonstrations. Expecting the situation to calm down quickly and not wishing to add oil to the fire started by the electoral fraud, the regime was content simply to impose a media blackout on the events in Belgrade for the first few days. However, as soon as it appeared that the protest was starting to subside, when the number of people in the streets was obviously reduced compared with the previous days, the police turned up in unreasonably large strength, wishing to show who was the "boss." After that, the game of "who is the master of the street" between the demonstrators and the police continued for days, until the police withdrew before the students walking with the Serbian Patriarch.

3. We must note that this research was done in the first half of December, after only about 20 days of the protest, so that the data stated here are not entirely adequate. Namely, at that time, the whistles were not yet widely sold, and the banging on pots, pans and the like at 7:30 p.m., during the broadcast of the state TV daily news, had not yet become a daily routine.

4. Even when the regime tried to organize a counter-rally (December 24, 1996) and demonstrate its legitimacy to the world, bringing into a seething Belgrade tens of thousands of its confused supporters from outside the capital, there were no large-scale incidents, and it all ended in occasional clashes between supporters of two rival groups.

5. New modernization theories do not define the concept of the mass precisely enough; this obviously refers to the part of the population which counters the ruling elite.

6. In this context, we could propose a hypothesis of the primarily class nature of the protest, in view of the clear over-representation of the new middle strata and a remarkably small number of industrial workers who account for the largest share of the employed. However, it appears to me that the class theory cannot fully account for all the relevant aspects of the 1996–97 protest, and so I have not used it as a framework for data analysis here.

7. More than that, precisely an infatuation with the West is interpreted as a motive for modernization. However, we must also note the views that socialism, too, had a modernizing character. Theoreticians of modernization, however, mostly believe that the socialist society had a quasi-modernizing character (Sztompka, 1995).

8. Previous protests in Belgrade and other towns in Serbia were nationally covered to a much larger extent, although that could not have been avoided given the situation in the territory of the former Yugoslavia at that time.

## Bibliography

Balcerowicz, L. (1995): *Socialism, Capitalism, Transformation*, CEU Press, Budapest, London and New York.

Lazić, M., ed. (1995): *Society in Crisis*, Filip Višnjić, Belgrade.

Marković, J.P. (1996): *Beograd izmedju istoka i zapada 1948-1965* (Belgrade between East and West 1948–1965), Službeni list SRJ, Belgrade.

Sztompka, P. (1994): *The Sociology of Social Change*, Blackwell, Oxford, U.K. and Cambridge, Massachusetts.

Zbornik (Collection of papers) (1994): *Srbija u modernizacijskim procesima XX veka* (Serbia in modernizing processes of the 20th century), INIS, Belgrade.

# Social and Political Consciousness of Protest Participants

*Vladimir Ilić*

An attempt to look into the ideological preferences and the wider meaning of a practical political effort implies the use of two key analytical concepts: that of a vision of a desirable society, i.e., desirable directions of social change; and the perception of the public enemy, i.e., the most important obstacles to the intended practical objectives. Since the questionnaire used in the research was not essentially designed to look into the problems we are dealing with in this article, it has almost completely failed to grasp the problems related to the latter key analytical concept, while its coverage of the former is substantially limited. Nevertheless, the available evidence is sufficient for at least a partial interpretation of this specific subject. I believe that, if the analysis left out the ideological dimension of mass political protests which were held in the streets of Belgrade for months, it might strengthen the influence of daily politics and the Manichaean logic in the sociological research of this specific phenomenon. Furthermore, the decision to carry on with this line of analysis was reinforced by the increasing tendency of denying any ideological character to political events in present-day Serbia, recently manifested in numerous works of domestic political scientists. These scientists show an obvious inclination to ideologically neutralize the events in this country and present them as a mere struggle for power of competing elites. This approach—although understandable if applied in practical politics or insufficiently elaborated social integrative thought—becomes highly dangerous in cognitive terms if allowed to act as a factor channeling sociological analysis. It largely reduces a scientific study of political phenomena and processes to ideological support of a specific practical policy and thereby not only instrumentalizes the scientific analysis itself, but also limits its scope without actual scientific justification. On the other hand, examination of the ideological dimension of the political phenomena observed enables us to detrivialize the problems. The study of this aspect looks beyond the struggle for power of the competing elites to uncover the profound social divisions and the real conflict of interests among the opposing smaller and larger groups. This reveals events and processes that are much more lively and substantial. Their social consequences are, in the Balkans, often incomparably more brutal than they may seem to the actors or analysts of these events who either make no effort or fail to establish the necessary distance from the political consciousness of the participants themselves.

It hardly needs emphasizing that the study of the ideological dimension of a specific political phenomenon or process observed remains a mere description unless it accounts for the link with the real interest-based group divisions. The background material collected for the purpose of this research gives no specific evidence relevant for these divisions. However, the data on the most important social characteristics of protest participants provide the guidelines for establishing a number of important points.

## Outlines of protest participants' social profile

The introductory part of this article explains the need to include the study of this subject into a wider collective research effort. The fact that this collection includes specific articles dealing with the social basis of the protests allows me to avoid dwelling on this subtopic in great detail. The Belgrade protest is an essentially civil protest, primarily because it represents a movement of the urban middle strata, with hardly any workers or peasants. The absence of peasants may be partly explained by the location of the protest, while the negligible participation of workers clearly reveals the social background of the protagonists. Suffice it to mention only a few data:

Out of the total number of participants, only 2 percent[1] were industrial workers, while 4 percent were manual workers in the services sector. A relatively high share of pensioners should not deceive the analysts: as many as 55 percent of the total number of interviewed pensioners were retired professionals, and only 7 percent of them had intermediate education. Studies of voters' behavior in the Republic of Serbia usually point out that the pensioners provide the mass base for the ruling coalition. However, they invariably forget to mention that the pensioners are, strata-wise, a highly heterogeneous group and that efforts to define their position on the stratification ladder with respect to their previous profession and/or position of their family in the class-strata structure are fairly justified. This piece of information indicates that by far the largest number of pensioners who took part in the protest belonged to the middle class. As for intragroup divisions, we should certainly point out that an otherwise very small group of interviewed workers did not include a single one without intermediate education, i.e., skill. The Belgrade protest was marked not only by a class but also, by a highly pronounced urban, character. An overwhelming 84 percent of its participants lived in the very center or central districts of the capital. In view of these characteristics, the protest revealed itself as isolated from groups in the lower part of the social structure in both social and spatial terms.

## Consistency vs. confusion

The link between the social composition of actors of political phenomena and processes, on the one hand, and their ideological affiliations, on the other, although disregarded in recent times, is far from simple or direct. Members of the same social groups may, for different reasons, pursue mutually discordant and occasionally even opposite social objectives. In any case, before we examine the ideological contents advocated or supported by protest participants, the analysis should, at least briefly, address the consistency of their basic convictions. Namely, people often participate in events whose real meaning they find neither clear nor transparent. Thus the fact that the undesired consequences of one's choice substantially depart from the consciously selected objectives is not unusual in social life. One need only recall the large number of voters with a nationalist orientation who rejected the pacifist policy of the Yugoslav prime minister in the 1992 elections and actually voted for the Dayton–Paris peace accords which, at least temporarily, put an end to the militant Serbian policy. The awareness of the real purpose of political elections is, as a rule, a rare phenomenon, by the very fact that this implies an insight into the undesirable or unintentional (but necessary) consequences of one's own political behavior (Weber, 1921).

This article will consider the consistency of attitudes toward some key ideas on the basis of two examples, available in view of the contents of the questionnaire. About 34 percent of the total number of respondents expressed their complete agreement with the view that justice cannot be achieved without material equality. But as many as three-fifths of the respondents who fully accepted an expressly egalitarian view were in complete agreement with the statement that social progress can rest only on private property. Obviously, many respondents declared their complete agreement with two statements that express completely opposed views. In order to outline the phenomenon discussed as clearly as possible, our attention is focused on respondents who asserted the maximum degree of agreement with both positions. Equality in material terms and affirmation of private ownership are clearly mutually incompatible not only for impartial analysts of social relations but also for those who promote different variants of liberal ideology. This is obviously not so for a fairly large number of respondents who participated in the protest and is revealing of their inability to perceive undesirable consequences in the event that their endeavors succeeded.

Similar results are observed by comparing the answers to the questions on the desirability of building a Western-European-type system with reactions to the already mentioned statement concerning the inseparable link between material equality and (social) justice. As many as 93 percent of the total number of respondents opted for the construction of a social system for modern Serbia similar to those now existing in Western Europe. But among these respondents with a pro-European orientation, only 29 percent completely rejected affirmation of equality in material terms, as opposed to as many as 34 percent who accepted it completely. Substantial characteristics of Western European societies may be perceived in different ways, but they certainly do not include the affirmation of egalitarian values. It is obvious that a large part of protest participants was completely unaware of the real meaning of their own strategic options concerning alternative lines of social development.

## Profession and social-political consciousness

One may rightly assume that the profession of respondents largely determined their political beliefs and behavior. The overall social profile of participants clearly reveals the civil, urban and middle-class nature of the protest. However, the interpretation of findings related to this sub-topic is rather problematic not only due to the realized structure of the sample by professions but also because of a largely fragmented frame-work for classification. It is much more difficult to analyze nuances in the acceptance or rejection of specific ideological contents within the same wider stratum than on a sample consisting of a sufficient number of members of different social classes. The distribution of the realized sample, therefore, defines the technique of the analysis. In that sense specific attention will be devoted to answers that express the complete rejection of certain statements by some professions, since this may sharpen the focus necessary to carry out the given task.

For the purposes of this article, certain characteristics of group con-sciousness which are, otherwise, directly addressed by socio-psycho-lôgical research are observed as dimensions of the protesters' ideologi-cal options. In that context, the concept of ideology is understood in its neutral meaning, namely as denoting a specific social-political conscious-ness of respondents, without going into the truthfulness of its contents (Mannheim). One such dimension of the protesters' consciousness is authoritarianism. This characteristic was examined by measuring the respondents' agreement with two statements. The first proposed that the most important thing for the success of a group was to have an energetic and just leader whom everybody would obey. This statement elicited complete disagreement from 29 percent of respondents and complete agreement from 28 percent. According to professional distribution, highly educated professionals led in the rejection of this statement, followed by managers and the unemployed, who also registered above-average re-jection of this view. All other groups rejected this statement to a lesser degree. Particularly interesting is the fact that the share of secondary-school and college students in this group (18 percent) was lower than the one of pensioners (26 percent). The second statement that may serve as an indicator of authoritarianism is the one that a nation without a leader is like a man without a head. While this position was rejected by 31 percent of the total number of respondents, 35 percent completely agreed with it. Complete rejection was most pronounced among entre-preneurs (44 percent). Secondary-school and college students completely rejected this position in only 21 percent of cases. On the other hand, 56 percent of pensioners completely agreed with it, while the intensity of acceptance of other groups was about average. These findings do not

*Photo:* Perica Vujanić

*Photo:* Dejan Tasić

*Photo:* Draško Gagović

*Photo:* Perica Vujanić

*Photo:* Perica Vujanić

*Photo:* Boris Subašić

*Photo:* Imre Sabo

*Photo:* Perica Vujanić

*Photo:* Miroslav Petrović

*Photo:* Draško Gagović

*Photo:* Vesna Pavlović

*Photo:* Draško Gagović

*Photo:* Miloš Bicanski

require any specific comment at this point. Suffice it only to point to a small share of extremely authoritarian secondary-school and college students in their own subgroup (about a fifth). It is also interesting that an ambivalent relation of respondents toward authoritarianism was coupled with a high acceptance of parliamentarism, measured through the view that a state president must be subjected to Parliament. This statement elicited agreement from a decisive 83 percent of respondents, although the respective shares of groups consisting of secondary-school and college students, the unemployed and technicians were somewhat below the average. The widespread firm commitment to parliamentarism reflects a concrete historically conditioned acceptance of a dogma characteristic of all lines of the present-day Serbian opposition, since it does not have a single personality who could compete with Milošević as a political leader. Bearing in mind the responses to previous questions, one gets the impression that the parliamentary orientation of protest participants was largely influenced by daily politics and that the appearance of a credible opposition leader may substantially change it.

The authoritarianism of protest participants is definitely not a situationally conditioned phenomenon. Numerous research studies by B. Kuzmanović reveal that "a paternalistic leader is required—a model of a just, strict and energetic father," and that the social consciousness of the Serbian population has long been marked by a "craving for leaders and idealization of the leader's role" (Kuzmanović, 1997: 15). In research carried out in 1989–1990, the statement that a nation without a leader is like a man without a head elicited the agreement of as many as 77 percent of Serbs in Serbia (Kuzmanović, 1995).

The view that a nation that does not cherish its tradition deserves to perish may be indicative of traditionalism in the context of this analysis. It elicited complete disagreement from 7 percent of respondents and complete agreement from as many as 65 percent. Complete rejection of this statement was the most pronounced among professionals, while pensioners (85 percent), clerks (81 percent) and entrepreneurs (72 percent) took the lead in accepting it completely. On the other hand, xenophobia was substantially less widespread among protest participants than broadly defined traditionalism. The statement that a man should not trust foreigners too much met with complete disagreement from 22 percent of respondents and complete agreement from 29 percent. Those who fully rejected this statement did not display large differences according to professions, while pensioners led among the xenophobic group (a resounding 48 percent fully agreed with this statement). It is interesting that the respondents, although divided on the xenophobic statement, manifested a remarkably pro-European orientation. An overwhelming 93 percent agreed with the statement that Serbia should build a social system similar to those in Western Europe, displaying only minimum differences between members of specific professions, although entrepreneurs were still far ahead of others with a share of 100 percent.

These results, observed as a whole, outline the social and political consciousness of protest participants, which is heterogeneous and even controversial. Six-sevenths were firmly in favor of parliamentarism, but less than a third manifested remarkable authoritarianism. Traditionalists were nine times more numerous than radical anti-traditionalists, while almost all of them expressed a pro-European orientation, accompanied by a high degree of xenophobia. Inconsistency in responses indicates that the political consciousness of protest participants was not fully conceived and suggests that they could be manipulated considerably.

A deeper analysis demands observation of responses concerning the preferences related to the acceptance of egalitarianism versus private-ownership (pro-capitalist) orientation. Overall findings in this respect have already been mentioned. But we should recall that the frequency of complete disagreement with the egalitarian statement amounted to 29 percent in the whole sample. Entrepreneurs were the most numerous in their thorough rejection of egalitarianism (47 percent), while appropriate frequencies for the (few) workers in services and industrial production were low, as expected (11 percent and zero percent of their total number in the sample, respectively). In this sense, responses to this question according to the profession of respondents suggest the class character of the Belgrade protest, although we must not lose sight of the fact that complete acceptance of the egalitarian statement in the whole sample was higher than its rejection (34 percent : 29 percent).

This subtopic becomes even more interesting if we, once again, take into account the responses to the statement that social progress can rest only on private property. This statement was completely rejected by only 5 percent of respondents, compared with 52 percent who completely agreed with it. However, we must note that entrepreneurs (72 percent) and pensioners (71 percent) were far ahead of others in agreeing completely with this statement, while secondary-school and college students and the unemployed supported it in only 44 percent of cases. This clearly reveals that the firm pro-capitalist orientation is interest-based, and the high share of the retired may only be surprising if we disregard their educational profile, as explained above. From this angle, we may single out a core of protest participants which, in social terms, had greater awareness of its interests and perceived a practical, particular advantage in the overthrow of the existing social order more clearly than other groups. With this observation in mind, some other research findings appear less surprising, however unexpected they may seem at first sight, e.g., the proportionally lower share of secondary-school and college students than pensioners among the supporters of radical authoritarianism.

## Radicalism and pragmatism

Radicalism in political demands is structurally only partially defined; it depends more on the practical evaluation of possibilities for efficient action under the given circumstances. While considering the perception of protest demands by profession of respondents, we have taken into account only the demand the respondents rated first (in order to facilitate this review). The responses have been classified into minimalist demands, namely those requiring that electoral results be honored, and radical ones, including requests to change the regime and depose Milošević. This classification gives us a frequency of 51 percent of minimalist demands compared with 27 percent of the radical ones, bearing in mind that, as already noted, we only took into account the first response of the respondents, and they may have listed a number of others. Professionals are proportionally the most represented in the group of minimalists. Pensioners are their polar opposite: only 32 percent of them insisted primarily on the respect of electoral results. Pensioners, on the other hand, had a leading share in the group voicing radical demands (31 percent of this group's members). In their case, the real interest was coupled with the fact that their advanced age leaves them less time to wait for the desired change. The usual treatment of pensioners as being outside the class-stratal structure is unfounded, as is revealed by the responses concerning the wishes for the expansion of protest demands. Opposition to the expansion of protest demands was expressed by 60 percent of respondents, as opposed to 13 percent who were in favor of their radicalization. However, even 25 percent of the total number of interviewed pensioners expressed support for expanding the demands, i.e., radicalizing the protest.

Radicalism of protest participants may also be observed at an individual level through the answers concerning the participants' reasons to join the protest. Sixty-one percent of respondents stated that the main reason for their participation in street events was their desire for justice and freedom of vote, 22 percent mentioned their desire to overthrow communism or depose Slobodan Milošević and 14 percent a wish to build a society similar to the ones in Western Europe, etc. Radicalism manifested through the demand for the overthrow of communism or Milošević's rule is unevenly distributed among respondents of different professions. It was manifested by less than 20 percent of professionals but by 39 percent of entrepreneurs along with 37 percent of managers. One almost gets the impression that members of intellectual professions were, in this respect, characterized by idealism of a specific kind, while the well-off strata demonstrated a sober understanding of their own narrow group interests and— at least when their representatives who took an active part in the protest are concerned—an active wish to see them implemented as soon as possible. The fact that many members of the socialist managerial strata transferred to a new bourgeois class accounts for their interest in the overthrow of socialist rule (cf. Lazić, 1995).

The reasons for joining the protest were, in the consciousness of participants, certainly linked with the images of concrete advantages expected from the establishment of a new, more desirable social system after the downfall of the existing regime. The most frequent responses to this question have been classified in two groups: one includes those who emphasized the importance of the dignity and freedom they expected to gain in post-Milošević Serbia, while the other includes those expressing expectations of a growing social standard and a higher degree of safety for the respondents and their children. The first type of response could be conditionally assigned an idealistic motivation in the neutral meaning of the concept, while the second type may serve as an indicator of pragmatism. At the level of the whole sample, these two types of answers had almost equal shares (45 percent : 42 percent). The pensioners were exceptionally pragmatic: 35 percent wished to enjoy freedom and dignity after the collapse of the current authorities, compared with 48 percent who stressed practical advantages. Strongly pragmatic were professionals in social services who shared in the two types of answers with 22 and 72 percent, respectively. It is interesting that the otherwise small group of industrial workers among protest participants demonstrated what might be conditionally called an idealistic orientation in 20 percent of cases, compared with the pragmatic one in a decisive 70 percent of cases. It is, therefore, obvious that expectations from the outcome of social and political processes, manifested through the Belgrade protest in a condensed form, were diverse and dependent on group membership. In order to sustain the political potential of protest participants, it was necessary to have an ideological orientation in which both elements mentioned above would have to be prominent so as to preserve the unified action of this large and in many ways heterogeneous group of people. However, the manifested diversity of expectations, as well as the narrow real interests of groups of protest participants, did not jeopardize the previously outlined middle class and urban nature of the protest. We would like to emphasize that the political unity of protest participants was not a static characteristic and that their differences were a challenge for the ideological and manipulative skills of leaders of the rival political blocs and their professional advisers. I will address their success in using this skill in the concluding remarks.

## Parties and the Belgrade protest

Examination of the influence of parties on the social-political consciousness of protest participants is substantially limited by the contents of the instrument applied, the small number of party members among the respondents and a large diversity of the sample with respect to the party identification of its members. All that notwithstanding, the importance of this subtopic imposes the need to undertake an additional risk and, using the analysis of certain views of members and sympathizers of specific political parties, try to deepen the understanding of the basic problem.

In view of the definitely insufficient number of supporters of the Civic Alliance of Serbia and the Serbian Radical Party in the sample, the analysis focuses on members and sympathizers of the Democratic Party (DS), the Serbian Renewal Movement (SPO) and the Democratic Party of Serbia (DSS). The unevenly developed ideologies of these parties reveal the coexistence of various conservative, liberal and modernized conservative ideological contents in variants reflecting their specific characteristics in the Balkans. Indicators of the social-political consciousness used in previous interpretations proved unevenly discriminatory with respect to party identification of the interviewed protest participants.

In terms of the observed characteristic, there seem to be no differences in the participants' rejection of xenophobia. Complete disagreement with the previously mentioned statement taken as an indicator of xenophobia was manifested by 27 percent of members of the DS, 21 percent of the SPO and 22 percent of the DSS, or 23, 20 and 19 percent of these parties' supporters respectively. Answers to the questions concerning the link between private property and social progress are so scattered that they are not worth quoting. On the other hand, some other questions revealed greater differences. The statement used to measure traditionalism elicited complete agreement from 40 percent of members of the DS, 78 percent of the SPO and 87 percent of the DSS. The corresponding frequencies for sympathizers of these parties are 59, 75 and 71 percent, respectively. It is interesting that complete disagreement with the statement used to measure egalitarian orientation was manifested by 47 percent of DS members, 24 percent of SPO members and 22 percent of DSS members, while the corresponding results for sympathizers of these parties were 30, 18 and 45 percent, respectively. The responses to the last two questions show that the Democratic Party was the only one whose members among the protest participants had mature ideas and expressed views relatively consistent with the party program. This may indicate good prospects for this party to take the leading role in opposing the current regime. As for political radicalism, which is (let us recall) measured by the readiness to expand the protest demands, members of the DSS were in the lead, as expected. Members of this party felt less obliged than others to observe the requests of protest organizers, because the DSS executives were not included in the leadership of the protest. Only 22 percent of this party's members opposed the expansion of protest demands, compared with 57 and 53 percent of the DS and SPO members, respectively. But the radicalism of the DSS supporters substantially declines if the analysis incorporates responses of sympathizers of this party, 64 percent of whom opposed the expansion of protest demands, while the corresponding percentages for the sympathizers of the DS and the SPO were 55 and 63. The widespread public image of the DSS as an extremely nationalist party has been confirmed by the responses of its members to the question about the most important objection to Milošević. Failure in resolving the national question as Milošević's biggest mistake was mentioned by 7 percent of the DS, 18 percent of the SPO and 44 percent of the DSS members. But, while anti-socialist radicalism, traditionalism and pronounced nationalism of the interviewed members of the DSS appear to be in harmony with the program of this party, the situation is different with the previously mentioned low level of explicit anti-egalitarianism among them. We should repeat the general impression that, judging by the results of this research, the DS is the only party with a large membership whose members have relatively consistent social and political consciousness. This particular finding is more important for the evaluation of the potential of this party to take the leading role in a possible new social movement than is the total share of supporters of individual parties among the protest participants. Moreover, the discord between the diffuse and often controversial social and political consciousness of the movement's participants and the relatively consistent party consciousness of the DS members is certainly not seen as handicapping the latter. Historical experience in many ways suggests that small, tightly integrated parties may take the lead of mass political movements, especially if these unfold largely spontaneously and take on the characteristics of street events.

## Concluding remarks

The examination whose findings have been presented in this article had to assume the nature of a secondary analysis. A more demanding undertaking would involve the verification of assumptions developed in advance through a specifically devised tool. Secondary analysis always involves a danger of using *ad hoc* explanations of appropriate nature. In any case, this risk was taken consciously, and it is up to the reader to judge how rewarding it was in terms of the knowledge acquired.

The social and political consciousness of participants in the Belgrade protests turned out to be largely underdeveloped and controversial. This basic finding should not come as a surprise. Actors of political events, especially the highly condensed ones, are rarely generally aware of the overall social meaning of their own engagement and all of its relevant consequences. The Belgrade protest, in these terms, appeared more rational than most other similar social movements. This is due to the fact that it was triggered by a clear motive: to challenge the obvious falsification of local election results in Belgrade and certain other Serbian towns. The clearly visible motive of the protest reduces the possibility of conscious manipulation with its participants, while the absolute majority orientation toward moderate demands, focused on the undoing of the electoral fraud, acts as an additional but highly important rational factor in this context. There is also an obvious impression that, despite all inconsistencies and even contradictions in deeper ideological strata of the social political consciousness of protest participants, they display an almost general strong conviction that power positions in Serbia today may be won, retained or lost only in elections. The importance of this basic conviction can hardly be emphasized enough, since it represents the basis for a rational, legalistic, political climate which is, under the present conditions, a necessary basis for the development and modernization of the entire society. Political leaderships of the rival blocs have a historical responsibility not to disregard this fact. The immediate future will show whether and to what degree they can rise to this challenge.

## Note

1. In this article, percentages are given as round numbers.

## Bibliography

Kuzmanović, B. (1995): "Authoritarianism," in: M. Lazić, ed., *Society in Crisis*, Filip Višnjić, Belgrade.

Kuzmanović, B. (1997): "Autoritarnost kao prepreka razvoju demokratije" (Authoritarianism as an obstacle to the development of democracy), *Dijalog* (Dialogue), No. 3–4.

Lazić, M. (1995): "Transformation of the Economic Elite," in: M. Lazić, ed., *Society in Crisis*, Filip Višnjić, Belgrade.

Manhajm, K. (1977*): Ideologija i utopija* (Ideology and utopia), Belgrade, Nolit.

Weber, M. (1921): "Politik als Beruf," *Gesammelte politische Schrifen,* Drei Masken Verlag, Munich.

# The Walks in a Gender Perspective

*Marina Blagojević*

In a patriarchal society every social phenomenon has genderness clearly imprinted on it. Everything is coded and pervaded with genderness. The basic idea of this article is to address the genderness of the 1996–97 Belgrade protests in different spheres, on different levels and with different methodological procedures, i.e., to examine the ways of its manifestation and possible conclusions related to the further development of civil society and the feminist movement. The study of the link between gender and protest is equally important in cases when differences between men and women are small and when they are large. Every one of them reveals an essential aspect of the dynamics of societal relations among genders.

Gender dimension will, in this article, be traced along a number of lines. First, we will look into the participation, behavior and attitudes of women protesters. The main assumption related to this aspect of genderness is that the participation of women and men, their behavior and even their attitudes did not display substantial differences. On the other hand, we will also examine whether the protests revealed the regular practice that, the higher the level of decision making, the less women are represented.

The second line of examining the gender dimension of the protests relates to the symbolic/communication sphere, i.e., the use of sexual symbols and messages in the media and artifacts produced during the protests. This part serves to detect the strength of patriarchy in the sphere of culture and the reproduction of power in the sphere of politics.

The link between the two lines indicates the reshaping of patriarchy and its adjustment to the society "in transition" whereby it increasingly abandons the "lower" levels of domination, such as the family,[1] in order to focus or retain the concentration of patriarchal power in the spheres which are of key importance in forming the general structure of power. The patriarchalism of a society must always be empirically examined in order to see its specific characteristics.

The third line of study of the protest's genderness is certainly the most difficult to grasp and empirically verify. Still, this aspect is also the most relevant for further development of the civil society and the feminist movement in its context. That is so because of the mutual influence of the women's movements and the protests on one another. The underlying assumption in this case is that both the protest and the women's movement helped each other in opening the society and establishing real democracy, as opposed to the current quasi-democracy, which operates with the almost complete exclusion of women. The protest actually resulted from a long struggle for civil society that has been going on in certain "islands" of this civil society, including the women's movement, an element of particular interest for this article. It is also assumed that the accumulated experience in protesting will result in an increased activism of women in the coming period, providing, of course, that a new dictatorship does not obstruct it.

These three lines of examination of the protest's genderness shall, in this article, be based on three different types of information. Namely, I will start from the "hardest" data obtained in the survey-type research carried out during the protest, continue using "softer" data acquired through observation and analysis of contents, and end with the "softest" data of all—resulting from participant observation. In the conclusion of this article, the scientific analysis necessarily intertwines with my activist position. In this respect it is important to note that, in the spirit of the feminist methodology, I consider an insider's approach, an engaged approach, a legitimate one. Besides, I believe that only this kind of approach is useful in evaluating the basic characteristics of this movement.[2] This engaged insider's view happens to be highly relevant for understanding and even predicting future societal development.

I do not intend to be an "objective" scientist. "Objective" science with "scientific" methods was quite incapable of predicting the protest. Nevertheless, the miracle happened! Miracles like this are impossible to either predict or fully explain by academic sociological knowledge which ignores an activist's perspective. More power means better predictions. Thus the link between "predictability" and power should not be ignored.

Activism gives power, and in that sense it enables greater sensitivity for future events, while the academic, sociological knowledge has a basically static, structural, general view even on so dynamic a social movement as the protest. The activist approach understands and provokes social change by analyzing the steady, small, multiple, step-by-step efforts in building civil society. Committing these efforts to memory is an important part of empowerment of future civic initiatives.

## Participation, behavior, attitudes: Gender lines

Empirical investigations[3] made during the protest allow us to create a rather precise picture of women's participation. Findings of the surveys on the student and civil protests show that women were very much included in both. In fact, one could say that they were involved on an equal basis. A survey of the students (Čičkarić, Jojić) speaks of 49 percent of women participants, while another one (Popadić) establishes the presence of female students at 46.7 percent. As for the civil protest, women protesters accounted for 44.9 percent.

Female students came, just as men did, from an urban, middle-class background. Half of them were living with their parents, meaning that they had urban origins. Their fathers (just like the fathers of male students) had university degrees in 65 percent of cases. This basically urban background largely accounts for the style of the student protest, with its obvious lack of kitsch. The 1996–97 student protest, as well as the one of 1992, was a remarkable cultural event with sophisticated and humorous political messages. A revealing difference between male and female students appeared in relation to the support they were getting from their parents with respect to their participation in the protest. Parents of female students were more supportive than those of male students (58.1 percent and 49.0 percent, respectively), but they also opposed the protest more often (13.4 percent and 9.9 percent, respectively). However, men, much more than women, answered that their parents felt "it was their own business whether they protested or not." These data reveal quite clearly the different socialization patterns for boys and girls within the family. The greater independence of men is still something desirable, while female students are more dependent on their parents' support.

While students in the protest represented a young generation, the age differences between men and women involved in the civil protest are both significant and indicative. The average age of women in the civil protest was 41.3 years, while men were younger—38.5 years. Men were over-represented in all age groups from 19 to 39 and over 60, while women were over-represented in the age group from 40 to 59. This age difference was no accident. While male protesters were younger, and thus not fully integrated into the societal structure of Serbia, women protesters were middle-aged, employed and educated, but not supportive of the ex-communist regime. The lower involvement of younger women (19-39) could also be explained by their responsibilities toward their families (motherhood).

Age differences connected with the differences with respect to the public/private sector of employment reveal some important dissimilarities between men and women involved in the protest. Women protesters, although well educated, remained on the margins of the public sector for most of their careers. It is highly likely that they were not protesting for themselves alone, but also for improved living conditions for their children. Younger men, who were often employed in the private sector, were protecting their own right to live better.

Not only did women take an equal part in the protest, but they also had similar experience in previous protests. As many as 77 percent of men and 61.6 percent of women had some protesting experience. Some forms of organization of the student protest included 20.7 percent of male and 17.8 percent of female respondents. These data reveal that the student protest had a widely diversified organization, based almost equally on both men and women. Women included in the 1996–97 civil protest claimed—even more often than men—that they had some previous experience in protesting. More than 80 percent of both men and women had participated in a protest before, but women had done so somewhat more often than men. This, of course, can be attributed to the difference in the age distributions of men and women demonstrators. Still, it seems that one of the keys for successful protesting, in fact, for the creation of civil society—and the one that fortunately cannot be annulled—is the cumulative experience of protesting.

Both men and women participating in the civil protest were involved in the protest from the very beginning. Women attended the protest as often as men did. It is interesting that women joined the walks somewhat more often than men, but they did not listen to the leaders as often as men did. This is most probably due to their generally less enthusiastic attitude toward institutional political life, also shown by the fact that they were less frequently affiliated to political parties than men.

Despite the absence of major differences between male and female students in terms of identifying the protest's demands, it is interesting that another research on the student protest (Popadić) shows that male students had more demands than female students. While as many as 60.2 percent of female students did not have any additional demands (at the beginning of the protest, except for those for the recognition of the victory of the *Zajedno* coalition in local elections), 63.9 percent of the men had additional demands. This was the most pronounced difference between men and women in the 1996–97 student protest. Male students also expressed a greater readiness to continue to protest until their demands were fulfilled (82.4 percent compared with 77.8 percent) and a greater readiness to "go out into the streets" (which later proved to be a very successful strategy) than to stay in university buildings (as was the case in the 1992 student protest). They also participated more than women in the 1996–97 civil protest. All these facts indicate somewhat more politicized and more radical attitudes and behavior of men than women in the 1996–97 student protest.

As expected, male students were more likely to be members of political parties than were female students (12 percent compared with 4.6 percent), although the overwhelming majority of both were not party-affiliated. Consequently, male students took part in the 1996–97 civil protest much more often. As many as 75 percent of male students attended the civil protest, compared with 57.7 percent of female students. Still, many believed that their protest should be "political, but not party-spirited" (76.3 percent to 78.9 percent). This fact indicates the emergence of civil political engagement outside the "polluted" political scene, which is highly disorganized, manipulative and manipulated, as well as very corruptive.

Relevant data about women's inclusion in the hierarchy of the student protest were given to me by the organizers.[4] On the one hand, female students obviously played a very important part in all the organizational activities (such as press, information, public relations, program organizing and security), constituting at least 50 percent of those involved (and in some faculties even more than that). On the other hand, women were heavily marginalized on the higher levels of the student protest's public representation. The protest was headed by an Initiative Board, which counted 11 members and one chairperson. Only one of them was a woman. In the Main Board, consisting of the representatives of different faculties, women accounted for about 30 percent. Since the Initiative Board was the very body which, being more operational than others, actually passed the decisions, the role of women at the highest levels of decision making was clearly marginal. However, of greatest importance is the fact that, out of three spokespersons of the protest, two were men and one a woman. But since only men were outspoken in their public appearances, the student protest became symbolized in the public eye by its special "leader" Dušan Vasiljević, more than it was the case with the civil protest, where an almost ritual equal participation of its leaders—two men and one woman (Zoran Djindjić, Vuk Drašković and Vesna Pešić)—was manifested. In this sense, the appearance of Dr. Vesna Pešić in the political life of Serbia represents a significant turning point for women. Pešić is the promoter of a new role model for women in politics, by demonstrating the independent political engagement of a woman, outside the usual pattern in which the only influential women in politics are "the wives."[5]

Empirical data from the surveys prove that men and women in the student protest had very similar demands. However, male students expressed somewhat clearer and more precise demands. This reveals the well-known difference in attitudes toward institutional politics and women's traditional reluctance to get too involved. There are firm grounds to believe that the radicalization of the 1996–97 student protest, which occurred several weeks after it started and provided major moral reinforcement to the civil protest, should be attributed to male much more than female participants in the protest. On the other hand, women should be given the credit for advocating non-violent methods more than men. This was especially visible on the level of the leadership, where Vesna Pešić represented a symbol of civil, nonviolent resistance to the recent war.

The general level of optimism in the civil protest was higher than in the student protest. Still, a significant number of men and women alike expected their demands to be fulfilled only partially (50.6 percent and 45.4 percent, respectively). Women in the civil protest indicated they were as prepared as men to "see it through" (99.5 percent and 97.3 percent respectively). This readiness can be understood only in the context of their previous experience. Since many of the demonstrators had some experience in protesting, they were also very much aware of the fact that every previous failure had disastrous effects. Although the overwhelming majority of participants advocated nonviolence, women were somewhat more supportive of nonviolent methods than men. But women were highly verbally aggressive and were also ready to hurl eggs and even stones at certain buildings that became the symbols of citizens' oppression (the TV building, the Republican Parliament, the Presidential Palace, etc.).

It is no surprise that the attitudes of protesters were rather critical. In fact, with their above-average education levels, these people were quite capable of fairly precisely identifying the institutional collapse. They also knew what was happening with the dissolution of the former Yugoslavia, under the cynical labels of "democratization" and "self-determination." Most institutions of the system were rated extremely low. Some of the relevant differences between men and women were registered with respect to the legislature and church and scientific institutions. While male students believed more in "conventional authorities" such as the legislature and the church, female students rated "science" the highest. In the context of the university, this appreciation of science does make sense. However, as the church was extremely traditional and conservative, especially concerning abortion, female students manifested much greater skepticism toward it than males.

But students in the 1996–97 protest were also very skeptical toward opposition leaders. As many as half the female students did not consider any opposition leader good enough. In general, opposition leaders got better ratings by male students than by female students. This is closely connected to another fact revealed by the survey: women in the 1996–97 student protest, more often than men, wanted to be independent from the other protest, the civil protest. Although the vast majority of both men and women agreed on this issue, this fact is another indication of a somewhat different understanding of "politics" that women in today's Serbia have in comparison with men. Similarly, women did not want any workers' or union organization to be involved with the student protest, but preferred that each stayed independent. Male students had different strategic ideas about the protest in the sense that they wanted to see it spreading, "contaminating" others. This once again reveals much deeper differences in women's and men's understanding of political action today and should not be treated as accidental. Women are, even within the feminist movement in Serbia, very reluctant to get involved in "dirty" politics and do not show much willingness even to support other women leaders, although women participants in the civil protest gave Vesna Pešić's political activity higher ratings than men did (on a scale of 1 to 5, women gave her 3.9 and men 3.5). Women are more inclined to fight for "idealistic" goals, leaving the "political arena" to men.

Empirical data from the surveys analyzed here indicate that gender differences on the level of actual participation and behavior during the protests were small, while they were greater on the level of attitudes. But even when small, they were indicative of the "genderness" of activism. However, the most pronounced "genderness" existed on the level of political presentation of the protests, especially of the student protest, where female students were very much marginalized in decision-making and public representation. The gender pattern within the organizational structure proved unmistakably patriarchal—the higher the level of decision-making and the more prestigious the position (e.g., public representation of collective bodies of the protest), the more visible and influential men were. But men in the student protest were also more strategically oriented and displayed a more sophisticated, analytical and realistic approach than women. On the basis of my interviews with student protesters, without any specific survey data, I had the impression that a "spontaneous" division of labor had been made along gender lines. Women were not making coffee but were very much engaged in both organizational and creative activities. On the other hand, men were more oriented toward defining "pure" political strategies and political representation of the student protest.

## Sexism in the protest

It is quite clear that both protests were largely based on a ludic element, on carnivalization, irony and sarcasm. Yet some of the metaphors were not always devoid of pejorative gender characteristics. As the protests themselves changed over time, becoming increasingly civil, so did the symbols change in a sense. The initial symbol—the eggs, deriving from the idea that the authorities were "egg thieves" or that they lacked "eggs" (balls)—was relatively quickly substituted with a more neutral symbol, a whistle.

Just how clear the male symbols were is evident from a series of protest paraphernalia (slogans, posters) using the male sexual organ or its symbol (the middle finger). The first issue of the humor paper *Krmaca*, which appeared on December 5, 1996, carried a picture of a truncheon over broken eggs on its front page. The symbolism is clear. Yet this same paper, ending a quotation from a speech by President Slobodan Milošević, cites its author as "Slobodan Milošević (husband of Mirjana Marković)," hinting at his increasingly subordinate role in politics compared with that of his wife.

One interesting difference between the student protests in 1992 and 1996–97 is that in the latter Mirjana Marković frequently appeared as an object of ridicule. Given that her political engagement in 1992 was not so strong (at least visibly) as it is today, it is quite clear that she does not appear in the role of a "wife" but rather in that of a "politician." Still, we should note that allusions and metaphors, slogans and effigies concerning Mirjana Marković were often directed at her female attributes. Thus, a demonstrator in outlandish drag, sporting a black wig, a pair of falsies and the already legendary flowers in his hair (an ornament Marković uses quite often) carried a banner: "I am the prettiest Russian academician." Symptomatically, it does not say "the cleverest" or "the most educated" Russian academician, but "the prettiest."

However, the most drastic case of sexism in the protest was undoubtedly the contest for "beauty queen of the student protest" organized by the daily paper *Demokratija*, the mouthpiece of the Democratic Party and one of the key sources of information (along with Radio B92) for the participants and sympathizers of the protest. Since the protest took place in winter, the student candidates appeared in photos fully dressed, and most of them were presented in portraits. However, considering the editorial approach of the paper, which publishes a few photos of scantily clad women in every issue, one may rightly assume that the beauty contest would have been presented differently had the protest taken place in summer. Thus women, although they are participants in a political protest with a clear demand for the defense of civil electoral rights, are primarily treated as dolls who merely decorate a men's happening. The patriarchal cynicism of the "Miss Student Protester" contest was laid bare when it was followed by a competition for the "king," naturally a policeman. Thus, the female students and policemen found themselves on the same side, treated as "the other."

However, the symbols used in the protests were, over time, increasingly freed from gender identifiers. Some played with gender in order to overcome it; consider the self-deprecating slogan: "Even the blondes have got it," carried by two blonde women, which alluded to the complete transparency of the lie and fraud with the electoral results. The symbols seen at the beginning (eggs, "egg thieves") corresponded to the "macho" and even aggressive onset of the protest, which resulted in some tangible damage. As the protests grew peaceful, better organized and in favor of nonviolence and nonconfrontation, these gender symbols "evaporated." Instead of a "male" symbol, the egg became, as a students' slogan stated, a "symbol of the birth of a new world which has to crack the shell in order to come out."

## Feminist movement and women's activism

Both the 1996–97 student and civil protest, just like the 1992 student protest, have characteristics of new political movements. That is why they are close and similar to, for example, the women's movement in terms of their objectives and the manner of organization as well as models and means of communication. As already mentioned, the relevant data indicate that both male and female participants in the protest had largely participated in previous protests. This suggests not only the continuity of resistance to the current regime but also the existence of a process of learning civil resistance. In addition, a diffusion of methods, communication models and actions from one protest to the other is quite obvious. One could even say that the methods and actions used by various other groups—initiatives, protests, demonstrations—are quite successfully transported and extended to similar but (in terms of their nature) new political movements. This was apparent, for instance, in the use of bells and noise, or the idea of "awakening," actually launched by the Center for Anti-War Action at the beginning of the civil war in Yugoslavia.

Although less inclined to participate in institutional political life or to join political parties, women are not apolitical. This is where a parallel between the student protests and women's participation in the protests is in order. In the 1992 and 1996–97 student protests, women tried to remain detached from the parties, thus affirming a new form of political action, nonparty, supraparty, extrainstitutional political action—actually a new form of political activism close to civil society. The political objectives of both the student protest and the women's movement in Serbia are basically related to the problems of daily life, concern for the individual and the quality of life. The specific *politicism* of women implies not only "street" action, but also a series of micro-actions to influence a specific problem in a specific environment. The apolitical trait in women is actually a specific kind of "universal *politicism*" based on the feminist axiom that "the personal is political." Women's political activism, placed outside official institutions, within alternative groups and organizations, or simply a series of individual actions, is an activism which is the necessary corrective of institutional policy, a constant pressure on that policy. The dilemma—politics or no politics—is a false dilemma for the women's movement. Women have to engage in politics, but in the way they want to, which does not necessarily have to be institutional.

Although at this point in time there are no systematic analyses of the autonomous women's movement in Belgrade, the abundance of documentation, as well as the personal insight of the author, enable this movement to be linked with the 1996–97 student and civil protests. Even before the war, independent women's initiatives related to UJDI (Association of the Yugoslav Democratic Initiative) and ZEST (Women's Party) attempted to show resistance and oppose the imminent catastrophe of the war. The ZEST program, for example, clearly supported the idea of a civil society with a developed "welfare state," in which a high degree of regional autonomy was to help relieve ethnic conflict and avert a civil war.

It is not possible in this article to deal with the multitude of actions and reactions of autonomous women's groups and initiatives to the war and violence over the past few years. The important thing is to say that "the experience which many women and, naturally, a number of men who had joined them acquired in conflicts with the police, in mass media distortions of what they had gone through with the institutions of power and the system, provide a valuable basis for the growth of a future new movement which would express the authentic needs, interests and demands of female and male citizens." ("Žene za žene," 1993: 53).

This is precisely what happened. The resistance to war and manipulation of national interest have been learned over time, primarily through different autonomous and/or related initiatives, reactions, appeals to the public and symbolic actions (e.g., throwing of war toys into garbage bins), as well as through the establishment and activity of new groups for resisting the war or assisting the victims of war. Resistance to the war gradually spread the civil initiatives. Women organized a whole series of autonomous women's groups (SOS phone line, Women in Black, Center for Women's Studies, Women's Lobby, Women's Parliament, Autonomous Women's Center for Struggle against Sexual Violence, Women's Safe Houses, women's autonomous "flea market" sales, Incest Trauma Center, SARA Center for the Young, Group for Support to Disabled Women, Women's Legal Group, Arkadija/Labris, etc.). They also actively participated in conceiving and implementing various peace-movement actions (the "Yellow Ribbon," the "Bell," the "Black Ribbon,"[6] etc.), either as individual actors through the Center for Anti-War Action or as collective participants in demonstrations and happenings. For instance, during the 1992 student protest they organized "women's workshops" at the Faculty of Philosophy in Belgrade as a specific contribution of the feminist movement to the protest.

The link between different movements was made in the 1996–97 protests. The feminists of Belgrade were in the streets in both protests. In their public appearances, proclamations, leaflets and articles, they reminded the public of the continuity of their resistance to war and violence and, at the same time, "welcomed all forms of self-organized civil nonviolent protests against the violation of principles of a legal state," supporting the "incorporation of women's human rights into all institutions of civil society." The Belgrade women's lobby printed a leaflet indicating that "whistling" was not only a form of organized civil disobedience but also a proven method of women's self-protection against violence.

## Conclusion

The participation of women in the 1996–97 protests, their representation, behavior and views as well as the link between their activism—manifested through the feminist movement—and the protests reflects the paradox of the women's position in the period of transition quite well. On the one hand, women already have a sufficiently strong position in the public sphere, no doubt attributable to the socialist era, and have indeed strengthened their position in the private sphere ("self-sacrificing micro-matriarchy"). On the other hand, the patriarchal culture is becoming increasingly misogynist. At the symbolic level, sexism is remarkably present, as confirmed by the existence of patriarchy as a stable structure of power which is increasingly generated through culture, especially the mass media. Sexism is reinforced as a negative relationship toward "otherness" during the transition.

These two facts, that of the real empowerment of women on the one hand and a real increase in sexism on the other, are logically connected, since patriarchy, as it loses its positions, grows increasingly aggressive. These two facts are also well correlated with the examined phenomenon—the participation of women in the 1996–97 protests. Thus the equal participation, similar behavior and similar attitudes of men and women reflect the real share of women in the public sphere. On the other hand, their absence at the highest level of decision making in the student protest reveals the obstacles which ordinary women—those who rely on male resources (their fathers or husbands)—have to face in their social mobility.

The way out of this obvious division of patriarchy can only be sought in a new "gender contract," the kind of a contract that would balance the positions of men and women in the private and public spheres, both in concrete daily life and the symbolic sphere. This new "gender contract" would be a relief for a large number of men who are currently on the margins of a patriarchy they themselves are not responsible for. The feminist movement, in this sense, represents an unavoidable part of creating the civil culture and, in the final instance, learning to respect and tolerate those who are different.

## Notes

1. For the phenomenon of "self-sacrificing micro-matriarchy," see: Blagojević, 1994.

2. To explain my epistemological starting point even further, I will list the multiplicity of roles I have "naturally" found myself in during the protest. As a university professor, I took an active part in the protest, as did most other professors. As an active feminist, I also took part in a number of different feminist actions aimed at expressing support for both the civil and student protests. As a sociologist, I analyzed the survey results during the protest and was one of the authors of this book. I was not only a participant in the protest, but like most other social scientists, I was also a participant-observer. And, finally, over the three to four months of the protest, I was a passionate believer, a "graduate" noise-maker during Radio Television Serbia Evening News and one of hundreds of thousands of people who really enjoyed the protest.

3. The relevant data were taken from the following three research efforts:

— research on the students (second week of the student protest, sample: 383, author: Popadić),

— research on the students (second week of the student protest, sample: 585, authors: Čičkarić, Jojić),

— research on citizens (fourth and fifth week of the protest, sample: 483, authors: Babović, Vuletić, Cvejić).

4. Data were collected in the Press Center of the student protest.

5. Slobodan Milošević's wife, Dr. Mira Marković, and Vuk Drašković's wife, Danica Drašković, are especially politically influential. The difference is that Dr. Mira Marković founded her own party/coalition bloc, "JUL" (meaning the Yugoslav Left), which is in coalition with the Socialist Party of her husband, Slobodan Milošević. Meanwhile, Danica Drašković is active within her husband's party, the Serbian Renewal Movement. However, both wives are often blamed by the public for the erring of their husbands. In a patriarchal, misogynous culture such as Serbia's, politicians like the above two are considered to be "seduced" by their vicious wives and therefore relieved of responsibility and excused. This is especially pronounced in the case of Slobodan Milošević.

6. These are peace actions with a symbolic meaning. For instance, the "Bell" was an action at the outset of the war aimed at "awakening" Belgrade and Serbia. The bell later became the symbol of the Civic Alliance, the party headed by Vesna Pešić. The "Yellow Ribbon" was designed to symbolically express disagreement with the increasingly widespread pressure on the non-Serbian population of Belgrade. The protesters carried a yellow ribbon encircling the Federal Parliament. Another action of this kind, the "Black Ribbon," gathered a

large number of Belgraders and was organized during the first days of the bombing of Sarajevo. Citizens carried the black ribbon as a sign of mourning and solidarity with the people of Sarajevo. The column of Belgraders moving through the center of the city was a few kilometers long. Carrying the black ribbon, they sounded the sirens signaling the danger of air attacks and played the sounds of bombing.

## Bibliography

Blagojević, Marina (1994): "War and Everyday Life: Deconstruction of Self/Sacrifice," *Sociologija* (Sociology), No. 4, Belgrade.

Gelb, Joyce (1989): *Feminism and Politics: A Comparative Perspective,* University of California Press, Berkeley and Los Angeles.

Kuzmanović, Bora *et al.* (1993): *Studentski protest 1992* (Student protest 1992), Institut za psihologiju, knjižara Plato, Belgrade.

Lazić, Mladen, 1995: "Osobenosti globalne društvene transformacije Srbije" (Characteristics of the global societal transformation of Serbia), in: Bolčić, Silvano, ed., *Društvene promene i svakodnevni zivot: Srbija početkom devedesetih* (Social change and everyday life: Serbia in the early '90s), ISI FF, Belgrade.

*Republika* (1993): "Studentski protest 1992" (Student protest), special issue, Belgrade.

Stojanović, Ljiljana (1995): *Socio-kulturna analiza studentskog pokreta 1991-92* (Socio-cultural analysis of the 1991-92 student movement), FPN, Belgrade.

*Žene za žene: protesti, apeli, izjave, informacije autonomnih ženskih inicijativa* (Women for women: protests, appeals, statements and information on autonomous women's initiatives), (1993), Grupa izdavača, Belgrade.

# PART II

# Value Orientations
# and Political Attitudes of Participants
# in the 1996–97 Student Protest

*Bora Kuzmanović*

Observation and study of social movements and events that involve a large number of participants require us to distinguish between a few levels of facts related to the course of events and the meaning of the participants' behavior: 1) the explicit, official objectives, demands and statements made in official communications which are formally backed by the legitimate leadership of the movement concerned (if it exists) or a group which initiates, organizes and seeks to channel the social event; 2) less formal, more spontaneous products which also have a specific meaning linked with the nature of events, such as spontaneously created slogans, catch phrases, authorial texts published in mouthpieces of the movement, artistic and cultural products (e.g., artistic solutions which symbolically manifest certain positions); 3) outward, open and mass behavior of participants (spontaneous display of emotions and views in a gathering, various forms of approval or disapproval of the views expressed by others, participation in specific actions); 4) intimate beliefs, attitudes, value orientations; 5) unconscious aspirations, motives and objectives of participants in the movement or the social event concerned.

If a movement is properly articulated and organized, a certain harmony between these levels is expected—for instance, that the official demands of the protest are expressed, elaborated and interpreted in various informal products and also that the overall behavior of participants serves the function of attaining the basic objectives. In such a case a harmony between deeper political and value orientations of participants and the official demands and objectives of the movement is also expected. Moreover, mass meetings (rallies, demonstrations and protest gatherings) are merely an open, more precise and energetic way of expressing the attitudes and values which have already been formed and for whose attainment the citizens are gathering. But there are also cases

of converging interests of highly diverse social groups and political organizations which, despite different ideological and value orientations,
find a common interest in specific demands and actions—for instance,
to depose a minister (or entire government), to introduce certain social
policies and the like. After such an action is completed, whether successfully or not, these groups disperse, and the wider entity (or whatever
acted as one) disappears, lacking a common system of values and an
ideology (namely a joint political program) to keep it unified. In that
case, the social event has a quite specific motive, and the participants
have a concrete common objective which, once realized (or given up),
eliminates the reasons for their further gathering.

There are also cases when developments go beyond the concrete
motives and turn a relatively heterogeneous gathering or a protest into a
more lasting movement. This is possible if there are sufficient binding
elements—latent common interests, similar views, values and objectives—which are revealed in the event itself and may serve to articulate
a more precise program. Finally, there is also a possibility that unconscious aspirations and objectives of the participants differ from the official, explicit demands and what the participants directly manifest in their
behavior. Authors taking a psychoanalytical perspective often doubt the
full harmony of unconscious aspirations and the official program.[1]

Whatever the case, the intimate moods, views, attitudes and value
orientations of the participants of a social event (especially a protest
gathering) should be examined, since the purpose and future of social
events cannot be properly understood or anticipated without such knowledge. This is particularly important if a social movement (in the widest
meaning of the word) has not sufficiently formed long-term objectives
or articulated its views on essential social issues, especially when there
is uncertainty over whether the official communications express the beliefs and attitudes of a large number of participants and sympathizers.
Moreover, given their nature, official positions relate to merely some
(usually current) issues and do not adequately express other attitudes
and orientations the participants may also find important.

In the case of the 1996–97 student protest (and also the citizens' protest gathering), the question is primarily whether the protest may grow
into a more lasting movement with long-term objectives. The protest
started for a specific reason and focused on highly pragmatic demands,
but the analysts (and even participants) have, from the very beginning,

wondered whether it expresses more than that, namely whether there are conditions for it to grow into a new student movement. The student protest was not organized by a student organization which had a rallying point among them and a clearly articulated program (a fact which makes it somewhat different from the one in 1992). Instead, it was initially a largely spontaneous reaction to something that had happened outside the university, regardless of the fact that the idea for the student movement might have come from the outside, from a political organization. That is why we have to see whether there are some objectives, attitudes and values which make the students in the protests (and students in general) sufficiently homogenous and which are relevant for social engagement and therefore represent a basis for developing a movement. In this sense it is important to look into the essential attitudes and value orientations of the participants in the 1996–97 student movement.

In this text we will present some of the most important findings of research carried out on a sample of 402 students, participants in daily protests on the plaza in front of the Faculty of Philosophy. The interviewers (psychology students) completed the survey on December 19, 20 and 23, at the time when the students gathered to take their "walk." The sample itself was a convenience-type one, but the interviewers managed to question students from various faculties, although not all of them are equally represented. In our view, the sample is sufficiently representative of those who gathered there and then. Male and female students accounted for 53 and 47 percent of the sample respectively: 44 percent of them were residents of Belgrade, 28 percent came from a medium-sized or larger town, 16 percent from smaller towns and 6 percent each from very small towns and villages. It is obvious that these young people generally came from highly urban environments (mostly Belgrade), but that is generally true of students at the University of Belgrade. Two-thirds of the respondents identified themselves as Serbs (67 percent), 19 percent as Yugoslavs, 7 percent as nationally unaffiliated, 2 percent as cosmopolitans and 2 percent as Montenegrins. Most of them classified their families as belonging to the middle class: lower middle class (49 percent), upper middle class (23 percent), working class (15 percent) and higher (upper) class (2 percent), while only 1 percent categorized their families as farmers. Ten percent stated they could not determine which class they belonged to. Data on the profession of parents confirm that these students generally came from a middle-class family, since, for example, 40 percent of respondents stated that their fathers were professionals with a degree of higher education.

The main findings of this research related to value orientations are outlined below.

## Democratic orientation

Since the student protest officially appealed for the respect of the free choice of citizens, democratic elections and free media, it was necessary to check to what extent the sample of "ordinary" participants accepts this value orientation. For this purpose we have used a reduced (six-point) scale of democratic (or non-democratic) orientation we recently used on a sample of employees from two Belgrade firms. Thus there are six statements the respondents reacted to by selecting one of five modalities of answers ranging from full agreement to disagreement. To prevent respondents from tailoring their answers to what sounded more socially acceptable, all statements referred to political democracy (most often a multi-party system and political liberties) in negative terms, meaning that the democratic orientation of respondents was revealed in their disagreement with these statements.

It turned out that most respondents indeed accepted the democratic orientation. The average result on the whole scale is 24.12 or, narrowed down to a scale of five points (which is the range of one statement), 4.06 (indicating that a decisive majority supported democratic views), as opposed to the employees of the two enterprises mentioned above, who had an average of 2.65, indicating that they are predominantly disinclined toward democracy. If we divide the total range of the scale into five equal segments, we may note that 44.4 percent of respondents fall into the category of those with a strong democratic orientation, while 33.1 percent show a moderate democratic orientation. In addition, 18.9 percent are in the vacillating or undecided category (wavering between a democratic and non-democratic orientation), 3 percent reveal a moderate non-democratic orientation and only 0.5 percent (two respondents in the whole sample) display a strong non-democratic orientation.

Students' attitudes toward democracy may be illustrated by their reactions to specific statements. For instance, the statement, "However important political democracy may be, it should be postponed for better times" obtained the approval of only 2.8 percent of respondents. Those who were undecided accounted for 4 percent, while as many as 93 percent disagreed (79 percent of them very resolutely). Respondents who agreed with the statement, "The appearance of the multi-party system brought our society more harm than good," were somewhat more numerous (16 percent), while 14 percent were ambivalent and 71 percent rejected it. An even higher percentage (27 percent) agreed with the statement, "Many people should be denied the right to vote," while the vast majority rejected this view. The largest number of respondents (43 percent) agreed with the following statement: "Some parties which are active in our country should be prohibited," but most of them rejected this statement (51 percent). Naturally, there are grounds to assume that the respondents who agree with this statement were thinking of extreme parties intolerant of others. Nevertheless, it is a restrictive position that might be conducive to a situation in which the one who has the power may prohibit the parties he does not like. In any case, preliminary checks show that this position fits into the set of positions used to measure democratic orientation.

On the whole, most respondents displayed a democratic orientation, although the percentage of its supporters is somewhat reduced as we move from the general level toward concrete questions.

## Authoritarian orientation

When considering attitudes toward democracy, there is good reason to examine the question of authoritarian orientation, since it is logical to expect that authoritarianism implies aversion to democracy. Authoritarianism itself is generally understood as a complex feature or syndrome of features of a personality (Adorno et al., 1964) based on an uncritical attitude toward authority and the principle of hierarchy (Fromm, 1963 and 1964). It involves the simultaneous appearance of authoritarian submissiveness (uncritical submission to persons who occupy a higher place in the hierarchy, or uncritical glorification of leaders) and authoritarian dominance and aggressiveness (crude and intolerant attitudes toward those who are lower in hierarchy, or the impotent). Authoritarianism may also be understood and examined as a value orientation if it is operationally defined through statements that manifest support for specific patterns of behavior, refer to the respect of authority as a specific value or exaggerate the importance of leaders or special groups in society. Since authoritarianism, according to many researchers, is formed (or at least starts forming) in early childhood, it becomes an important psychological basis for the adoption or rejection of social positions and values formed in adulthood (such as national views, democratic orientation, etc.).

Our research uses a short six-point scale which is one of the many variants of a revised Adorno's scale (Kuzmanović, 1984 and 1990). Again in this case, the respondents answered by choosing one of five offered alternatives to express the degree of their agreement or disagreement. Using this scale (with a theoretical range of 6 to 30), we obtained an average of 14.09 (or, reduced to the five-point scale, 2.35), which ranks among the lowest average values obtained in our country. Thus there is no doubt that most students participating in the 1996–97 protest do not display authoritarian value orientations.

We will compare some answers given by this group of respondents with the results obtained on a sample of the general population. For instance, the statement "The young need strong discipline and have to be ready to do the tasks they are given by their family and social authority" elicited agreement from 56 percent of respondents among the general population of Serbia in 1993 (Kuzmanović, 1995), or 44.4 percent only a few years later (1996), while the acceptance of this statement in our sample of students was only 13 percent. But this is undoubtedly where the specific position and interests of respondents play a certain role. The statement "Obedience and respect for authority are the most important values children should learn" was accepted by 74 percent of respondents in the general population in 1993, compared with a third (34 percent) of the sample of 1996–97 protest participants. Students who participated in the 1996–97 protest come the closest to the general population in their reactions to the statement "Whoever harms our honor has to be punished." Adorno and his associates assumed that this statement was indicative of authoritarian aggressiveness and preoccupation with power. Here, however, it probably indicates rigid adherence to the traditional values of honor and dignity and the heroic code. This statement elicited agreement from 57.8 percent of citizens in 1993 and 57 percent of students in the 1996–97 protest—an almost equal number. At the same time, this is also the item that accounts for the largest difference between the participants in the 1992 protest and the 1996–97 student protest. While the sample we have been examining here gave an average of 3.41, the sample of the 1992 protest had an average of only 2.17 (clear rejection of the statement). This discrepancy may be partly explained by the differences in social situations at the time of the two surveys. In 1992 the international community imposed strict sanctions against Serbia and Montenegro. Many were already fed up with war, and the insistence on respecting "our honor" may have appeared as support for confrontation with the world community, which is precisely what the participants in the 1992 protest wanted to avoid. Students today probably link the issue of honor and dignity with the relation of the authorities toward the people. Still, on the whole, authoritarianism was lower in 1992: the average result was only 10.29 on a scale of 6 to 30. This is the lowest average we have ever established here. Although the average result on the sample of participants in the 1996–97 student protest was higher (14.09), it also belongs in the category of low authoritarianism. There are some who will recognize a violent Dinaric type in the demand to punish anyone who hurts "our honor," but the actual behavior of students in the protest did not display violence or intolerance. Quite the contrary, the students avoided conflicts and displayed their wit, charm, and a good sense for expressing nonviolent forms of resistance to power. This may be a specific form of "punishment" for those who injured their honor and dignity. In any case, it is wiser. Otherwise, the correlation between authoritarianism and democratic orientation is statistically significant and negative ($r = -041$), which supports the thesis that authoritarianism is essential in providing the psychological basis for a non-democratic political orientation.


## Equality or freedom?

The issues of equality and freedom and their mutual relationship take the central place in all large ideologies. Some researchers believe that ideologies may be successfully classified and differentiated precisely on the basis of their relation toward these values. Rokeach (1973) considered the texts written by representatives of various ideologies: socialist (primarily Fromm and authors with similar theoretical orientation), communist (Lenin), fascist (Hitler) and capitalist (Goldwater). He came up with the idea of a two-value model for classification of ideologies. These four ideologies may be represented in a coordinate system consisting of freedom and equality as the abscissa and ordinate. Communist ideology, on the extreme left, is characterized by its emphasis on equality as opposed to freedom. Socialist ideology (as left-oriented) is characterized by a high valuation of both equality and freedom. However, capitalism (meaning liberal capitalism), as a moderate-right ideology, assigns low importance to equality and high importance to freedom. Finally, fascism, as an extreme-right ideology, places little value on either equality or freedom.

Rokeach's analysis and subsequent studies of these and other values prompted other researchers to deal with the issue of the acceptance of equality and freedom. Some of them intentionally set these two values against each other, and the respondents are asked to choose between them. Our research used a question of precisely this type, taken from Inglehearst (1977) and already used in research work here (Golubović, Kuzmanović, Vasović, 1995). The respondents were asked to opt for either equality or freedom from the following alternatives:

a) If I had to choose between freedom and equality, I would say that personal freedom was more important—the opportunity for everybody to live in freedom and to advance without limitations;

b) If I had to choose between freedom and equality, I would consider equality more important—that is, a situation in which no one is privileged and that social differences are not large.

On the basis of these formulations of opposing alternatives, 84 percent of respondents chose freedom and only 16 percent equality. Our examination of the sample of the general population in Serbia in 1993 revealed that the citizens were split: 50.6 percent selected freedom and 49.4 percent equality (Golubović, Kuzmanović and Vasović, 1995). But even at that time an almost identical number of students (82.6 percent) chose freedom. Therefore, it is a general orientation of students rather than a specific characteristic of participants in the 1996–97 protest. Otherwise, attitudes toward equality and freedom largely depend on education, profession or the overall social status of individuals. Notwithstanding the fact that the research of some 20 years ago did not use exactly the same tools, a review of comparable data shows that social equality was appreciated among the students much more than before and that it ranked among the first or even first on the list of values (cf. Tomanović, 1977).

Social equality occupied a prominent place in normative presentations of socialism, although different groups understood it in somewhat different ways: the poorer more often perceived it as material equality (egalitarianism), while the more educated and affluent understood it as equality of opportunity (see Vasović, 1992). The political elite manipulated this value by organizing occasional campaigns both for greater social equality and against excessive egalitarianism (leveling). As of the mid-1980s, the erosion of this value has been noted along with the weakening of belief that it may be realized (Popović et al., 1988). The downfall of socialism as a system was accompanied by a decrease in the number of citizens who upheld this value, although many believed that the years of economic crisis, hyperinflation and pauperization of citizens would reinforce the demand for equality, especially for equalization of salaries.

In order to identify the attitude of the students in this protest toward egalitarianism as a specific form of social equality, we asked them a question that had already been used in previous investigations into the attitudes and values of the young: "What should be the ratio between the lowest and the highest personal incomes in our country?" Table 1 gives these results along with the previously noted views of the young (Stanojević, 1979).

Compared with previous generations of the young, a much higher percentage of students participating in the 1996–97 protest reveal a nonegalitarian disposition. Stanojević notes that at that time more than 50 percent of students were in favor of a small ratio (of maximum 1:3), while the current research registers only 24 percent of respondents sharing that view. Still, we may note that a substantial number of students participating in the protest support moderate ratios of 1:3 to 1:5 (41 percent). We may also note that egalitarianism is now substantially less accepted than it used to be (probably not only among the participants of the protest but also among the students in general), but that there are also large variations. According to a more liberal interpretation of the analyzed data on the "freedom or equality" dilemma, it would seem jus-

*Table 1*
Attitude on the ratio of salaries

| Responses | Belgrade youth | Students participating in 1996/97 protest |
|---|---|---|
| | % | |
| a) All salaries should be equal | 9 | 1 |
| b) Up to 1 : 2 | 24 | 5 |
| c) Up to 1 : 3 | 21 | 18 |
| d) Up to 1 : 4 | 8 | 14 |
| e) Up to 1 : 5 | 2 | 9 |
| f) Up to 1 : 6 | 1 | 3 |
| g) Up to 1 : 7 and over | 0 | 4 |
| h) The ratio should not be limited | 22 | 45 |
| i) No answer | 13 | 0 |

tified to say that the students prefer individual freedom, but many of them do not disregard material equality understood as an issue of social justice, with respect to the level and ratio of incomes.

## Conformist orientation

If the participants of the 1996–97 student protest prefer individual freedom over equality, one would expect that they are not inclined toward conformist behavior, i.e., uncritical acceptance of the majority view and excessive adjustment to the requirements of the group. This research has also looked into the conformist orientation, that is, the consciously accepted strategy of fitting into a group, adjusting to the thinking of the majority and giving up one's own views and style of behavior in case they diverge from the dominant behavior in a group. It is a strategy and tactic of behavior which is accepted as "wise" and useful, and to this extent we may speak of life and value orientations. However, some real conformists will probably fail to manifest their conscious support of this orientation, even if, in practice, they behave in a conformist way. In any case, the (five-point) scale applied here was not intended to measure overall conformist behavior (which requires a kind of experiment and a test situation), but precisely conformism as an accepted orientation.

It turned out that the respondents in our sample indeed predominantly rejected the conformist orientation. The average we obtained is 12.82 or, reduced to the five-point scale, 2.13. For instance, only 7.7 percent of respondents agree with the statement, "Whenever important social problems are concerned, a man is best advised to keep silent and wait to see what others think." But 29 percent agree with the following sentence: "I do not like people who stick out from the group and behave differently from others," while 37 percent endorse the statement "I try not to be different than others as much as possible." Many researchers have noted that the young often behave like nonconformists compared with others or their wider environment, but are fairly conformist compared with their age group (especially the adolescents). Certain analysts have even noted that the participants of the 1996–97 student protest also often behaved in a conformist way. But this assessment is dubious, since a certain uniformity of behavior is the result of real agreement of views and moods as well as the pressures of the situation more than the result of uncritical adjustment of one's own opinion and behavior to the requirements of the majority. In any case, this sample, for the most part, fails to demonstrate the tendency of conscious positive valuation of conformist behavior.

A correlation has been established between conformism and authoritarian orientation ($r = 0.41$), since in both cases there is a non-autonomous view and behavior of individuals, in the first case toward authority and in the second case concerning dependence from the group. A certain negative link has also been noted between conformism and democratic orientation ($-0.23$), which means that conformists are more inclined to reject the idea and principles of democracy. For democracy to develop, it is highly important that its supporters be nonconformists, since only then do the people support the full freedom of opinion of individuals, and there is a chance that the democratic decisions are real ones, i.e., that they are not reduced to mere conformist adjustment to the views and demands of the majority (often only assumed, since in a situation where many do not behave autonomously, the dominant minority can present itself as the majority). Common decisions would have to result from a serious discussion and a competition among the opinions of participants who, at the same time, show appreciation of both the independent views of individuals and of democratic procedure.

## Openness to the world

Our research also included an instrument to study the overall attitudes toward the national problem—a shortened version of Pantić's scale (six-point) of openness or closure to the world. Pantić reckoned that this dimension "subsumes the classical dimension of internationalism-nationalism" (Pantić, 1981: 39). He says: "We arrived at the terms 'openness' or 'closure' to the world by searching for an expression that would most completely express the rich variety of concepts which imply various relations toward ethnic belonging—from the closest local community to the widest community of the world, all humanity" (*ibid.*). Extreme forms of closure include ethnocentrism, localism, national exclusivism, chauvinism, tribalism and xenophobia, while according to Pantić, extreme forms of openness include not only internationalism, cosmopolitanism and overall human links, but also xenophilia and negative national identification (identification with other, so-called large nations). It seems highly problematic to refer to these other forms as being "open to the world," which is why, in our scale for examination of maximum openness, we retained only the statements that man feels best as a citizen of the world, or that mankind should make it its objective to eliminate divisions into nations. Three items on the scale speak in favor of being closed to the world (i.e., strong national affiliation), and three speak in favor of openness. The respondents were asked to express the degree of their agreement or disagreement with each of them.

Research results show that in the sample of participants in the 1996–97 student protest, openness toward the world prevails. The average is 20.10 (or 3.35 when reduced to a five-point scale). This figure is almost identical to the result obtained using the same scale in a survey of secondary-school children carried out in 1994 (20.19) in Belgrade, Valjevo and Leskovac (Kuzmanović, 1995). It seems that after the horrors of the civil war, young people are again showing increased openness to the world, and their national exclusiveness is growing weaker. A few years ago (1993), with a somewhat different scale, we found a substantially larger degree of exclusive nationalism on a general population sample, but even then, most students had a non-nationalist orientation (Golubović, Kuzmanović and Vasović, 1995).

The kind and degree of the students' openness to the world may be illustrated by their responses to a few typical questions. For instance, the statement, "It is necessary for every nation to be open to the world and the influence of other cultures" elicited agreement from 89 percent of respondents (while only 6.7 percent rejected it). Another statement, "Openness to the world brings a nation greater harm than good," was rejected by 80 percent of respondents, compared with only 12 percent who accepted it. However, the division was more marked concerning the statement, "It is better to be a citizen of the world than to belong to a certain nation," which met with the approval of 48 percent of student protesters and the disapproval of 37 percent. Therefore, many would like to link with the world, but without neglecting their national identity. This is even more obvious from the answers to the statement, "Mankind must make it its objective to eliminate divisions into nations," which was accepted and rejected by 41 percent and 43 percent of respondents, respectively (15 percent were undecided). The experience of civil war has, for some people, resulted in a wish that nations as social groups would disappear. However, a fair number of these people still find this group an important basis of their social identity. This is revealed by responses to a special question in a survey (also of students in the protest) done by D. Popadić, who asked the respondents how important their national affiliation was for them personally. Twenty-seven percent stated that they considered their national affiliation highly important, and another 31 percent found it fairly important (Table 2).

*Table 2*

Importance of national affiliation for participants
in the student protest

| How important is your national affiliation to you? | Protest '96/97 (366 respondents) % | Protest '92 (374 respondents) % | General population 1993 (1555 respondents) % |
|---|---|---|---|
| Very important | 27 | 12 | 31 |
| Fairly important | 31 | 27 | 30 |
| Somewhat important | 21 | 27 | 21 |
| Fairly unimportant | 11 | 16 | 10 |
| Unimportant | 11 | 18 | 8 |

We note that this group finds national affiliation more important than did the participants in the 1992 protest. Students taking part in the 1996–97 protest are closer to the general population of Serbia surveyed in 1993 (Golubović, Kuzmanović and Vasović, 1995) than to the general student population of Serbia surveyed that same year.

The importance of national affiliation for participants of the 1996–97 student protest is revealed by answers to yet another question. The respondents were given a list of five social groups and asked to indicate which they considered most important. The largest number of them opted for nation (43 percent), followed by profession (16 percent) and generation (14 percent). Only 5 percent opted for class, while 3 percent chose religion (even though, when specifically asked, 42 percent identified themselves as believers).

The importance of national identity for many respondents does not lead to the conclusion that they are all characterized by national exclusivism and chauvinism. Many of them think of national identity as an element of patriotism or assign psychological importance to their attachment to a recognizable social group; this does not prevent them from making simultaneous demands to be linked with the world. The wish to be linked with the world is revealed by the fact that 43 percent of respondents completely agreed that Yugoslavia should join the European Union sometime in the future, while 38 percent approved of the idea fairly strongly.

As for national feelings and attitudes, we should note that conflicts between nations on the territory of the former Yugoslavia created mistrust and fear of others, which was reflected to some degree in the answers of our respondents. Thus, while many express considerable openness toward the world, 42 percent of respondents simultaneously agree with the statement, "One should be cautious and restrained with respect to other nations, even when they are friendly toward us." This, again, should not be immediately interpreted as hatred and hostility toward others, but primarily as fear and uncertainty of a people who were exposed to an unpleasant experience. This has led to a paradoxical situation (previously noted in certain other parts of the former Yugoslavia): a fair number of people simultaneously express both considerable openness to the world and mistrust toward the nations which until yesterday they considered the closest. Paradoxes of this kind also include the fact that, when asked about the solutions for Kosovo and Metohija, 36 percent of our respondents supported the abolishment of any autonomy, however democratic they appeared on the relevant scale. Other responses to this question show the acceptance of other solutions as follows: current status of the province (14 percent), confederate status within Yugoslavia (11 percent) division into Serbian and Albanian parts (11 percent), status of the province such as existed in line with the 1974 constitution (8 percent), and creation of an independent state, by itself or unified with Albania (only 1 percent). Although there is a correlation between openness to the world and the position on the solution for Kosovo (C = 0.40), abolishment of any autonomy is supported by a substantial number of those who expressed considerable openness toward the world. Kosovo has become a painful problem for the Serbs, and many people who are often democratic and rational stop behaving rationally when discussing it.

## Social activism as value orientation

In order for the participants of an ongoing social action to be able to form a more lasting movement, they need more than specific value orientations and political attitudes. They also need a sufficiently strong motivation, a potential for long-term engagement. Over the past years the analysts have often pointed to the apathy of the young, and systematic research efforts indicated that interest in social engagement was decreasing (Kuzmanović, 1995). In this particular case we used a reduced scale to examine social engagement or social activism as a value orientation (Kuzmanović, 1984, 1995).

This scale revealed that participants in the student protest predominantly accepted social activism as a value orientation and rejected passivity. The average we obtained was 20.48 (or reduced to the five-point scale, 3.41). By way of comparison, let us mention that by using this same scale on a sample of 12th graders in Belgrade, Valjevo and Leskovac in 1994, we obtained an average of 15.50 (or 2.58), which indicates a predominant rejection of activism as a value orientation. For instance, 69 percent of protest participants approved of the statement "I would find it very hard if I did not have the possibility to discuss various social problems," while a remarkable 72 percent rejected the statement "I prefer to let others attend to social problems, so I can deal with something else." In answer to a direct question: "Are you interested in politics?" 27 percent stated they were very interested, 51 percent were fairly interested, 16 percent were "not particularly interested" and only 6 percent said they were not interested at all. Thus, interest in politics does exist, but it is not intensive with all participants, and a small number of them, regardless of the fact that they come to protest, are not interested in politics (perhaps they do not experience their engagement as being political).

The potential for engagement of students is also reflected in their relation toward the so-called Promethean way of life, which is described in the following manner: "One has to be constantly active in changing the situation and relations in the environment and society in general; to fight for distant objectives and ideas even when faced with resistance from one's environment; to be ready to make major sacrifices for the ideas one believes are right." This way of life is considered desirable by 53 percent of respondents, but only 19 percent of them would very much like to live that way, which is only understandable, since this is a kind of life which requires major efforts and a readiness to take risks and make sacrifices. Close to a third (30 percent) of respondents are undecided, while 17 percent would not like to lead that kind of life. It is likely that a certain (not negligible) number of protest participants experience their participation as normal social engagement for elimination of certain injustices and the protection of basic civil rights, rather than as a romantic fascination with ideals and idealistic struggle for objectives which are difficult to reach (something characteristic, for example, of many participants in the 1968 student protest).

An essential psychological condition for social engagement is that the actors are optimistic that their common action may cause a shift or accomplish some change, or at least initiate the desired change. This minimum condition was met in the case of participants in the 1996–97 student protest. When asked "Do you think that it is possible that the citizens with their actions (such as demonstrations, rallies and protest) and their pressure will bring about or accelerate some change?" exactly one-fifth of respondents said it was quite possible, close to two-thirds (64 percent) "believed that it was, even under the circumstances, possible," while 7 percent were undecided and 8 percent had serious doubts as to this possibility. Only 0.7 percent did not believe this was possible at all. Naturally, this is, to a degree, attributable to "participant optimism," but it is in any case a suitable basis for persistence in action.

## Self-perception of global
## political orientation

General political orientation is often presented in characteristic dimensions—e.g., "liberalism-statism," "radicalism-conservatism," "political left-right." However, although the concepts of the left and right may have lost their clear meaning today, or here obtained special connotations, we wanted to see how the participants perceived themselves in these dimensions. The results we obtained were somewhat surprising (cf. Table 3), because the number of students who classified themselves to the right is large (55 percent of the total). The fact that few of them see themselves inclining to the left (4.3 percent of the total) is not surprising, because the notion of the left has a negative connotation for the students (primarily linked with the Union of the Yugoslav Left), while members of the left mostly did not take part in the protest. However, it is amazing that few of them saw themselves as members or sympathizers of the political center, although the members of the *Zajedno* coalition (or at least some of them) have, of late, presented themselves as parties of the center. But the findings remain. It may be that for the students the position of the political center does not imply a sufficiently critical relation toward the ruling parties.

*Table 3*

Self-perception of the participants' own
global political orientation (%)

| | |
|---|---|
| Extreme right | 9 |
| Right of center | 18 |
| Moderate right | 28 |
| Center | 21 |
| Moderate left | 3 |
| Left of center | 0.5 |
| Extreme left | 0.8 |
| I don't know | 12 |
| I am not interested in politics | 8 |

# Conclusion

The survey carried out on a sample of 402 participants in the 1996–97 student protest revealed that the largest number of them accept a democratic orientation, prefer individual freedom to equality and overwhelmingly reject extreme egalitarianism. Furthermore, they display low authoritarianism and a disinclination toward conformist behavior. This group finds social engagement an important value orientation and is more interested in politics and social problems than other segments of the population are. The students who in late 1996 and early 1997 protested in the streets of Belgrade demonstrate a high degree of openness to the world, but many of them simultaneously attach importance to their national identity. This, in our view, in most cases does not imply national exclusiveness, but rather a kind of national self-awareness. It is what is known as divided national affiliation—simultaneous attachment to one's own nation and humanity, the world community. Certain elements of nationalism and mistrust of other nations (primarily those who live close by) should be understood as a consequence of everything that happened in this territory over the past 10 years or so, especially since the beginning of the destruction of Yugoslavia and the war.

At the outset of this text, we wondered about the existence of conditions—related to elements of the common value system—for this protest to grow into a lasting movement. On the basis of the research findings, we can say that such conditions do exist (at least insofar as value orientations and binding elements are concerned) and that we are already witnessing the beginning of a modern, democratic movement led by an educated young generation. But its further destiny, namely whether it will continue to grow or die out like some before it, will also depend on the specific circumstances and other social actors.

## *Note*

1. A famous sentence from Freud reads: "We are worried what the Soviets will do once they exterminate the bourgeois". Freud simply did not believe in the goodness of human nature and thought that the use of violence for declared humanistic ends often concealed utterly egoistic and aggressive aspirations.

## Bibliography

Adorno, T.W. et al. (1964): *The Authoritarian Personality*, I–II, John Wiley and Sons, New York.

Fromm, E. (1941): *Escape from Freedom*, Farrar & Rinehart, Inc., New York, 1941.

Fromm, E. (1955): *The Sane Society*, Rinehart, New York.

Golubović, Z, B. Kuzmanović, and M. Vasović (1995): *Društveni karakter i društvene promene u svetlu nacionalnih sukoba* (Social character and social change in the light of national conflicts), Institut za filozofiju i društvenu teoriju i Filip Višnjić, Belgrade.

Inglehart, R. (1977): *The Silent Revolution*, Princeton University Press, Princeton.

Kuzmanović, B. (1984): "Motivaciono-vrednosna osnova odnosa prema samoupravljanju i učešća u samoupravljanju" (Motivational-value basis of the attitude toward self-management and participation in self-management), *Psihološka istraživanja* (Psychological research), 3, pp. 465–546, Institut za psihologiju, Belgrade.

Kuzmanović, B. (1990): "Vrednosne orijentacije učenika završnog razreda osnovne škole" (Value orientations of students in final grades of elementary school), in: Havelka, N. *et al., Efekti osnovnog školovanja* (Effects of elementary-school education), Institut za psihologiju, Belgrade.

Kuzmanović, B. (1995): "Autoritarnost kao socijalnopsihološka karakteristika" (Authoritarianism as a social-psychological characteristic), in: Golubović, Z. et al., *Društveni karakter i društvene promene u svetlu nacionalnih sukoba* (Social character and social change in the light of national conflicts), Institut za filozofiju i društvenu teoriju i Filip Višnjić, Belgrade.

Kuzmanović, B. (1995a): "Društvene promene i promene vrednosnih orijentacija učenika" (Social changes and changes in value orientation of students), *Psihološka istraživanja* (Psychological research), 7, pp. 17–47, Institut za psihologiju, Belgrade.

Kuzmanović, B. (1996): "Stepen i činioci autoritarnosti" (Degree and factors of authoritarianism), manuscript.

Pantić, D. (1981): *Vrednosne orijentacije mladih u Srbiji* (Value orientations of the young in Serbia), Izdavački centar SSO, Belgrade.

Popović, M. *et al.* (1987): *Društvene nejednakosti* (Social inequalities), Institut za sociološka istraživanja Filozofskog fakulteta, Belgrade.

Rokeach, M. (1973): *The Nature of Values*, Free Press, New York.

Stanojević, R. (1979): *Idejno-politička opredeljenja i društveno-politička angažovanost mladih u Beogradu* (Ideological-political orientation and socio-political engagement of the young in Belgrade), GK SSO, Belgrade.

Tomanović, V. (1977): *Omladina i socijalizam* (Youth and socialism), Mladost, Belgrade.

Vasović, M. (1992): "Svest o socijalno-ekonomskim nejednakostima u jugoslovenskom društvu" (Consciousness of social-economic inequalities in the Yugoslav society), doctoral thesis, Filozofski fakultet, Belgrade.

# Student Protests:
# Comparative Analysis of the 1992 and 1996–97 Protests

*Dragan Popadić*

The struggle of man against authority is the struggle of memory against oblivion noted Milan Kundera in one of his novels. The desire to save from oblivion, in as precise a form as possible, an event which, when it happened, was immediately hushed up and used for manipulation inspired a group of researchers of the Institute of Psychology to engage in a study of the 1992 student protest. Another motive was their strong intellectual curiosity—the awareness that we were witnesses to an important and relatively brief social event which, while it lasted, offered the opportunity for a close study of important socio-psychological phenomena. The student protest that started in 1996 presented an equal challenge to the researchers and elicited identical reactions. Due to a media blackout, the likes of which would not have been conceivable even during the war year of 1992, the need to preserve for future study as much information on the protest as possible was still greater. Scenes observed during the initial days of the new protest stirred the memories of those who had witnessed the 1992 protest: packed amphitheaters, slogans on windows (some even with identical contents), various services organized by the students, walks through the streets, the same dilemmas in continuing talks, the same pulsing of positive energy. At times one could hardly believe that this was not the same protest continuing after a brief pause, but an altogether new event. A substantial number of participants in the later event had no direct experience with the former. Many of them were finishing elementary school at that time! The astonishing similarity of some details, as well as the awareness of essential differences, inspired us to make the comparison of the two student protests as presented in this text.

The two student protests, though are not the only ones which took place in the recent past, were subsequently analyzed and mutually compared. Let us mention a few such protests at the University of Belgrade, such as, the equally famous student protest of June 1968 and a lesser-known protest in 1954, as well as the demonstration in front of the Federal Parliament in February 1989, the so-called Terazije protest in March 1991, the protest of March 1992, etc.[1]

It is very difficult to collect the data on events at the time of their unfolding, especially if they happen suddenly and unexpectedly and their end or duration cannot be predicted. A researcher who undertakes to do this faces a number of limitations posed by various practical problems as well as the lack of insight into the entirety of the phenomena. This renders the comparison of data depicting the two events difficult and uncertain. But despite these reservations, some collating is both possible and useful. This text will aim primarily at comparisons based on certain findings of surveys carried out during both student protests. In addition to the empirical data collected this way, I will also draw on the available written material, primarily press reports.

The basis for this comparison are the results of a survey carried out in 1992 on a sample of 374 students interviewed on the 12th day of the protest,[2] when it was already well under way and formed and when it had, in a way, reached its zenith (for more detailed results, see Kuzmanović, 1993; Popadić, 1993).

A number of surveys were carried out during the 1996–97 protest. The first one was done on the 13th day of the protest, December 4, 1996, and the respondents were students participating in the protest. The second survey followed a few days later, in the period from December 8 to 11, encompassing the participants of the student and civil protests as well as students and citizens who did not support the protests. The third survey, the findings of which are analyzed in the text by B. Kuzmanović (see p. 131 in the present volume), was carried out from December 17 to 19. In order to facilitate the comparison of the findings, some questions were retained in the same form they had had in 1992. It would be difficult to specify the exact stage of the protest registered by these surveys, but we could at least say that the first one was done at the time when the protest was gaining momentum (when it was faced with a complete media blackout and started obtaining the organized support of professors, etc.).

Student protests, just like all profound social events, do not have permanent participants. In a situation when the number of participants changes on a daily basis, or from one action to the next, when even the criteria for distinguishing participants from non-participants are vague and subject to daily change, in other words, when it is impossible to identify all those who make up the population of protest participants, selecting the sample for such an indefinite population presents a major problem. Under such conditions, as it was impossible to use the standard methods to design and secure the sample or even to subsequently check its representativeness, we decided for a convenience sample where the interviewers would try to ensure as diverse and representative a sample as possible. The first survey was done in the afternoon and evening hours when the student and citizens' walks were over and the students gathered at their faculties to rest, hear the latest news or attend organized talks. A large number of student-interviewers "covered" all faculties where the students gathered.[3] As a result, the first survey included 391 students from over 20 faculties and high schools. For the purpose of this comparison, we have singled out the responses of student protesters collected in the second survey, which aimed to examine the participants and non-participants in both protests. The respondents were sought not only at faculties but also in student dormitories, in their apartments and in the streets. The overall sample consisted of 180 students who took part in the student protest on a regular or temporary basis.

## What did the students demand?

Demands posed by the students in 1992 appear substantially more ambitious than those of four years later. The protest of 1992 took place immediately after the UN Security Council had introduced sanctions against Yugoslavia, and it reflected wider dissatisfaction in society, as well as a conviction that radical reorganization of the highest political institutions was required in order to find a way out of this situation. The main demands of the students included the disbanding of the Serbian Parliament and government, resignation of Serbian President Slobodan Milošević, formation of a government of national salvation and the scheduling of elections.

The protests of 1996 emerged as a result of a gradually uncovered fraud at the local elections and the increasing awareness of the public that this theft of votes had been organized and concealed by the authorities. Soon after they started protesting, the students formulated three demands. The basic one was for the immediate establishment of a commission which would establish the electoral results objectively. This request was later (on January 9, 1997) changed into a demand for the recognition of the electoral results, their proclamation in line with the OSCE report, as well as initiation of a procedure to establish responsibility for the electoral swindle. In addition, the students demanded the replacement of the rector and student-vice-rector, whose statements and acts objectively worked against rather than for the students whom they represented.

## How the participants perceived the protest

We will start this analysis by comparing the answers given by students in 1992 and 1996 to identical questions related to their expectations of the further course of the protest, their willingness to continue participating in it and the support they received from their families.

The review of students' expectations of the outcome of the protest (Figure 1) reveals that their participation, even during what we could conditionally call the protest's peak, was not accompanied by a firm conviction that the protest would end in the fulfillment of the demands they had put forward. Such expectations were regularly noted only with a small minority of students. At least as many students (twice as many in the 1992 protest) suggested that the protest would end in failure, either by petering out without the demands being fulfilled or being terminated by force. In both cases the largest group expected that the protest would end in a kind of a compromise or at least in a way which would be neither a complete success nor a total washout.

Changes demanded in 1992 were so thorough that it was unrealistic to expect that the students themselves would be able to bring them about by boycotting classes. Furthermore, the general situation, in which the entire state mechanism, from the military to propaganda organs, was set in motion to promote the Bosnian war, could hardly encourage optimistic expectations of a sudden about-face. In addition, the struggle for the fulfillment of protest demands was complicated by the fact that the replacement of the political leadership was demanded for different reasons and often from diametrically opposed positions. Some accused Milošević of causing the war, while others accused him of inferior abili-

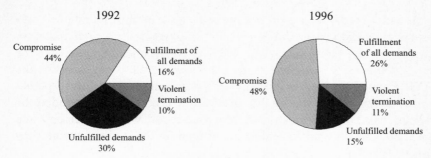

*Figure 1.* How will the protest end?

ties and insufficient resoluteness in conducting the war. The students supported the demand for deposing the authorities, but without stating their reasons, so as to create as wide and as unified a front as possible. They carefully avoided the topics which required an explanation of their positions, primarily concerning the responsibility for the war and the introduction of sanctions. But this, in turn, deprived their demands of the support of additional argumentation and specific facts and thereby reduced their weight.

On the other hand, the subject of the 1996–97 protest was the theft of votes on local (thus not crucial) elections, which was quite obvious and substantiated by material evidence. The fulfillment of the protesters' demands, i.e., the acknowledgement of the genuine electoral results, could have been attained without contesting the authority of the ruling circle. Moreover, citizens all over Serbia reacted angrily and in an organized manner from the very beginning, thus making it clear that they would not accept the theft of votes, and the international community had already signaled that it would not tolerate the electoral fraud. If we also take into account that the students' initial demand was not the acknowledgement of the second round of elections, but merely the formation of a commission to investigate what had actually happened, I would say that the task the students in 1996–97 assigned themselves was a very easy one and that the fact that only 26 percent of them believed that the demands would be met indicates their remarkable faintheartedness.

However, these differences in anticipation of the protest outcome did not substantially influence the students' intentions to continue their engagement: a large majority of respondents stated that they intended to

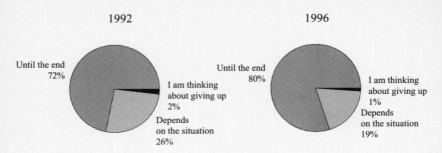

*Figure 2.* How long do you intend
to participate in the protest?

stay in the protest until the end, whatever happened (Figure 2). Those
who were convinced that the protest would fail should be sought primarily among the students who did not take part in the protest; they were
disheartened by the feeling that an action of this kind was futile. But
many with pessimistic expectations were, nevertheless, ready to participate in the protest until its end.[4]

Just as they express somewhat more resoluteness and more optimistic expectations, the students in 1996–97 also obtain greater support from
their environment (Figure 3). The largest number of participants in the
1992 student protest thought that their parents had no objections to their
decision to demonstrate, while only 18 percent believed that their parents were opposed to it. (This is a significant piece of information, since
one of the most important propaganda instruments of that time—not
used in 1996—was to keep repeating that parents were against their children's activities and were calling on them to go back to their studies.) In
1996–97 the largest number believed that their parents supported them.
Statements about having one's parents' support should not be understood as mere guessing. Parallel with the 1996–97 student protest, a
mass civic protest with the same basic demands unfolded throughout
Serbia.

In addition to these differences in estimates, we should also take into
account the fact that the 1996–97 student protest after the survey (thus
in the period that would better correspond to the 1992 survey) was substantially more massive and had greater prospects of success than at the
time the survey was carried out. Based on all this evidence, we may
conclude that the participants in the 1996–97 protest were more numer-

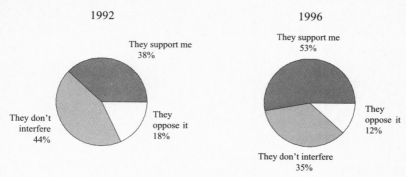

*Figure 3.* Parents' views

ous[5] than their colleagues in 1992, that they manifested greater resoluteness and more optimism and also that they enjoyed wider support in their surroundings. However, if we look at the both groups of students' demands, it is surprising that this difference is not even higher. To be more precise, from the vantage point of the present day, the optimism and enthusiasm of students in 1992 might appear surprisingly large.

## Relation toward the civil protest

Neither the 1992 nor the 1996–97 student protests developed independently. Both evolved in parallel with larger civil protests organized by opposition political parties. In 1992, it was the St. Vitus' Day Convention, the largest opposition gathering in Belgrade until that time, organized by DEPOS,[6] while in 1996–97 it was a protest organized by the *Zajedno* coalition, which developed from November 20 onwards and was also triggered by the falsification of the results of local elections. This is no coincidence, but rather a rule, which applies almost without exception. In 1991, the Terazije student protest was a continuation of the violently discontinued opposition protest of March 9. The demands the students posed in March 1992 were identical to those voiced by the Democratic Party at the same time. The protest organized in front of the Federal Parliament on February 27, 1989, was initiated by the students, but they were soon, and in an organized manner, joined by other citizens voicing demands that reflected the policy of the Serbian leadership of that time.

The parallel unfolding of their protest with that of the parties normally required the students to declare their position toward the party protest. The first reaction was usually a distancing from the parties and a public insistence that the student protest had a non-party nature. Just as the party leaders were prohibited from addressing the citizens gathered around the Terazije fountain in 1991, so were the members of the DEPOS council told that they did not belong in the student march in 1992. In 1996 a decision was taken that the students gathered on the plaza in front of the Faculty of Philosophy should not be addressed by party figures, while professors who were known to be members of certain parties could not address their students even in the amphitheater of the Faculty of Philosophy (although these limitations were subsequently waived). The reasons for this kind of distancing are numerous. On the one hand, the students were defending themselves from the regime by reducing their vulnerability to attack in a situation when opposition parties were vilified (which has been happening ever since the introduction of the multi-party system in Serbia). A link between the students and these parties would have intensified the negative stereotypes and grave accusations as a prelude to the use of repressive measures. This logic was bolstered by a widespread belief that politics and party involvement were dirty work, something which was bad in and of itself ("struggle for power"), just as youth was, again in a stereotypical way, invariably equated with progress, purity and incorruptibility.[7] From this point of view, a possible link with opposition parties may only be perceived as a situation in which these parties stand behind the students, namely that the students are naïve and manipulated children.[8] A non-party (or supra-party) position is, furthermore, the only possibility for rallying mass support for the same objectives from students who may be members or sympathizers of various parties and from those who are distrustful of anything with a party or political label. And, finally, a supra-party approach provides protection from the parties themselves, and gives the students the possibility for an organizational autonomy, especially in a situation when it is feared that the students, who are not real actors in the political struggle, are being used by parties merely to increase the pressure and secure a better position in negotiations on their own interests.

It is interesting that, as a rule, the regime, faced with parallel protests, has the same needs. It seeks to set the two apart either by continuously repeating (through various comments, presentation of views of "ordinary people" or statements of parties and student organizations close to it) that the students should be beyond the parties (under a slogan which might be formulated as "politics for politicians, studies for students") or by publicizing the fact that the students are distancing themselves from the parties.[9]

However, the very fact that the student protest developed in parallel with the party one, especially since their demands were essentially the same, may cast some doubt on their non-party nature. But both in 1992 and 1996–97, the protests were non-partisan in terms of their demands, to the extent that they voiced demands posed by a coalition of diverse parties, thus demands which did not reflect particular interests of individual parties but were shared by all of them. In addition, the main demand of the 1996–97 protest, although the parties had already posed it, had to do with defending the principle of the legal state and the role of citizens, something which is above any party affiliation.

In any case, both times the students were faced with the dilemma of how to position themselves toward the party protest and, on both occasions, it was solved in the same way. The students did not collectively join the St. Vitus' Day Convention in 1992 or the *Zajedno* coalition protest in 1996–97. Judging by the responses to our survey, the students in 1992 were divided on this issue, although the majority supported the idea of collectively joining the opposition's protest. At that time, 50 percent of respondents stated that they should join the Convention collectively, 21 percent were undecided, while 29 percent opposed the idea. It appears that in 1996–97, reservations toward the party protest were much higher. A solid 86 percent of students believed that the student protest should remain as independent as possible from the protest of the *Zajedno* coalition, while only 14 percent expressed support for firmer links. Furthermore, only 4 percent stated that the student protest should be a political and party protest, while 77 percent believed that it should be political but not party-related and 18 percent thought that it should not even be political. These views coincide with the students' perception of the protest itself: 6 percent of students described the 1996–97 protest as a political and party protest, 82 percent as a political but not party protest, while 12 percent believed that it was neither party nor political protest. (It is obvious that a number of students attached too narrow, if not slightly pejorative, meanings to the term "political.") The students were also divided over whether the party personalities should be allowed to address them, with 44 percent and 56 percent supporting and opposing the idea, respectively.

This kind of distancing should not be understood as opposing the protests of the *Zajedno* coalition. On the contrary, a large number of participants—86 percent—had a positive opinion about the coalition's protest, while 10 percent had neither a good nor a bad opinion, and only 9 percent expressed a negative opinion. Moreover, support implies not only a positive opinion but also active participation. Thus 22 percent of participants in the student protest stated that they regularly went to *Zajedno* coalition protests, while 46 percent of them did so occassionally.[10] Therefore, we believe that their insistence on the independence of the student protest was primarily due to the awareness that this independence implied numerous advantages of autonomous organization and more positive attitudes of the regime and the public toward the protest. The need for a different way of fighting for the same objectives was particularly emphasized in the first stage of the protest, when the participants of the party protest—in contrast with the strategy of the students—were invited to express themselves by hurling eggs. In addition, a large number of students, despite the common demands, did not identify themselves as party-affiliated. Sixty-seven percent of them (62 percent in the second survey) did not consider themselves sympathizers of any specific political party.

## Attitude toward political parties

The insistence of the students on the non-party nature of their own protest did not mean that they detached themselves from all parties, especially not to an equal degree.

We looked into the party preferences in both 1992 and 1996–97 by giving the respondents a list of the most important parties and asking them to rate their attitudes toward specific parties on a scale from 1 to 5. Average ratings of the parties are presented in Figures 4 and 5.

The students expressed explicitly negative attitudes toward the parties in the ruling Left coalition. These parties—the Socialist Party of Serbia (SPS), the Union of the Yugoslav Left (JUL) and New Democracy (ND)—actually reached the bottom: almost everyone rated them the lowest. This is only one indicator of the huge mistrust of the young

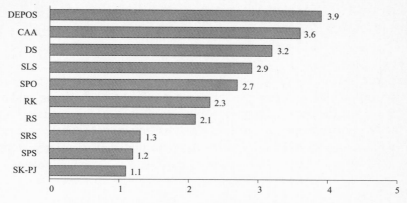

*Figure 4.* Average ratings of political parties, 1992

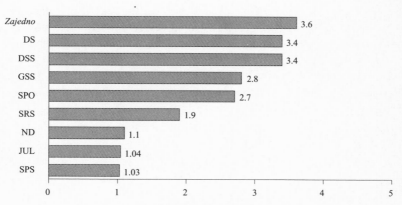

*Figure 5.* Average ratings of political parties, 1996

toward the leading state institutions. Since the ruling parties (primarily the SPS and the Yugoslav Left) presented themselves as the parties of the left, it turned out that the authorities' attempt to cover the entire political space left of center did not bring them the expected votes of the young, who might otherwise lean toward such ideas. The regime merely managed to discredit the ideas of the left, since they were, in the consciousness of the young, linked with the ideological deceit and corruption of those in power.

The second bloc consisted of parties of the democratic opposition. The best-rated among them were the Democratic Party (DS) and the Democratic Party of Serbia (DSS). Next came the Civic Alliance of Serbia (GSS) and the Serbian Renewal Movement (SPO), although with these parties grades of 1 and 2 prevail, in contrast with the DS and the DSS, which were assigned higher grades (4 and 5) by most respondents. The *Zajedno* coalition was also rated better than its member parties; in fact, a quarter of respondents gave it the highest grade. The heterogeneous party affiliation of student participants is clearly indicated by the fact that the grades given to all these parties range from the lowest to the highest. In other words, each one of them had both fervent supporters and opponents among protest participants.

In between these two groups of parties was the Serbian Radical Party (SRS). The SRS was rated the lowest by almost half the students, but the range of grades given to this party goes all the way to the highest one. The low rating of this party is probably the consequence not only of ideological disagreement but also of reactions to the negative statements of the SRS about the student movements in 1992 and 1996–97.[11]

The picture of 1992 is not easy to compare with that of 1996–97, primarily because of the extremely rapid changes on the domestic political scene. Some widely known parties die out or are forgotten, while new ones are established. In addition, although the names of some parties have remained the same, their leaderships, membership and programs may have changed. Still, a careful analysis indicates that the situation in 1992 was very similar to the one of 1996–97; only the list of parties important at that time was different. The lowest rating at that time was assigned to the SPS and the League of Communists-Movement for Yugoslavia (SK-PJ), with the SRS close by in the second-lowest position. At that time, the SRS was not perceived as an opposition party. Furthermore, Šešelj, referred to by the students as "the red duke" (the title of a commanding officer in the Chetnik movement), had a much harsher attitude toward the students than those who were the direct target of the student protest. The best-rated was DEPOS, along with the Center for Anti-War Action (CAA), which confirms the tendency of students to support coalitions and associations that fight for wider social objectives. The Republican Club (RK) and the Reform Party (RP), which later grew into the Civil Alliance of Serbia, although closely linked with the CAA, were given a substantially lower rating than the one the GSS enjoys today.

Paradoxically, the SPO, which was the strongest party in the most popular coalition, DEPOS, was given lower ratings by the students than two other important parties in the democratic opposition due to the substantial percentage of those who rated this party the lowest. However, we should recall that of all opposition parties, the SPO was the subject of the most frequent media condemnations.

## What has remained the same?

Writing about the 1992 student protest, B. Kuzmanović made the following conclusion: "Someone has somewhat pathetically noted that the student protest was like a phoenix rising from the ashes. At this point in time it is once again in the ashes, and we will have to see when it will rise again" (Kuzmanović et al., 1993: 194). Four and a half years later, the student protest did rise from the ashes once again in a still more dramatic form. But, despite the inevitable differences, the similarities between the two protests appear much more conspicuous, as if we were really talking about the rekindling of the same protest. The changes we may note are primarily the consequence of different demands and the changed social contexts rather than differences in basic political options or inclinations toward different strategic and tactical decisions. In the first place, the student protest retained the same basic goal as before. This accounts for the largest difference between it and the party protest with which it shares the same objectives and the same destiny. While the opposition parties at their rallies seek to link and reinforce their own membership, to increase its confidence and numbers, the students try to win over the public and expand the circle of like-minded persons. The parties tend to reinforce their positions by closing ranks and address their active and potential membership. Students, on their part, address others, those who are undecided or of different minds, and even their opponents, trying to win them over.

The most efficient means for that purpose are those for which the students happen to be well cut out. The important thing is not to accept the language of hatred, fear and threats, but to be witty, cheerful, charming, creative and open toward others, to devise ever new and headline-grabbing actions and do so with enthusiasm and optimism.

The students applied this strategy during the so-called velvet revolution (in March 1991). It was commonly used in 1992 and perfected during the most recent student protest (there was certainly enough time to do that). Witty slogans and posters, performances, links with other universities, winning artists and public personalities over to their side: all these elements had been "patented" in the 1992 student protest but were not used to their fullest until 1996–97.[12] The walks, which were the most attractive element for the citizens and most dangerous for the authorities, appeared as an alternative to the rallies used in the 1992 student protest (the students were not permitted to walk through Dedinje either at that time or on two occasions in 1996–97).

## Postscript

Belgrade protests will be remembered not only for their manifestations but also their results. Many participants of the 1996–97 student protests have, later on, repeated that only their protest was successful, as opposed to previous student protests, especially the one in 1992, which ended in failure. However, it would not be entirely correct to say that the 1992 student protest was a flop. Although its ambitious demands were not fulfilled, the protest accelerated social events; these could have provided a chance for the democratization of society, but further development along these lines did not depend on the students. The authorities failed to break the student resistance, and many students got a taste of freedom in the difficult days of war. In addition, they also developed and tested numerous instruments for the successful organization of such protests. Judging by the fact that all of its demands were finally met, despite the enormous resistance of the regime, the 1996–97 student protest was no doubt a success. More importantly, the protest was a valuable three-month "school of democracy" for the students, in which they formed their own identity and established links between themselves and with the world. But subsequent social events have seriously endangered the hard-won achievements of the students, through no fault of their own. The two student protests seem highly similar in this respect, in that the subsequent events, largely beyond the influence of the students, will determine whether the future will consider them winners or losers.

## Notes

1. Some of the studies and articles analyzing and comparing these protests include the ones by Arsić and Marković (1984), Popov (1990), Popadić (1992a), Popadić (1992b), Kuzmanović et al. (1993) and Popov (1996).

2. In addition to this one, a group of psychology students carried out three surveys in the period from June 17 to 27, in order to examine the attitudes of participants toward the student protests and the current political events (see: Baucal et al., 1993).

3. Interviewing and preparation of data for statistical processing was completed by psychology students Ana Altaras, Ivana Damjanović, Hana David, Nataša Doševska, Biljana Jokić, Zoran Krstić, Ana Mihajlović, Tatjana Mihajlović, Jelena Mirković, Sanja Omčikus, Ivana Orolicki, Milica Panić, Dragana Perović, Ana Popovicki, Jelena Prokić, Tatjana Ristanović, Suzana Stanović, Sandrina Špah, Dejan Videnović and Dragan Vučićević.

4. This time the missteps of the authorities should be given most of the credit for retaining and increasing the motivation (for instance, the rector's statement of November 28 that the classes were being held under normal conditions and that only a few students were involved in the protest; the termination of Radio B 92 and Radio Index broadcasting on December 3; the regime's efforts to organize its own Independent Student Movement consisting of its supporters on December 11; attempts to stop the walks using police cordons from December 28 onwards, etc.). Four years before, the regime did not react so nervously; on the other hand, the intensity of that protest was lower.

5. While press reports on student actions in 1992 estimated the number of participants at a few thousand or 10,000 in the most numerous of its actions, they spoke of tens of thousands of participants when the 1996–97 protest was concerned.

6. DEPOS (an acronym for a Democratic Movement in Serbia), is an association formed on May 23, 1992, for the purpose of unifying the democratic parties and prominent non-party personalities. Soon after its establishment, DEPOS formulated its demands, which were almost identical with the ones of the student protests at that time; they were also voiced at the St. Vitus' Day Convention.

7. See the analysis by I. Čolović (1996). The question is only to what extent the students consciously used this black-and-white categorization or shared these views themselves.

8. The daily *Borba,* in its commentary of December 2, 1996, characterized an alleged manipulation of the students on the part of the *Zajedno* coalition as the "height of inhumanity" and found "the acts of the insane group unheard of and inhuman, comparable only with fascist manipulations and abuse of chil-

dren by the separatists in Kosovo." Dragan Tomić, president of the Republican Parliament, was a bit less emotional when he said that the worst thing about the *Zajedno* coalition demonstrations, which bore all the characteristics of pro-fascist groups and ideologies, was their manipulation of children, which he found reminiscent of Hitler's tactics (*Naša borba*, December 3). The students responded by saying: "It is wonderful that you care for us, Mr. Tomić, but where were you when young men of our age were being killed in Vukovar and other battlefields, on orders from the regime you belong to? When you were spilling our blood, you did not care about our age."

9. For instance, reports published in the daily *Politika* stated on a number of occasions that the students had distanced themselves from the rallies of the *Zajedno* coalition. Describing the action of building a wall in front of the offices of the Serbian Presidency (*Politika*, December 6, 1996), the daily even wrote that by doing so, the students "were once again distancing themselves from the *Zajedno* coalition rallies," because "they build, while supporters of this coalition destroy Belgrade."

10. Data on the views concerning the civil protest have been taken from the second survey.

11. True, in 1996–97 Šešelj appeared more restrained than four years before, when he appeared with a gun and called out the names of students he accused of being foreign mercenaries and traitors. This time he was content with the statement that the Serbian Radical Party did not approve of the student protest, because its demands were political and unrelated to the problem of the university and studies (*Politika*, December 27, 1996).

12. In 1992, the students successfully popularized and developed the forms of activities applied before them by the few peace associations in organizing their civil actions (e.g., lighting of candles in front of the offices of the Serbian Presidency as a sign of protest against the war, carrying a black mourning ribbon 1300 meters long through the streets of Belgrade to manifest grief over and protest against the bombing of Sarajevo or the action called "the Bell" in front of the Yugoslav Parliament, etc.).

*Bibliography*

Arsić, M. and D. Marković (1984): *'68 Studentski bunt i društvo* ('68 student revolt and society), IIC SSO Srbija, Belgrade.

Baucal, A., D. Marković, D. Havelka, J. Pešić and R. Vulić (1993): "Studentski protest i prateća politička zbivanja vidjeni očima učesnika protesta" (Student protest and accompanying political events seen through the eyes of protest participants), in: B. Kuzmanović *et al.* (1993): *Studentski protest*

'92 (Student protest '92), Institut za psihologiju Filozofskog fakulteta, knjižara Plato, Belgrade.

Kuzmanović B. et al. (1993): *Studentski protest '92* (Student protest '92), Institut za psihologiju Filozofskog fakulteta, knjižara Plato, Belgrade.

Popadić, D. (1992a): "Prvi i drugi deseti mart" (March 10, first and second), *Republika* (Republic), No. 41–42, Belgrade.

Popadić, D. (1992b): "Studentski protest '92" (Student protest '92), *Republika* (Republic), No. 49–50, Belgrade.

Popadić, D. (1993): "Stranačka opredeljenja studenata" (Party orientations of students), in: B. Kuzmanović *et al.* (1993): *Studentski protest '92* (Student protest '92), Institut za psihologiju Filozofskog fakulteta, knjižara Plato, Belgrade.

Popov, N . (1996): "Univerzitet u ideološkom omotacu" (University in ideological wrapping), in: N. Popov, ed.: *Srpska strana rata* (The Serbian side of war), BIGZ, Belgrade.

# A Generation in Protest

*Andjelka Milić, Ljiljana Čičkarić*
*and Mihajlo Jojić*

Day after day, for months, an enormous procession of young people passed through the streets and squares of Belgrade. At the head of their column was a large banner reading "Belgrade is the world." Students who walked behind the banner were actually using a symbolic language to say that *"hic at nunc"* they were that "world" into which they were returning Belgrade (their country and nation) from the exile, humiliation and hatred it had been exposed to until recently. Thus it seems that the slogan carried at the head of the students' column did not reflect merely the vanity of the young or the romantic trance of a generation pressured by cruel reality, but it showed that this message was a purposeful step into the future. This step, taken by launching a protest against the unprecedented lawlessness of the authorities, announced that the "world" was not over there or somewhere else and was not different from us; and that if we wanted to live in that world and with it, we should not run from here to go there, to a foreign land to be foreigners, migrants or guest workers and to live in exile and seek asylum. Instead, with this act of refusal to accept abuse and manipulation, we show that we "are" the world. The transformation was not the consequence of external pressure or need, unconsciously or accidentally, but we achieved it as a conscious product of human and civil liberation. Indeed, those who walked in the column of students these days could almost feel the fresh breath of this unbridled, peaceful but resolute, joyful, lively and spontaneous flow of humanity swelling and reshaping on the inside.

This empirical research seeks to describe, interpret and clarify the actors of this undertaking and the shift it brought, after which it will hardly be possible to return to the traditional and regressive models of collective behavior and action dominating the scene of Yugoslavia's disintegration and war. Since the actors are naturally recognized and presented in the image of the protesting students, this might be the end of the story. Student protests have occurred ever since there have been students and will probably transpire in the future, and the general and synthetic knowledge based on accumulated scientific studies in the world, as well as here, could prove sufficient to satisfy the superficial curiosity of the public and the media. But a response obtained that way would leave some of the key questions open. How could one explain that, despite the large variety of the student gathering itself and over such a long period, the protest has managed to preserve its indisputable internal coherence? What accounts for the stubbornness and almost fanatical attachment of the participants to the protest's objectives, their mutual solidarity and extreme discipline, without the existence or imposition of a specific external authority or leadership?[1] One of the available conceptual explanations, which will be discussed in greater detail in the conclusion, relates to the concepts of the "political generation" and "generational mission" (R. and M. Braungart, 1984; Milić, 1987).

But before we give the explanation, there is a question of how empirically to approach the examination of the actor of the protests—what should be taken as the main reference point of observation? Students are young people in a double status: on the one hand, they are of age, citizens, legally responsible subjects and independent and already formed personalities and, to that extent, personalities and individuals who belong to the adult world. On the other hand, they are still children, immature and not independent; their economic existence still hinges on others (family, state, university); they are still maturing as personalities and are in the position of those who learn and are continuously exposed to evaluation, criticism and control by their teachers, parents, and society. They are, therefore, still on the doorstep of the adult world and largely belong only to the world of the young as a specific modern social substructure (Milić, 1987). In brief, the students can be defined as young people who are at the height of the socialization process in which the forming of their individual and social personalities is completed in a specific way.

Starting from this view of the students' population, we have defined both the objective and the characteristic approach to the participants of the student protest in this empirical research. The purpose was to arrive at the personality of protest actors through the consideration of the socialization process and its main agents the participants were exposed to.

The process of socialization develops within a general social framework, which determines all individual agents of socialization. This framework is, in the specific case of actors of the student protest, formed by the dramatic historical events that brought about the breakup of the former Yugoslavia, civil war and the total failure of Serbia and the present-day Yugoslavia to join the Central European "convoy of transition." The atmosphere of disintegration, moral decay, existential danger and insecurity provides the framework in which this generation of students is growing up. Within that framework two socializing agents are especially important for empirical observation: 1) family in its various aspects (structural, functional, developmental-psychological, interactive-educational), where it acts as the primary framework and bearer of socialization of personality of an individual, while at the same time being caught in the maelstrom of historical drama and defeat itself; and 2) student protest as the most mature form of socializing generation practice. The protest as a self-made generation collective produces and forms individual participants, although the participants are simultaneously self-actualized and produced as social personalities and thereby also define the edges of a new social time-space frame (Giddens, 1990).

Given the financial and time limitations in which the research was carried out, it was not possible to probe deeply into the action of the designated socializing agents. Instead, we had to reduce the efforts and focus only on the most important phenomena and relations in that context. The contents of the research had to be adjusted to the research technique (survey), but not at the cost of endangering the objective of the research. The questionnaire consisted of three thematic parts. The first one concerned individual characteristics of protest participants: this was needed to evaluate the nature of the protest as well as the participants themselves as its bearers. The second part had to do with the influence of the family and parents in the process of the respondents' maturation and with certain important social characteristics of the families the participants came from. The third part addressed the characteristics of the organization of the protest and the subjective relation and experience of the protest and one's engagement in it. The main focus of the research was on the family of respondents for the following reasons: first, the family is undoubtedly the most important agent of socializing development of an individual; and second, socialization in a family preceded the engagement of respondents in the student protest and has, therefore, in a way determined participation or non-participation in it.

The sample was operationalized pursuant to this main idea of the research. It consisted of two groups of protest participants and a control group of students who did not take part in the protest. We decided to call the first group of participants "protagonists"; it represents the core of the student protest. It includes all members of the Initiative and Main Boards of the student protest, consisting of representatives of all faculties at the University of Belgrade (61 in all) and a sample of students engaged within four services of the student protest (student security, logistics, medical emergency service and public relations-promotional department). The group of protagonists numbered 107 students.

The second group of protest participants, the one we refer to as "walkers," consisted of 118 students, picked at random, from the mass of students who participated every day in the manifestations of the student protest (daily walks, attendance of rallies at the plaza in front of the Faculty of Philosophy, street manifestations, actions such as the "cordon against cordon," etc.) and who accounted for the most numerous, but surprisingly persistent and stable body of the protest.

The third control group of students, "non-participants" in the protest, consisted of 110 students, again picked at random, outside the spaces where the protest took place (in libraries, student dormitories and cultural centers as well as other locations in the city). The examination of this group was intended to facilitate the specification of individual differences and characteristics of the socialization process the participants had been exposed to.

The whole sample comprised 335 students. Although small in terms of numbers, this sample proved representative for the mass of protesting students in terms of its essential socio-demographic characteristics. A comparison with some socio-demographic features of our sample with the samples of students in another investigation (cf. text by B. Kuzmanović in this collection) does not reveal substantial differences. The sample includes students from all faculties of the University of Belgrade. Gender distribution is close to balanced, with only a slight domination of men—56 percent (with the exception of the group of protagonists, which reveals a substantial difference in this respect). Most students were born in Belgrade (52.5 percent) and other urban centers in Serbia (only nine respondents said they were born in a village). National composition shows that most identify themselves as Serbs (79 percent). In addition, students mostly define themselves and their families as members of the middle class (63 percent) and less frequently as members of lower classes (clerks, workers, farmers, etc.), owing to an above-average percentage of parents with the socio-professional status of professionals with high education (48.3 percent).

## Socio-demographic characteristics of respondents and their families

In order to describe the respondents and their families, we will, this time, take only some of the crucial selective characteristics that enable us better to perceive the action potential and orientation of the participants in the student protest. In this sense we believe that we should start from the characteristics which are essential for the students, such as the reasons for choosing a specific faculty or a study group they enrolled in, success in studies and plans after graduation.

As already noted, the respondents, on the whole, display a very large diversification by faculties or study groups; 37 different faculties and high schools were registered. Still, the largest group of students is studying social sciences, followed by students in technical and natural sciences, while the students of art academies are the fewest. The distribution of participants of the student protests according to the primary categorization of the sciences they study is by no means accidental. It shows a larger or smaller susceptibity to specific scientific areas of social events. Asked what made them choose a specific faculty or school, 68 percent of the protagonists said it was what they had "always wanted" to study, as did the walkers. Opportunistic responses, i.e., the lack of independence in choosing the faculty or school, are more frequent among the non-participants, who state such reasons as parents' advice, the possibility of better employment or higher chances of passing entry tests, etc. Although the differences are not so large, and the samples are rather small, they still suggest a greater presence of characteristics such as passivity, opportunism and perhaps even conformism among the non-participants.

Success in studies reveals interesting variations among the participants and non-participants. Among those who have very good or excellent grades, the sequence by groups is as follows: protagonists come first with 46 percent, followed by walkers with 38 percent, while non-participants again rank third with 35 percent of students with above-average grades. At the same time, adequate success among non-participants was registered in 13 percent of cases compared with only 3 percent among the protagonists. If we also consider that a third of protagonists had to repeat a year, compared with more than half of non-participants (57 percent), we can no doubt conclude that the student generation of participants is more successful, active and ambitious than that of non-participants. This conclusion is further supported by the differences related to the year of entry of a faculty or school and the difference in the average age of students of the three observed groups. We found that the student non-participants were the oldest part of the student population, have been at the university the longest and, on the average, had lower grades. Answers to the question concerning the plans after graduation also reveal the expected differences among the groups. But two-thirds of students in all three groups (although somewhat more in the group of participants) responded that they wanted to complete their studies on time, or as close to it as possible. Differences appear in the following modalities of answers: 17 percent of non-participants and 10 percent of participants respectively say they will not hurry to finish the studies, but the percentages are reversed in relation to intentions to continue post-graduate and doctoral studies, announced by only 6 percent of non-participants and 16 percent of participants. Likewise, more protagonists and walkers wish to obtain a fellowship to continue their studies abroad (10.5 percent compared with 6 percent of non-participants). As for going abroad after graduation, the difference between participants and non-participants is quite substantial: 11.2 percent of the former and 24 percent of the latter are in favor of it, which clearly displays the greater pragmatism or even utilitarianism of this group of students.

Thus far, the findings indicate a greater independence, ambition and success of participants in the protest compared with non-participants. They also show a greater inclination toward utilitarianism and conformism of the non-participants compared with the participants when studies and plans for the future are concerned. Should these obvious differences be attributed to some essential socio-demographic and socio-professional characteristics of the families the two basic groups of students originate from, and to what degree? We will try to explain this in the broadest terms.

Students at universities in Serbia have long been drawn almost exclusively from urban centers and city families (Tomanović, 1997). This is partly the consequence of a powerful process of social differentiation, which started in the former Yugoslavia, and partly of the process of demographic aging and marginalization of the rural environment. In the case of our respondents, regardless of their sample group, very few students (about 15 percent) have come from rural families. However, the difference between the participants and non-participants is manifested in two other modalities: student participants more often have parents who were born in Belgrade (about a quarter), while as many as 60 percent of participants themselves were born in Belgrade. By contrast, 11 percent of non-participants had parents who had been born in Belgrade, while 40 percent were born in Belgrade themselves.

The education and profession of parents are variables that could have a multidimensional effect in the process of socialization. However, we must note that, because of general processes of social differentiation, being a student has over the decades become the privilege of the higher social strata. This is why, generally speaking, the overall sample shows an above-average educational distribution of parents. Therefore, it is important to note the differences among the two groups of students concerning the level of education and profession of their parents but also to establish the difference in the homogeneity or heterogeneity of these characteristics if both parents are observed. Protagonists have the highest share of parents with university education, master or doctoral degrees including both father and mother. They constitute more than 50 percent of this group. In the group of walkers the share of parents with high education decreases, as does the share of each of the parents with this degree of education (about 30 percent), while parents with intermediate education prevail. Among the non-participants the percentage share of parents with high education ranges between 40 and 20 for each of the parents individually. This constitutes the greatest heterogeneity in the educational distribution of the parents. In addition, non-participants, unlike the other groups, register a substantial share of parents with elementary education.

In view of variations in educational profiles, there are also differences in the structure of families by the socio-professional status of parents for the three groups of students. Basically, the differences are as follows: the group of protagonists most often have parents who are both professionals (about 70 percent) of all profiles (social, technical and natural sciences). In the case of walkers, the percentage of the modal combination of the previous group drops to less than 5 percent, while the modal combination here is that of a professional father and a clerk mother, and about 10 percent have housewife mothers. In the group of non-participants, fathers who are professionals are predominantly of technical vocation (36 percent), but there are also a lot of fathers who are clerks, workers, and pensioners. Among mothers the share of housewives increases to 20 percent. On the basis of these results one may conclude that, regardless of the above-average higher education of both parents in all three groups of students, substantial stratal differences are manifested among these groups. The group of protagonists, to all appearances, consists of families who belong to the upper middle class or a social and cultural elite of society. Walkers belong to families from the middle class, but with a substantial presence of members of the lower layers of this stratum, while non-participants come from families that are, for the most part, dispersed across the strata, since they are found in middle as well as lower strata and in marginal groups of the population (such as the retired).

In line with the strata differentiation comes the differentiation of students according to the amount of average family income. The group of protagonists is the most equalized in terms of income, since most of them (69 percent) belong to two medium income groups (1000–2000 and 2000–5000 dinars a month), and with a share of 8.44 percent in the top income category (above 5000 dinars a month). Walkers register lower incomes; the majority are concentrated in the income group of 1000–2000 dinars, while non-participants register the largest dispersion across income groups with 10 percent in the category of up to 500 dinars, 30 percent in the income group of up to 1000 dinars, and 6 percent in the group with income of over 5000 dinars.

Out of the range of family characteristics of potential importance for predicting engagement in the protest we will indicate only one determinant with significant political implications. It has to do with the membership of parents of the former League of Communists of Yugoslavia, a party which was an important actor of social mobilization of individuals (Milić, 1986). Although we arrived at this data through the statements of their children, we believe that the data are authentic, since only a small minority of respondents left the question unanswered or responded with "I don't know." We counted only the membership of respondents' fathers. In the case of protagonists' fathers, we found a 50 : 50 ratio between members and non-members. A similar situation was established with the walkers' fathers, although with a somewhat larger share of non-members. However, among non-participants' fathers, members of the Communist Party dominate over non-members (42 percent). The presence of the former party members in so high a percentage among parents of all three groups of students is due primarily to their educational-professional profiles, since the transformation of the Communist Party substantially influenced the change in its membership. However, we must note that membership itself does not say a thing about the actual party involvement of the parents, let alone their ideological profiles. Even where the statements of students concerning party membership of their parents coincide with the statements on their religious belief or atheism, there is a discrepancy between adherence to traditional religious rites (such as celebration of patron saint days, Christmas, Easter, etc.) in the families of respondents. The protagonists show the largest discrepancy between the membership of their parents in the LCY and adherence to religious customs: as many as 74 percent of respondents in this group note that their parents observe these customs. This percentage drops to 62 among the walkers and is the lowest among non-participants, amounting to a mere 57 percent. All three groups show a discrepancy between practicing of religious rites and fathers' membership of the party, but this is still, in terms of percentages, the most conspicuous in the group of protagonists. At this point, we cannot explain the degree of importance of this family ambivalence in such an important ideological sphere for the process of development of the participants' own identities or its influence in channeling their conceptual-ideological maturing. We can perhaps only ask whether this ambivalence has already been reflected in a certain detour toward "fundamentalism" manifested in some phrasing and iconography of the protest.

## Family as a framework for socialization
## —educational influence

The use of a survey method with mainly multiple-choice questions does not allow for a more detailed examination of family conditions for growing up and the nuances in the relations within it. However, the general frameworks of family relations and the upbringing of the respondents have been established, providing a basis for drawing conclusions on the possible influence of the family on the social activity of the young and the direction of this influence.

The first family variable to take into account is the birth sequence in the family. The relevant literature includes numerous indications of a link between this variable and the behavior and attitudes such as preference for power and control over others, autonomy, maturity, privacy, etc. (Handel, 1986). Our study, too, revealed statistically important variations between the three groups of students according to this characteristic. In this respect the highest percentage difference was for only-child status, which accounts for 24 percent of the group of protagonists and only 7 percent of non-participants. In the category of the elder/eldest child in the family, the three groups do not display significant variations, as opposed to the category of the younger/youngest child in the family, which is represented in the non-participant group much more (43 percent) than in the group of protagonists (26 percent). This accounts for the specific difference between the protagonists and non-participants: the former are most often the only or elder/eldest, while the latter are divided between elder/eldest and younger/youngest siblings.

This kind of grouping according to the sequence of birth among the protagonists indicates that they can be expected to have a greater degree of autonomy, freedom in decision making and support from their parents, but also a higher degree of responsibility than would be the case if children younger by birth sequence prevailed.

Another fact which speaks in favor of greater maturity and the faster gaining of independence of student participants in the protest—which derives more from their family status (as only children, elder or younger children) than from the year of their birth—is the average age of the three groups of students, which is 22.8 years for the protagonists, 21.4 for the walkers and the highest, 24.2, for non-participants.

A characteristic that may indicate the differences in family influence among the three groups of respondents was the characteristic style of upbringing by parents. We decided to differentiate between democratic, authoritarian and permissive (laissez-faire) models. The democratic style of upbringing is found most often and in equal proportions in all three groups (about 50 percent of the respondents in all three groups), but the differences appear with respect to the authoritarian and permissive styles. The authoritarian style has been noted twice as frequently among the non-participants (40 percent) than among the protagonists (24 percent), while the relation is reversed in the case of the permissive model of upbringing. The group of walkers is midway between these two, although the variation with respect to specific styles within the group itself tends to be closer to the group of protagonists than non-participants. In brief, these findings suggest that the group of protagonists was less exposed to the pressure by parents in the process of socialization than the group of non-participants, which concurs with previous findings on the manner of upbringing of an only child or older children in the family.

We tried to check whether and to what extent the student participants in the protests have also been exposed to pressures, limitations and control by the parents compared with those of the same age in the group of non-participants. For this we asked a series of questions related to the explicit prohibitions and control by parents in specific domains of their children's lives. The majority of respondents, regardless of the group they belonged to, stated that they had not been limited or restricted by their parents in any domain before they were 18 and still less after coming of age. The exceptions were curfews, restrictions on smoking and drinking, and rules about homework. However, parental restrictions decrease slightly from the group of protagonists to the non-participants. The parents appear to have raised the students more permissively than is usual in Serbian families (Vrcan *et al.*, 1986). This allows us to deduce that the differences in the styles of upbringing among the three groups of respondents were manifested in some other sectors of behavior of the respondents and in ways which are difficult to reveal using a survey method. This, however, does not mean that there are no pressures, tensions, anxieties, unbalanced or maladjusted behavior or relations in the families of the students observed.

The first direct statements on this situation were obtained from the responses on the question concerning the disagreements and conflicts between the parents, which are related precisely to the content and method of the parents' educational influence on children. Although most respondents said there were no disagreements or conflicts in the family concerning their upbringing (60–70 percent depending on the group), the remaining 30–40 percent of respondents acknowledged such disagreements and conflicts. In this context it is also important to note that there are differences between families depending on whether such disagreements of parents were openly stated, and if so, whether they caused any conflicts, or if conflicts were suppressed and covered up. Both variants are present in the observed families, although there is no statistically important difference in their distribution among the three groups of students. It may be that the use of these tactics by parents in case of such disagreements is somewhat more pronounced in the group of student participants (protagonists and walkers). All in all, these data indicate that the family relations in terms of conditions of upbringing are not so ideal as one may think, given the absence of prohibitions and strict control by the parents of respondents. But the responses obtained could, in this case, be assigned to a trend which leads toward a neutral perception of the activity of parents or else dismissal of unpleasant experiences which creates a more positive image of reality.

Responses to the next two questions, which are directly related to the specifics of family life and problems the respondents were facing, provide a different insight. The respondents were asked to give as straightforward an answer as possible to the question on important problems a family had to face and did not succeed in resolving. About a third of respondents in each group said they had encountered no problems in their family life, while another third of each group thought it necessary to mention two problems they had faced in their family life. Therefore, while a third of respondents assert that they live without any problems, another third is burdened with more than one problem. Naturally, this should not be surprising in view of the social-historical context of the observed families in the stage of intensive socialization of their offsprings. Most frequent references were made to the so-called "objective problems," mostly related to the lack of funds or some material resources (such as an apartment). Forty-five percent of student participants and about 36 percent of non-participants reported having these kinds of problems. Twelve to 15 percent of students (depending on the group) acknowledged related problems. The lowest share is that of problems related to family disturbances (such as illness of family members, death, divorce, disruptions in the behavior of members, etc.), which comes to 12 percent. However, taking also into account the respondents who mentioned two problems in the family, the frequency of families which register not only "objective" material problems, but especially problems in the sphere of interaction, and serious family dysfunctions and disruptions, increases. Generally, student participants more frequently mention problems of subjective nature, related to interactive relations within the family, while non-participants speak more often of family disruptions and dysfunctions.

On the whole, the analysis of statements on family difficulties and problems is not sufficiently convincing in terms of indicating the nature of influence of such situations on the socialization and overall behavior of respondents in social situations. It is obvious that there are numerous problems in the observed families, but in some cases, these problems succeed in mobilizing the respondents in social life, while in other cases, these had a demobilizing effect and made them passive both in private and social life.

However, answers to the question of how the respondents generally experience their family definitively reveal the character of family influence on pro-social behavior and the activity of the young. Responses referring to the family as an emotional community are found with a third of students in all three groups. More commonly, the family is defined with greater rationality, in the sense of a firm agreement and trust among family members. This response is found with 45 percent of protagonists, somewhat less among the walkers and least frequently with non-participants (37 percent). Although this difference is not statistically important, it still mildly emphasizes greater liberalism of the family among student protagonists than among non-participants, which is also in line with greater activation and orientation toward democratic values in society of participants in the student protest. However, the cardinal difference between the two groups appears in the case of negative experience of the family. While among the protagonists this experience is registered at 13 percent, it reaches as high as 30 percent among non-participants. If we take into account the previously cited findings on a roughly equal burden of problems for all three groups of families, as well as the existence of powerful dysfunctions in families caused either by disrupted interaction or the lasting absence of one of the parents (due to death, illness or divorce), which are generally equally represented in all three groups of students, it is obvious that the difference appearing in the last case has to do with a fundamental inability of the family as a group, or some of its individual members, to resolve their problems. Families who are not capable of resolving their problems exercise a powerful and constant pressure on their members, especially the younger ones, who experience that situation as a "cage" they wish to escape (Lane, 1969). This kind of family situation is seen from responses which show that family is experienced as a "passing community" that one would like to escape from or else indicate its collapse and the resulting neurosis. These families restrain the energy of their members, pulling them increasingly deeper into an inextricable web of problems, instead of giving them support to outgrow the problems and shake them off. These families do not provide the basis for social engagement of individuals, in contrast to families and parents who provide support which represents the "platform" for the development of an individual in all directions, including a forceful political identification.

## Student protests as identity practice

The second important theme of the survey had to do with the relationship of the students toward their own engagement in the protest through their identification with its specific elements and contents. In this context the role of the control group is taken by participants-walkers, since non-participants could not answer questions related to events they took no part in. This does not mean that they did not have views or positions concerning different elements of the events concerned, but these are not relevant in this case.

Among the protagonists 85 percent of students were in the protest from the start and performed the same function (61.7 percent); this applies primarily to the members of Initiative and Main Boards. About two-thirds of protagonists showed dedication to the common ideas and objectives, consciously accepting the entire burden of responsibility at the outset of the protest. By contrast, only half the walkers participated in the actions from the very beginning, supporting the initiatives of their colleagues from the group of protagonists. Compared with the protagonists they felt the burden of responsibilities and worries less and enjoyed the dynamism and imaginativeness of activity, daily walks and happenings in the streets of Belgrade more. By consciously undertaking the burden of leading functions from the very beginning, the protagonists stated more frequently than others that they enjoyed testing themselves in the new roles but also that they felt tired and sated in view of the duration of the protest and its intensity. Occasionally, it appeared that the students took on a major burden of responsibility out of proportion with their experience, knowledge and social position. This was confirmed by 79.4 percent of the protagonists, who identified the 1996–97 student protest as a movement aiming at the social reform of Serbia, while only 14 percent saw this protest as a movement of students intended to result in substantial changes at the university. Self-identification of protagonists with a wider social movement results from the common requirements of the 1996–97 student protest and the protest of the *Zajedno* coalition which developed in parallel. This is substantiated by the fact that two-thirds of students participated in both students' and citizens' protest walks. Yet the students felt their protest as strictly their own and autonomous, and manifested independence in almost all situations by insisting on a graphic and linguistic symbolic play on the word "pravo" as the essential determinant of the protest. Depending on the context, the word could have three meanings: "pravo" (straight), defining the direction of the movement, without turning left or right in political terms; "pravo" (right) in the ethical sense of a correct, truthful, proper deportment or standing, which in a sense indicates some elements of "fundamentalism" in the students' approach to themselves and society; and, finally, "pravo" (law) in the sense of legality, meaning the struggle for its observance in the face of the violation of electoral results. This symbolism is accompanied by the students' persistent adherence to certain initial principles, such as the non-party character of the protest, autonomy in the manner of its operation and duration compared with the civil protest.

In evaluating the effects of the student protest, a third of the protagonists express their full satisfaction with the success of the protest thus far, while as many as 62 percent are completely satisfied with their own engagement. For protagonists, participation in the student protest continues a process of political socialization that started in family surroundings, as they assume new, more complex and demanding roles. This fact has a decisive influence on the formation of the socio-cultural and political identity of the current generation of students and will leave a lasting mark on their personal identity.

The motivation of protagonists of the student protest as proponents of an expressly activist value orientation derives from unsatisfied social, political and cultural needs and their conscious non-acceptance of the marginalized position they have found themselves in, both as a special subgroup and as members of society in general. The awareness of the possibility to influence the change in the overall situation and open the prospects for the realization of their life plans forms the basis of an optimistic attitude manifested by a third of protagonists and walkers. Greater skepticism, expressed in the view that changes will happen but that their course cannot be determined, was noted by a third of protagonists and only a fifth of walkers. Doubts and a blurred perspective under difficult social and political conditions led some protagonists (27 percent) and just as many walkers to pessimistically judge that their participation in the protest would change nothing in terms of increasing chances for a better life. We may conclude that victorious optimism did not prevail among the students, but neither did fatalistic pessimism. In this respect again, the students—remaining consistent to their slogan of keeping away from the extremes—are sober and realistic.

The relationship between the participants in the protest and the protest, as their creation which defines them, is perhaps the best expressed by answers to the question about plans and life prospects. Life plans represent an essential aspect of self-determination of every individual, arising from his/her internal needs, the perception of one's own possibilities and the conditions for their achievement in society. In this sense the plans are a subjective expression of the dominant disposition of an individual. The answers about the extent to which the student protest has changed the life plans of participants reveal how much the respondents care about their personal autonomy even when the events they created are concerned. More than a third of both protagonists and walkers believe that participation in the protest did not change their plans, while 47 percent of protagonists and 44 percent of walkers note that it might be conducive to some change. A small number believes that it led to a complete change. On the whole, we may note that the participants resisted the challenge of events they brought about by sticking to their initial concepts and ideas.

# Student protest from the perspective of a "generational mission"

A study of youth revolts and unrest from the conceptual standpoint of a "political generation" implies an autonomous grouping of the young "by themselves," which includes a strong feeling of common belonging loyalty to common goals and values which are understood as a "generational mission" (R. and M. Braungart, 1984). Political generations result from a convergence of specific historical circumstances and generational mobilization for distinct objectives and tasks. It is therefore characteristic of generational politics to mobilize the dissatisfaction of the youth for a political action "authorizing itself ... to terminate with the past and change its previous political course" (Braungart, 1984). The same author draws on his own and other research works (Haberle, 1951) to identify four "waves"[2] of change attributable to political generations of the young over the past 150 years of world history, which gave rise to at least 40 different youth movements. Thus, although all four waves have highly different specific historical constellations, some generalization is still possible. In all situations the young faced critical conditions (foreign occupation, war, political absolutism, colonial repression, economic disaster, internal discrimination) which, in order to be overcome, required wide and profound social reforms which the social protagonists were not ready to carry out at the given moment, either because they were unable or unwilling to face the change or because they were unable to do so swiftly and efficiently. In brief, in all situations of this kind a political vacuum is established, and the reaction to this state comes precisely from the young, who feel the "staleness" of the social environment and emptiness of the existing political forms and orientations.

The social situation in Serbia and Yugoslavia is characterized by a significant degree of impotence of the main political actors to overcome the long, drawn-out crisis and social inefficiency. The protest obviously fills the vacuum created by the main actors' behavior. But this still does not allow us to speak of the appearance of a "political generation" on the social scene of Serbia. The very notion of a "political generation" is insufficiently articulated from the point of view of generational coverage. Should the term denote only the salient "core" of the protest, or also the supporters and sympathizers who belong to different calendar generations but are, nevertheless, "contemporaries" in Mannheim's sense of the term (Mannheim, 1967)? What should, in this case, be done with non-participants in the protest who belong to the same calendar generation? But independently from the methodological problems of defining the "political generation," we will try to use this concept to explain the actors of the 1996–97 student protest in Belgrade, bearing in mind less formal and more common substantial elements which might influence the appearance of a powerful idea and need for generational action.

Participants in the protests, both protagonists and walkers, entered the academic world in the crucial years of the tragic unraveling of the Yugoslav drama (1990–1993). This outcome drew some of them into its destructive maelstrom in an unexpected way. Thus, in this critical period of the country's disintegration and the start of war, 8.4 percent of protagonists were completing their compulsory military service, as well as 6.4 percent of non-participants and 5.95 percent of walkers. However, the element that substantially differentiates the protagonists from the other two groups is that they include 8.4 percent of those who volunteered during the war, who are not found in the remaining two groups. These circumstances reveal elements of their future devotion to social issues. Further social entanglement takes our protagonists through a few successive students' actions and protests with a changeable duration and demands of varying range. Namely, three-quarters of protagonists participated in one or more successive student protests and demonstrations in Belgrade since 1991 with a clear democratic character (March 1991 protest, May and June 1992 protest, strike of secondary-school graduates, peace actions and protests during 1992–93 and protests against recruitment for the army). By contrast, nonparticipants in the 1996–97 student protest in 50 percent of cases did not take part in any of these forms of protests. Protagonists appear to have the strongest inclination toward social activity and account for the group with the largest experience in these actions. The orientation towards self-determination and engagement of the protagonists for the resolution of the social crisis are, judging by some elements, reinforced by the knowledge and experience acquired within their family frameworks, as already discussed. This consideration may be substantiated by another fact, namely that in the case of protagonists, 38 percent of fathers and 36 percent of mothers participated in the student revolt in 1968 in the former Yugoslavia. This is also the case of a fifth of walkers' parents, while the percentages were the lowest for non-participants (12 percent and 14 percent, respectively). Thus the protagonists indicate not only a continuity of personal participation in successive social events but also a family continuity of radical engagement, which is transferred from parents to children.

Protest participants almost unanimously link the new order with the attainment of the following institutions and processes in Serbia: civic society, parliamentary democracy, legal state and individual rights and freedoms. In brief, the respondents place primary importance on the political change and political tasks and see the solution for the current crisis in Serbia mostly in the use of political and democratic means. This emphasis on the political aspect accounts for a substantial difference between the participants and non-participants who find economic ends and means (manifested in the alternative of a "fast economic recovery") more appropriate in approaching the change (almost 40 percent, compared with 10 percent among the protagonists).

The quality of a "mission" which may be ascribed to the 1996–97 student protest in Belgrade derives not only from the desired political shift demanded in the protest but also from personal dedication to the mission and identification of participants with the social troubles of their country. These aspects are precisely the ones that allow us to distinguish an active "core" consisting of protest participants from non-participants within the political generation. Namely, most non-participants do not express opposition to the protest. On the contrary, they, for the most part, have an understanding and sympathies for its actors and their objectives. However, they explain their failure to participate by offering reasons which reveal an absence of personal engagement and identification with political action. Thus, non-participants claim they "have no time" to participate, that they are "more interested in other things," that it is "boring" to "walk" every day. In contrast with this indifference of non-participants, the participants see their involvement in the protest as a kind of identification with the joint action and its political objective. This aspect of identification is symbolically expressed in the protest slogan mentioned at the beginning ("Belgrade is the world"). It is again a pun, since the word "svet" (world) can be read as "sacred," and may convey a message that the students are defending the honor of Belgrade (and Serbia), which has been tarnished by the electoral fraud and which the students intend to clear through their uncompromising struggle for a just and honest electoral result.

Furthermore, the protagonists, in their feeling of dedication to their country and its troubles, fail to show any significant degree of nationalist euphoria. Moreover, we may conclude that distancing from the nationalism is typical of the generation as a whole. All three groups of respondents are characterized by national and religious heterogeneity (80 percent : 20 percent for the majority nation and religion). In the same way, patriotism of most respondents (60–70 percent) in all three groups are predominantly linked with the use of democratic and civilized procedures and tolerance in resolving the accumulated problem critical for the existence of Serbia.

These overall generational features may lead to the conclusion that the decisive element separating the participants from non-participants is the "genealogical effect," i.e., differences in the process of political socialization of individuals. Regardless of the existence of the overall generational shift in the political visions and values which the young seek to attain by "disempowering" the older generations, protest participants still appear to be "good children" of their parents, not in terms of adopting their values and political views, but rather in terms of their family-induced inspiration and motivation for pro-social activity. The amount and intensity of this motivation are precisely where the key difference between participants and non-participants in the 1996–97 student protest is manifested.

In this case, we may conclude that the 1996–97 student protest in Belgrade (and other towns in Serbia) provides irrefutable evidence of the constitution and advance of a political generation of the young. But the "mission" this generation is taking upon itself is not the work of the whole generation, but rather of the parts thereof which, in the process of political socialization within their families, acquired the readiness, need and consciousness for social and political engagement.

## Notes

1. During the protest, few students from the leadership appeared in public as leaders, and, until the very end, many of them were not even known to have held important functions in the protests. They did not appear in public in that capacity, and the role of the mediator between the leadership of the protests and participants-walkers was mostly taken by spokesmen in charge of public rela-

tions. The apparent reason for avoiding the public and popularization of the leadership was not their wish for conspiracy, but rather their intentional and conscious decision to operate democratically, collectively and as a team. For that reason, we have decided to use the term "protagonist" to denote the group of students in the protest leadership, as it is better suited to their position in the protest.

2. The first is represented by the "Young Europe" generation of 1815–1843, intent on dealing with absolutism and the awakening of national-romantic awareness of non-free nations. The second wave appears in the post-Victorian era from 1890 to 1918, expanding the movement of the European youth to other continents, starting the germs of national-liberation movements. The third wave is connected with the period of the Great Depression of the 1930s in Europe and America (the American New Deal generation). Finally, the fourth one coincides with the rebellions and unrest of the early 1960s (the civil-rights movement and the Vietnam War), climaxing in 1968.

## Bibliography

Braungart, R. and M. (1984): "Generational Politics," in: *Political Behavior Annual*, Denver, Col.

Giddens, Anthony (1990): *The Consequences of Modernity*, Stanford University Press, Stanford.

Handel, Gerald (1986): "Central Issue in the Construction of Sibling Relations," in: A. and J. Skolnick, eds: *Family in Transition*, Little Brown and Co., Boston, 384–402.

Lane, Robert (1969): *The Political Thinking and Consciousness. The Private Life of Political Mind*, Chicago Publishing Co., Chicago.

Mannheim, Karl (1967): "Das Problem der Generation," in: Z. Friedenburg: *Jugend in der modernen Gesellschaft*, Klagenheuert Witsch, 33–48.

Milić, Andjelka (1987): *Zagonetka omladine. Teorija i istorija omladinske strukture* (The enigma of the young. Theory and history of youth structure), Institut za društvena istraživanja Sveučilišta u Zagrebu and Centar za istraživačku, dokumentacionu i izdavačku delatnost SSOJ, Zagreb and Belgrade.

Milić, Andjelka (1986): "Process of political socialization in the family and actual political commitment. Two empirical tests," *Sociologija*, special issue, 199–211.

Milić, Andjelka (1995): "Everyday family life in the maelstrom of social disintegration," *Sociologija*, No. 4.

Tomanović, V. (1977): *Omladina i socijalizam* (Youth and socialism), Mladost, Belgrade.

Vrcan, S. (1986): *Položaj, svest i ponašanje mlade generacije Jugoslavije* (The position, consciousness and behavior of the young generation in Yugoslavia), CIDID and IDIS, Zagreb and Belgrade.

Vučković, B., and S. Obradović (1988): *Kretanje i tendencije u strukturi članstva SKJ u periodu 1980–1985* (Developments and trends in the structure of Yugoslav Communist Party membership), Sveska br. 94, CKSKJ, Belgrade.

# PART III

# Protest as an Urban Phenomenon

*Sreten Vujović*

*Belgrade is the world!*
Slogan of the 1996–97 student protest

## Large towns, 1996–97 protest and movement

This text deals with the *urban character* of the civil and student protests as, thus far, rare manifestations of civil disobedience. Our attention is focused on Belgrade as the brain and heart of this country, but this is not to belittle the simultaneous actions of citizens and youth in many other towns in Serbia.[1]

On a few occasions in its history, modern Belgrade was a town of momentous initiative, manifested in mass protests and civic demonstrations of passionate social action. In such social events an entire city, striving toward freedom, reveals a high spirit. That is what happened, for example, on March 27, 1941; in June 1968; in March 1991; during the "velvet revolution" in 1992; and in the winter of 1996–97.

In the most general terms, a metropolis can be defined as a place of freedom. There is an old saying that "city air makes people free." We have to agree that "all large cultures are born of a city," that the "history of the world" is actually "the history of townspeople," and that the intellect and self-consciousness are forms of the urban rather than rural understanding of reality.

Large towns are no doubt the foci of progress: ideas, ways of life, customs and new needs are all created in the cities to spread over the rest of the country. When a society changes, it does so after the towns and by taking them as a model. The state of mind in the cities is naturally turned toward the future. No social space favors evolution of all kinds so much as a metropolis. Its essential feature is diversity.

The larger a modern town is, the more associations (secondary groups), social movements and actions of civil disobedience it includes. Their numbers and force increase in proportion with the size of the town.[2] To put it in Durkheim's terms, material density in a metropolis grows into a moral density of citizens causing the spreading of solidarity in the city, intercity, national and international spheres. Authoritarian rule is always suspicious of a large town, its diversity and secretiveness, because it can never fully control it, repression notwithstanding. A metropolis simply resists domination and manipulation.

If we accept a definition of a modern social movement as a collective, public, voluntary, mass and more or less spontaneous, diffuse and flexible action which derives from unsatisfied needs, reveals specific conflicting interests, moves to resolve important social problems and aims at small or large changes, then the months of actions by citizens and students in Belgrade may be defined as belonging to an urban social movement (Prpić et al., 1990: 117). This social movement does not have a class character and is more or less independent of the existing political parties. It also manifests some reservation toward strict ideological divisions ("left" and "right"). Its activity has been non-violent, and it uses new methods and forms of action (occupying the streets and squares, passive resistance), along with a new language, symbols and a media-friendly approach and, generally speaking, develops an opposition or alternative political culture (Vujović, 1997: 143).

In other words, civil disobedience, which has been manifested in Belgrade and other large towns in Serbia, is a public, non-violent, conscious political act, justified by a postelection social crisis caused by the huge injustice of altering the electoral will of citizens, and thus endangering an elementary democratic principle. The ensuing dissatisfaction is primarily of a moral and political nature. The dilemma is that of democracy or unrestricted personal rule (i.e., dictatorship), an independent or a biased judiciary, a legal or a party state.[3]

As for the internal structure of the movement, or rather its interests and actors, we could, in general terms, say that in contrast with the "happening of the people" characteristic of the populist (ethno-nationalist) movement of the late 1980s in Serbia, this time we have a "happening of the citizenry," who are, moreover, not submissive.

Urban development and citizenry have, in Serbia, been tragically discontinued: citizenry consisted of a small group and was short-lived and impotent. In addition it has, to this date, failed to impose itself as an actor of important social change, i.e., democratization and modernization. (The fact that there is not one properly constructed public city square in Belgrade is a specific confirmation of this thesis.) That is also why industrialization and urbanization are distorted and incomplete, and modernization is actually semi-modernization. Acquiring urbanity in the sense of forming the civic and the citizen has, for too long, been marked by "transitoriness," something mediocre and provincial in Serbia. Under such conditions, transition is an onerous and controversial process. The strongest resistance to the transition is mounted by the oligarchy in power, a symbiosis of new political and economic elites which, by preventing ownership and other changes in society, retain a monopoly on power and (of specific importance in the postelectoral crisis), also a monopoly on the media, especially the broadcast media.

But having emerged from years of stupor, vacillation, a propaganda war, international isolation, struggling for survival, hopelessness and lethargy, the citizens raised their heads and underwent a mass catharsis. The middle class, which prevails precisely in large towns, and the citizens of the capital sent a resolute message: "Nothing that concerns us can be decided without us!" That is why we consider this movement an urban phenomenon. The urban nature of the protest is confirmed by the data on its participants: 31.3 percent of demonstrators come from the city center or central districts of Belgrade!

What about the workers? Is a joint struggle of the middle strata and the workers possible? The workers are still struggling to secure a bare existence. They are largely engaged in the gray economy, on the black market and flea markets all over Serbia. Many are unemployed or underemployed and, in this situation, find the demands of the citizens and students an outright political luxury. On the other hand, both the previous (post-1945) regime and the current one have managed to abolish the workers' movement, to fragment the workers and their trade unions. The workers are today largely dependent on the state, and there is still an "unprincipled coalition" between a substantial part of the workers and the political-economic elite. These are essentially the reasons for the lack of wider participation of the workers in the 1996–97 protest.

Students, as a segment of the "free-floating intelligentsia," have mostly contributed to the rejection of the populist movement and the formation of another civil one. Their positive energy, wit and sharp imagination, as well as sound organization and resoluteness, have not only helped the civil protest in Belgrade continue for quite a long time but also made the hope of social change more realistic. A special value of the student movement is seen in the fact that it engaged in no political bargains with the regime. Bearing in mind that the student movement was joined by some secondary-school students, it is possible to speak of a 1996–97 youth movement.

By "instilling pride in us all," defeating brutality with humor, upholding human dignity, exposing hypocrisy and lie to ridicule and rehabilitating urbanity as civility, the student movement earned itself a 1996 tolerance award from the daily *Naša borba*. All in all, we could say that the 1996–97 student protest provided the backbone for the civil movement in Serbia.

As usually happens in other places, the civil movement in Serbia is challenged by a counter-movement, or rather by structural interests opposed to the civil protest and their organizational manifestations (counter-rallies organized by the Socialist Party of Serbia and the Union of the Yugoslav Left; the action of special police units—including using clubs, water jets and tear gas—to intimidate and prevent a nonviolent protest; and the unprecedented manipulation of public opinion by suppressing information on actual events, propagating semi-truths and lies, interviewing "passers-by" who outdid one another in condemning the "walkers" and publishing letters of loyalty to the president of Serbia).

In contrast with the diverse, Dionysian, ironic and auto-ironic, innovative, revolutionary, festive character of the student and civic movement, which is, in terms of the above-mentioned and other characteristics, modern and urban—the rallies of support for the president of Serbia and the SPS–JUL–ND coalition were essentially provincial. These rallies featured a routine, poor and stereotypical setting, monotonous slogans, socialist iconography, ordered and paid-for activities of heteronomous persons with a remarkably authoritarian syndrome (pledges and love of the leader, the slogan "Slobo, we love you") and speeches of "representatives" of workers, peasants and "honest intelligentsia" prepared in advance; all in all, a *deja vu*. One might say that "ordinary" participants in the civic movement and the counter-ralliers seem to belong to different civilizations more than they express different political attitudes. The worst thing about this action of the regime was that it caused a powderkeg situation and risked civil war by organizing a counter-rally in Belgrade in the same place (Terazije Square) and at the same time (December 24) as the *Zajedno* coalition. The narrow-minded regime chose a dangerous and arrogant way to celebrate the electoral swindle and manipulation in line with its position that all political opponents are "the fifth column." This counter-rally symbolically marked the twilight of a disastrous regime and its leader. This political twilight comes at a time when the state is conspiring against democracy.

It is more than obvious that the police have sided with the regime. The number and behavior of police officers have unfortunately showed us that we are living in a police state.[4] The army has kept its distance, while the church has, this time, actively supported the students and citizens. Many professional associations publicly demonstrated their support for the student movement, especially during the "cordon against cordon" action in Belgrade.

## What makes Belgrade so important to the regime?

The first multi-party elections in Belgrade after 1946, as well as the protests of citizens and youth in 1991, demonstrated that Belgrade is essentially an opposition city. That, in our situation, means a city tending toward social change and innovations. More precisely, the election map in Belgrade shows that the opposition was victorious in the central municipalities of Belgrade. These municipalities have the largest number of highly educated citizens and those with longer experience of urban-civil life. Something similar also happened in the local elections of November 17, 1996, although with an important difference: the representatives of the opposition coalition *Zajedno* also marked a victory in the Belgrade City Assembly. The essential importance of the City Assembly for the regime is revealed in the fact that even after an OSCE commission report (invited by the federal government) confirming the victory of the *Zajedno* coalition, the regime refused to acknowledge and accept it. What makes Belgrade and its assembly so important to the regime, given the authorities' claims that the city government only deals with the problems of utilities, housing and urban planning? Why does the city have so much importance, even after the centralization of power, which, over the past few years, transferred its key levers of power to the republic? The response to this question is complex. First, symbolically speaking, for a regime, especially an authoritarian regime, loss of control over the capital amounts to the loss or weakening of its power over the whole state. In addition, the mansion of the Belgrade City Assembly (the old court of the Obrenović dynasty) stands next to the offices of the Serbian Presidency, the headquarters of Slobodan Milošević at that time.

Therefore, it is a neighborhood with unfortunate political symbolism, especially since the tower of the Serbian Presidency building is still topped by a five-pointed star, while the one from the tower of the City Assembly was replaced with the former symbol: the two-headed eagle. Next, Belgrade is actually the most important political, economic and cultural center in the country. In the 1980s (and the situation has not substantially changed to this date) Belgrade accounted for 23 percent of the total population of Serbia (not including the provinces of Kosovo and Vojvodina, 40.2 percent in employment, 28.6 percent in industry, 55.1 percent in construction, 77.8 percent in transportation, 50.1 percent in trade and catering, 43.3 percent in crafts and 47.9 percent in other activities (Vujović, 1990: 72). In other words, Belgrade displays a conspicuous concentration of population and activities. Particularly important in the post-electoral crisis are those related to informatics, science, education and the publishing and printing industries. It is extremely important for the regime to control the media, especially the broadcast media.

A metropolis is a highly complex part of global society with almost all of its dimensions and therefore may be an autonomous social actor. It appears as a relatively independent, i.e., autonomous, subsystem within the framework of a specific global social system. That is what every regime knows and why the regime's interests have been endangered this time. The loss of the Belgrade Assembly amounts to the loss of control over the building lots and real estate, and this jeopardizes the megalomaniac projects of Europolis and the Chinese quarter launched by the authorities at the height of the economic crisis to offer the citizens false hope of fast economic recovery. This loss reveals the corruption and failures in urban policy[5] and denies the possibility to buy political loyalty by distributing apartments and business premises. The Belgrade City Assembly also carries financial importance: the sum the Belgrade City Assembly obtains from turnover taxes is about 4.5 times that collected by the 16 Belgrade municipalities taken together.[6] The financial centralism of the city of Belgrade in relation to its municipalities is obvious. All this explains (but does not justify) the stubborn refusal of the regime to relinquish Belgrade.

The regime is aware that the victory of the opposition in the largest towns, including the capital, has seriously shaken its position, that its monolith has been dented and that its chances in the next elections at all levels have been weakened.

## Belgrade as a moveable feast
## (a carnival, spectacle, festivity, play,
## laughter, noise)

*I think, therefore I walk.*
Slogan of the 1996–97 protest

During the protest the people of Belgrade both symbolically and liter-ally won the right to their own city, moreover its center, its historical core. They appropriated its squares and streets, turning the center into a kind of an agora, where the word is both the sword and the shield. Bel-grade became a moveable feast, a walking theater in the round. The street has been reclaimed as a common venue, a site of exchange, a public place *par excellence*. It is experienced (as in 17th-century cities) as an extension of the theater, a scene, a specific place to form opinions, express views and tastes, position oneself against the views of others, as a rhetoric of collective irony ...

For weeks, noisy, colorful and laughing protest columns of students, equipped with banners with the main slogan "Belgrade is the world," set off from a number of starting points (faculties) and converged on their destination (the plaza in front of the Faculty of Philosophy). At that spot they received new messages (addressed by professors and artists) and then left for their protest walks (most often limited to the very center, bordered by the route of the No. 2 tram) to return to their starting point after about two hours. On one occasion the gathering at the plaza started with the student hymn "Gaudeamus igitur," but later on it regularly opened with the "Hymn to St. Sava." The song played most often imme-diately before the walk was "On to Belgrade," composed by Vojislav Kostic for the film *Who Is Singing Over There?*

The procedure was similar in the protest organized by the *Zajedno* coalition. *Zajedno* protesters gathered at Republic Square and from there went for a walk which ended at different places in the city center, where they held their final rally with speeches by the coalition's leaders and their guests. With noise, banners, light and colors, the constant walks included whistling and booing for several minutes at the mention of the names of the Serbian president and his wife, especially in front of the Serbian Presidency building and the buildings of the TV ("TV Bastille"), the daily *Politika,* and others. In the "second part" of the demonstrations, the citizens gathered in various parts of the town (such as Banovo brdo, Vračar, Dorćol and New Belgrade) and formed columns to arrive at Republic Square. The rallies usually started by singing the hymn "God of Justice."

We should point out at least a few elements of tolerance noted at protest gatherings. After a few days, posters of party leaders and Draža Mihajlović (leader of the Chetnik movement in World War II) disappeared, to the acclaim of the citizens gathered ("We are not here to fight for the five-pointed star or the cockade, but for democracy and against dictatorship!"). On that same day (December 13) about 250,000 citizens at Republic Square observed a minute of silence in honor of Feriz Balakčari, a Kosovo Albanian and a victim of police torture. The widespread presence of children on the shoulders of their parents, in baby carriages or slings or led by the hand, tells us that the demonstrations were very peaceful. Asked why they brought their children to the protest, most parents stated that they "wanted their children to remember something of the newly awakened positive spirit of Belgrade" and also that their children enjoyed a happening of this kind (Radivojević and Kovačević, 1997: IV).

In time, the walks became a way of life for tens and hundreds of thousands of Belgraders. They were happening in plain view of all of Belgrade and the world. Only the cameras of Radio Television Serbia did not see them. The social, political and media effects of the walks were huge. The students clearly understood that their protest, if it developed only in the halls of their faculties, would soon die out.[7] Public revolt was manifested in outdoor spaces, befitting its nature. As time went by, communication among the walkers, as well as between the walkers and their fellow citizens in the windows and on the balconies and rooftops of the surrounding buildings, grew more frequent and intensive (waving, throwing confetti, displaying lights, signs, signals, creating noise…). Belgrade, just like any metropolis where people "do not know each other personally," has substantially changed in this respect. Sociableness increased, direct contacts became more numerous, new friendships were made and old informal relations renewed, and new sympathies and affections were born.

The carnivalization of political demonstrations, with condensed times of festivity, plays, laughter and noise, was one of the main characteristics of the civil, and especially the student, protest. A culture of "laughter and carnival," a feeling of the world as a carnival, established itself. It brought about, in a specific form, the resurrection of traditional urban festivities, carnivals, something that used to characterize our coastal towns, but not Belgrade. According to Mikhail Bakhtin, a carnival is a "synthetic representational form of ritual character." The carnival, as a "representational form," "liberated consciousness from the rule of the official view, allowing for a new perception of the world, without fear and veneration, completely critically but, at the same time, without nihilism, in a positive way, since it revealed a special material principle of the world—the existence and change, the irresistible and eternal triumph of the new, immortal people" (RKT, 1992: 341). Bakhtin believed that the "carnival feeling of the world" was characterized by the fact that one's relation to reality was experienced as a kind of inversion, an inclination to eliminate the clear boundaries between "up" and "down," the image of a humorous-ironic and grotesque reversal of the world. The basic characteristic of the "culture of laughter and carnival" is the "joyous relativity," or grotesque coupling of the fantastic and the real. Branimir Stojković rightly noted that "the basic logic of the protest image was the debasement and inversion of symbols of power and oppression" (Stojković, 1996: VII). The "debasement" of the dominant symbols develops according to the model used by Bakhtin in his analysis of the carnival on the example of Rabelais' *Gargantua and Pantagruel*. Of the wide range of striking examples of this procedure, a few are listed below:

— Slobodan Milošević: a life-size sponge effigy of Slobo, dressed in a striped prison uniform; a small head of Slobo done in modeling clay (like those in *Spitting Image*) and stuck on an umbrella; Slobo like a Pinocchio, his nose made of an inflated condom;

— Belgrade City Assembly, the dailies *Politika* and *Vecernje novosti*: an attack with eggs, red paint;

— Serbian Parliament: spraying rat poison and insecticide on the outside (in response to the postponement of the parliamentary session, allegedly due to the need for rat extermination);

— university rector: washing the rectorate building so that only the rector (who did not support the protests) would remain dirty;

— Radio Television Serbia: an attack with eggs, red paint and paper planes to conquer the "Bastille";

— the Supreme Court of Serbia: hanging one hundred condoms on the court building (condoms for lackeys action); mocking the court as the protector of justice (condom—protector) precisely on the World Day of Struggle against AIDS (Stojković, 1996: VII);

— counter-rally organized by the SPS, JUL and ND: using detergents to wash the area where the meeting was held, especially the part where the rostrum had been erected;

— cordons of special police blocking the protest walks: students carry shields with the lettering "I love you, too" (words Slobodan Milošević used to respond to his supporters who chanted "Slobo, we love you"); simulation of "truncheoning" among the students themselves and their going in circles with hands behind their heads in a "prison march"; "blockade of the blockade" or "carnival on wheels" by creating gridlocks using the cars of demonstrators which allegedly broke down in central streets and squares and then asking police for help;

— Belgrade University Board: washing of the facades of the Belgrade University Rectorate using detergent and water jets, after the hypocritical behavior of the University Board's members who first accepted the demands of the student protest, including the resignation of the rector, and then voted their confidence in him by a secret ballot;

— Serbian Parliament: two cordons of students along Terazije Square and the Street of Serbian Rulers. Between the cordons passes a car carrying a large sculpture of a brain and two life belts carved in ice, which the students wanted to give to the SPS deputies who, on that day, alone, adopted the *lex specialis* (slogan: "Tito had Rex, Slobo has lex") recognizing the authentic results of local elections of November 17, 1996.

Stojković notes two major actions which were not marked by Bakhtian "debasement": the offering of bread and salt to the Serbian president (although it reflects inversion, because it is the guests who are welcomed by bread and salt, and they do not bring the offering themselves—the message being you are not a good host) and the building of a thousand-brick wall in front of the Federal Parliament (the message: we do not destroy but build).

Wit (laughter, mockery, irony) is also the main tool of the civil resistance movements. Laughter has a dual function: it liberates from fear the one who produces it but causes "fear and humiliation" in those toward whom it is directed. According to Henri Bergson, "laughter conceals a thought of agreement, one would say almost a conspiracy, with others who laugh." Dead-serious dictators, gazing toward eternity and surrounded by flunkies, cannot stand laughter. They cannot conceive of being reduced to normal human size. In his essay "Laughter," Bergson supports the view that laughter is punishment. Created to humiliate, it must make those it refers to feel uncomfortable. Citizens have their revenge on those in power for taking liberties with the people and individuals. Laughter would not make its point if it included signs of sympathy or goodness, claims Bergson.

The civil and student movement may also be read as a spectacle. A spectacle is distinguished by a magnificent, showy, resplendent scene in a public place, aiming to attract as many people as possible. It is a complex phenomenon which is both art and entertainment, a place where these are performed, the audience and the social act of attending the performance. There were a lot of spectacles in numerous protest columns and rallies, but the mass meeting to ring in the New Year (1997) organized in and around Republic Square could rightly be called a first-class spectacle. The papers, naturally not the ones controlled by the regime, wrote of a "unique explosion of enthusiasm," of "the whole square lit by fireworks, love and happiness," of an "incredible happening which brought joy to thousands of people." One had to experience the miracle. One could feel and smell the good old spirit of Belgrade. Less fascinating, but very exciting and with an even greater attendance, was the burning of yule logs near St. Sava's Church. These events were followed by the festivity on the occasion of the Serbian (Orthodox) New Year, organized less successfully than the first, a religious procession on St. Sava's Day (the largest in the history of Belgrade) and the celebration of the *Zajedno* coalition victory. But the spectacle culminated in the "cordon against cordon" action in Kolarceva Street organized by students for seven days in succession ("the shortest street and the longest revolution"). In front of the police cordon, which was remanned on the hour, "cordons" of students, professors, artists (who even performed *Macbeth*) and members of various professional associations replaced one another. The awakened Belgrade supported its students to the last man. This brought back the spirit and humor of the cosmopolitan Belgrade, a city where in the 1970s a theater of the absurd flourished along with other forms of ridicule of the numerous absurdities of the communist dictatorship of the time. For instance, students wore bathing caps and played water polo on the asphalt in the rain. They placed mirrors in front of policemen, photographed them and drew their portraits. They tried to "hypnotize" the police, played chess, donned boxing gloves and pretended to spar with police officers and "fished" fish tins from the surrounding garbage cans. Throughout this time a discothèque, the "Blue Cordon," was open. The street resounded with rock music, and the playful girls invited the "men in blue" to dance. There was also a contest for the beauty queen of the student protest. All this provided a host of "genre pictures" which represented the civil ethos and urban humor. The students understood well Kierkegaard's maxim that "humor alone cannot be scandalized by the absurd and experiences it as something natural." Seven days later, the police withdrew, and the students were once again free to take a walk through their town.

Elements of play and traditional festivities, as well as their integrative and other social functions, were also noted during the 1996–97 protest. Play was recognizable as: 1. free (voluntary); 2. separated (time and space-wise); 3. uncertain (its course and outcome were unpredictable); 4. non-productive (creating neither goods nor wealth); 5. prescribed (subject to rules); 6. fictive (second-rate reality or complete unreality compared with everyday life) (Kajoa, 1965: 35). As for elements of traditional festivities, particularly prominent was the manifestation of "implicit examination" of (unconsciously) ambiguous relations a person in a given society maintains with his own social or symbolic universe: violation of bans and reduction of the social distance between individuals or social groups.

One of the most popular games was called "traffic lights." Participants in the game were demonstrators and policemen. As soon as the green light came up, the demonstrators would run into the street and start shouting: "It's green, look at the traffic lights." Then when the light turned red, they would go back to the pavement, crying: "Red bandits, give us our traffic lights back!" Two more games illustrate the continuing innovations of the civil resistance. The first is "noise against Radio Television Serbia Daily News" at 7:30 p.m., when citizens appeared on their windows or balconies creating noise in various ways. The other consisted of continuously calling ministries and other state institutions and the media in order to tie up their lines and "prevent their damaging work." These are also examples of Bakhtian "debasement" and inversion of the symbols of power.

Noise was also fashionable. Noisy people were the "awakened" people. (In traditional folk rites noise was used to chase evil away.) "The most important thing in the whole story is that one's whistle is not isolated because it would resemble the one of the police," noted Vesna Radivojević and Nada Kovačević, journalists from *Naša borba*. The whistle was the most popular gadget among the demonstrators. The slogan "The whistle came out of paradise" only confirms that.

Gorčin Stojanović writes on the multiple function of protest noise. Noise, in the first place, "melts the wax in the ears of those who pretend that nothing is going on." Noise also informs—the citizens are informed that the lies and the theft are aggravating and that the protesters will not keep silent about them. A sensitive director points out the symbolic meaning of noise, referring to J. Attali. He states that noise is a dialogue with death, with the end, the final. Thus the "drums, trumpets and whistles in the city streets are not merely meant as a support to the citizens' protest but also a response to the many violent deaths close by" ("Yes, this means talking of war, we will not and must not get rid of it soon") (Stojanović, 1996: XV). "Nice city noise" is, therefore, aimed not merely against injustice and the annulment of electoral results; it is a kind of collective absolution, a vast joint confession, a catharsis of a sort. It is not easy to break away from the shadow of war over the city.

The consequences of the civil and student movement, the urban nature of which has been outlined above, are hard to predict. Unquestionably, this movement and similar forms of self-organization of citizens are what sustains modern democracy. After this protest, Belgrade and many other towns in Serbia will think differently in political terms, and that in itself provides a sufficiently favorable environment for democratic social change. Whatever happens, the 1996–97 protest will be remembered as an important political baptism and stage of development, and a unique experience for hundreds of thousands of individuals.

## Notes

1. On November 21, 1996, an Association of Free Towns and Municipalities in Serbia was constituted. See: *Glasnik Saveza slobodnih gradova i opština Srbije* (the Association's Herald), No. 1, November 25, 1996.

The *Zajedno* coalition won the elections in 41 out of the total of 189, or 21.69 percent of municipalities in the republic. These municipalities account for 35.36 percent of the population of Serbia, 50.13 percent of the employed and 63.12 percent of employees with high education. These municipalities have 62 faculties (76.54 percent) and 33 high schools (63.46 percent). It is obvious that these municipalities hold most of the intellectual reserves of the country. See: *Godišnjak "Opštine u republici Srbiji 1994"* (Yearbook of Municipalities in the Republic of Serbia in 1994) and the *Official Journal of Serbia,* Nos. 17 and 50.

2. "Despotic authority always seeks to abolish, suppress or at least marginalize the strata between the potentate and his subjects. Once individuals start organizing into professional, interest-based or even leisure associations, when the so-called constituted bodies appear—the despotic rule is over" (Mimica, 1997: XIII).

3. Zoran Ivošević, justice of the Supreme Court of Serbia, in his public release, says: "I do not condone a submissive role of the court, which turns elections into self-appointment. I do not condone a dependent judiciary where the court 'launders' the daily policy instead of being the symbol of a legal state. I do not condone obedience to daily politics and refuse to judge in a way which indulges the political will of any party. I do not condone the election of justices who are loyal but incompetent. I do not condone defending the state from democracy, since democracy should be defended from the state, if it is not up to it. I do not condone silence on the disgrace of the judiciary, if I have to blush at the decisions which do the judiciary no credit." See *Naša borba*, December 3, 1996, p. 1.

4. For political use of the police against the civil protest in Serbia in 1996–97, see *Policija protiv protesta* (Police against the protest), Fund for Humanitarian Law.

5. For example, a law on the maintenance of residential buildings was not passed, as opposed to a law which enabled the purchase of apartments in buildings which are donated to the city and are as such protected by a special law concerning the preservation of architectural heritage and the like.

6. A decision to that effect was published in the "Official Journal of the City of Belgrade" No. 20, dated December 30, 1996, and has been effective as of January 1, 1997.

7. Dragoš Ivanović has noted that "Serbia was not only in the streets but also on the roads." Over 130 students from Novi Sad walked 80 kilometers to come to Belgrade and manifest solidarity with their Belgrade colleagues, while those from Niš and Kragujevac had to walk 290 and 120 kilometers, respectively.

# Bibliography

Bahtin, M. (1978): *Stvaralaštvo Fransoa Rablea i narodna kultura srednjeg veka i renesanse* (Works of Francois Rabelais and the popular culture of the Middle Ages and Renaissance), Nolit, Belgrade.

Kajoa, R. (1967): *Igre i ljudi* (Games and people), Nolit, Belgrade.

Mimica, A. (1997): "Srbija se umiriti ne sme" (Serbia must not be calmed), *Naša borba,* February 4, 1997, Belgrade.

Prpić, I., Ž. Puhovski, and Z. Uzelac (1990): *Leksikon temeljnih pojmova politike* (Glossary of basic political concepts), Školska knjiga, Zagreb.

Radivojević, V., and N. Kovačević (1996/7): "Vreme smeha i nezaborava" (The time of laughter not to be forgotten), *Naša borba,* December 31, 1996, January 1-2, 1997, Belgrade.

Stojanović, G. (1996): "Lepa buka" (Nice noise), *Naša borba,* December 21-22, Belgrade.

Stojiljković, B. (1996): "Retorika civilnog otpora" (Rhetoric of civil resistance), *Naša borba,* December 14-15, Belgrade.

Vujović, S. (1990): *Ljudi i gradovi* (Peoples and cities), Mediteran and Filozofski fakultet, Belgrade and Budva.

Vujović, S. (1997): *Grad u senci rata* (City in the shadow of war), Prometej and ISFF, Novi Sad.

Živković, D., ed. (1992): *Rečnik književnih izraza* (RKT) (Dictionary of literary terms), second revised edition, Nolit, Belgrade.

# APPENDIX

# Chronology of the Protest[1]

## Milica Bogdanović, Ljiljana Milovanović and Miodrag Shrestha

**Nov. 17, 1996**—The second round of elections for local authorities in Serbia ends. Initial, unofficial results from the electoral headquarters of the *Zajedno* coalition say that it has won the majority of seats in city assemblies in a number of municipalities, including large towns like Belgrade, Niš, Novi Sad and Kragujevac. That same night, citizens of many towns celebrate the victory of the opposition.

**Nov. 18, 1996**—The spokesman of the Socialist Party of Serbia (SPS), Ivica Dačić, confirms that the ruling party "fared worse" in Belgrade and some other large towns in Serbia, but that the Left coalition (SPS–JUL–ND), with its single list, won a majority in 134 municipalities in Serbia. According to the *Zajedno* coalition, this coalition has been victorious in 45 municipalities in Serbia and obtained the majority of seats in the city assemblies of Belgrade, Niš, Novi Sad and Kragujevac. A large rally to celebrate the opposition's victory is held at Republic Square in Belgrade, organized by the *Zajedno* coalition, whose leaders, after the rally, go to the City Assembly to warn the election commission not to tamper with the results.

**Nov. 19, 1996**—Election commissions announce preliminary returns of local elections. The SPS questions the regularity of elections in a number of constituencies where, according to preliminary results, the opposition coalition *Zajedno* has won. In Niš, supporters of the *Zajedno* coalition start a protest provoked by the election commission's attempt to falsify the results.

**Nov. 20, 1996**—The annulment of election results sets off protests in Užice, Pirot and Jagodina. Leaders and newly elected deputies of the *Zajedno* coalition invite several thousand citizens gathered in front of the Republican Parliament in Belgrade to defend their victory, the Constitution and the laws of Serbia. The *Zajedno* coalition addresses an open letter to President of the Republic Slobodan Milošević demanding that the original results recorded at polling places be honored. Leaders of the *Zajedno* coalition Vesna Pešić, Zoran Djindjić and Vuk Drašković meet representatives of a number of embassies and inform them of the SPS attempts to annul elections in most places where the coalition was victorious and hand them copies of original records.

**Nov. 21, 1996**—According to Reuters estimates, about 20,000 citizens in Belgrade respond to the invitation of the *Zajedno* coalition to hold a protest rally. The rally is followed by a protest walk.

**Nov. 22, 1996**—In Belgrade, an Initiative Board of the student protest is constituted. Its members appear before several thousand students to demand that the electoral will of citizens be respected. The members announce a general strike unless their demand is fulfilled.

**Nov. 23, 1996**—Daily protests continue in Belgrade, Niš, Kragujevac and other towns in Serbia, and the citizens are addressed by many prominent public personalities.

**Nov. 24, 1996**—The First Municipal Court in Belgrade annuls the election of 33 candidates of the *Zajedno* coalition to the City Assembly. The City Election Commission in Niš comes up with returns giving the SPS the majority of seats. The *Zajedno* coalition announces that it will not run in the third round of elections and will turn down all seats in municipalities where election results have been annulled. The Initiative Board of the student protest appeals to all students of the University of Belgrade to join the protest.

**Nov. 25, 1996**—The *Zajedno* coalition lodges a complaint with the Supreme Court of Serbia against the rulings of the First Municipal Court. The European Union withdraws trade preferences granted to Yugoslavia due to the non-observance of results of local elections in Serbia. During their protest walk, the citizens of Belgrade express their dissatisfaction by hurling eggs at the City Assembly and the buildings of Radio Television Serbia (RTS), Radio Belgrade and the daily *Politika*. Students from the University of Belgrade and of the University of Arts, who have started their boycott of classes today, gather at the plaza in front of the Faculty of Philosophy. There a students' proclamation is read, stating that they do not side either with those in power or the opposition but are fighting for a basic democratic principle—the respect of the freely expressed will of citizens—and request that a republic election committee be set up on a parity principle to establish the real results of the elections. Upon the insistence of protesters gathered at the plaza, the rally is followed by a protest walk. Students announce their intention to continue gathering at the plaza until their demands are met. Students of the University of Niš also start to protest.

**Nov. 26, 1996**—The Supreme Court of Serbia dismisses the complaints of the *Zajedno* coalition. The Actors' Association of Serbia issues a proclamation stating that it is joining the student protest. The Congress of Local and Regional Authorities—an advisory body of the Council of Europe—strongly condemns the decision of the authorities in Belgrade to annul some of the local election results.

**Nov. 27, 1996**—The third round of elections for local authorities is held. During the protest walks in Belgrade, some demonstrators, in addition to eggs, throw stones, breaking window-panes on the buildings of the RTS, Radio Belgrade and *Politika*. In his speech, Vuk Drašković, for the first time, demands the resignation of Slobodan Milošević. On the fourth day of their protest, the students try to walk to Dedinje (an elite residential area where Milošević lives) but are stopped by the police. The United States calls upon Milošević to revise his decision annulling the elections.

**Nov. 28, 1996**—The *Zajedno* coalition appeals to Belgraders not to throw stones. Citizens continue hurling eggs at media houses whose reporting on the events they find unsatisfactory. The rector of the University of Belgrade, Dragutin Veličković, tells the RTS that only a small number of manipulated students are in the streets, along with some secondary-school students and other young people and that university classes are proceeding normally. At the university, the Initiative Board for the Defense of Democracy is established, consisting of professors and associates of the University of Belgrade and the University of Arts. Thirty members of the Serbian Academy of Sciences and Arts pledge their support to the students.

**Nov. 29, 1996**—The Organization for Security and Cooperation in Europe (OSCE) expresses its "extreme concern" over the irregularities and deficiencies noted at the local elections in Serbia and states its readiness to provide assistance in the verification of election results, if necessary. The Council of Europe condemns the authorities in Belgrade for non-observance of the electoral outcome. The protest of *Zajedno* coalition supporters continues in Belgrade. During their walks, citizens also throw eggs at the building of the Supreme Court of Serbia. Students make an additional demand: the resignation of the Belgrade University rector, Dragutin Veličković, and the student vice-rector, Vladimir Djurdjević. In the course of their protest walk, students shower the building of the City Election Commission with rolls of toilet paper with the inscription "We've had enough of your crap." Representatives of all faculties and institutes of both universities join the Initiative Board for the Defense of Democracy. After the third round of elections, the SPS wins the majority of seats in Belgrade and Niš, while the

*Zajedno* coalition marks its victory in Kragujevac and Užice. *The London Times* and other papers say that 100,000 citizens of Belgrade were in the streets protesting, while the state television—the only source of information for the bulk of the local population—reports about the "demonstrations of a handful of provocateurs and hoodlums."

**Nov. 30, 1996**—The 11th day of the protest in Belgrade is marked by the largest number of demonstrators thus far. Estimates of various agencies range from 100,000 to 200,000. Along with eggs, citizens throw bags with red paint, yogurt and toilet paper. Protesters break a record in continuing whistling at the mention of Milošević's name by keeping it up for a full 20 minutes. Students gathered at the plaza in front of the Faculty of Philosophy are read a letter by the rector of the University of Arts, Darinka Matić-Marović, supporting the right of the students to express their opinions freely.

**Dec. 1, 1996**—Dragan Tomić, president of the Serbian Parliament, in his statement for the RTS, calls the *Zajedno* coalition protests "destructive, violent, and marked by everything that characterizes pro-Fascist groups and ideologies." "The worst of all is their manipulation of the children. We had an opportunity to see a scenario of this kind in Kosovo, as well as throughout our history—remember when Hitler came to power." The Serbian Ministry of the Interior issues a release stating that gatherings which have not been registered in advance shall not be tolerated by the police. In Belgrade, four persons are arrested on charges of taking part in destructive demonstrations. The student protest is marked by the struggle against AIDS. In their protest walk, the students "circle" the Supreme Court of Serbia and adorn it with condoms carrying a message "condoms for lackeys."

**Dec. 2, 1996**—President of the Serbian Parliament Dragan Tomić adjourns a session of the Serbian Parliament, scheduled for December 3, reportedly due to "disinfection, disinfestation and rat poisoning" of the Parliament's premises. The information service of the Secretariat for Internal Affairs of Belgrade announces that 32 demonstrators have been arrested and that four of them have already been sentenced. The *Zajedno* coalition appeals to the Federal Court. At the student protest in Belgrade is read the reply of the Initiative Board to Dragan Tomić's statement that students were manipulated. The reply says: "Where were you, Mr. Tomić, when young men of our age were being killed in Vukovar and other battlefields, on orders from the regime you belong to? When you were spilling our blood, you did not care about our age." A petition supporting the students' demands has been signed by over 1,000 professors and associates of the University of Belgrade and the University of Arts. Svetozar Marović, president of the Montenegrin Parliament, states that the will of voters is a foundation of democracy and that no man has the right to alter it.

**Dec. 3, 1996**—After being prevented from operating for a few days, independent Belgrade radio stations B-92 and Radio Index, as well as Radio BUM-93 from Požarevac—the only stations to report extensively on the student and civil protests throughout Serbia—are shut down. Five American congressmen take part in the protest walk in Belgrade. Leaders of the *Zajedno* coalition voice new demands for freedom of the press and the release of arrested demonstrators. A column of students passes by the Serbian Parliament building and writes "Rats out" on its walls to help the announced disinfestation. Several thousand students of the Novi Sad University gather in front of the Faculty of Philosophy in Novi Sad to support the students in Belgrade. The Student Association and the rector of the University of Montenegro express support for all efforts of students in Serbia. A number of judges of the Supreme Court in their letter to the public express their doubts concerning the work of election commissions and boards of judges. The United States and the EU increase their pressure on Milošević to refrain from the use of force and to respect the will of the people. The Independent Journalist Association of Serbia (IJAS) demands the resignation of Serbian government information minister Aleksandar Tijanić for suppressing the independent media.

**Dec. 4, 1996**—Mile Ilić, president of the Socialist Party branch in Niš, who was accused of falsifying the elections in Niš by *Zajedno* coalition leaders, submits an irrevocable resignation without any explanation whatsoever. Citizens of Belgrade participate in protest walks in the largest numbers so far. During their walk, students leave a loaf of bread and an open letter in front of the Serbian Presidency building, inviting the president to use his authority and power to take Serbia out of the post-election crisis. The initiative board of the student protest in Priština lends its support to the demands of students throughout Serbia. The municipal court in Belgrade dismisses complaints of the *Zajedno* coalition.

**Dec. 5, 1996**—Radio B-92 and Radio Index are back on the air. The director-general of the RTS, in a letter to the director of Radio B-92, informs him that the broadcasting of the radio's program was interrupted because of a waterlogged coaxial cable on the aerial. The City Election Commission of Belgrade asks the Supreme Court to reexamine the ruling of the First Municipal Court. For the first time, the protest column in Belgrade is headed by an effigy of Milošević in prison clothes with the number "17111996" printed on it. Under the slogan "We do not destroy—we build," the students put up a wall in front of the Serbian Parliament, reacting to state media reports referring to destructive demonstrations. Yevgeny Primakov, Russia's minister of foreign affairs, states that developments in Serbia are the internal affairs of the country, while Yegor Gaydar, president of the Party for Democratic Choice of Russia, supports the demonstrations. The White House, the French Foreign Ministry and the German Bundestag address new warnings to Serbian authorities, calling on them to refrain from the use of force and condemning their suppression of the media.

**Dec. 6, 1996**—Aleksandar Tijanić, minister for information in the government of Serbia, submits an irrevocable resignation. The mass civil protest continues, accompanied by carnival-like, festive atmosphere and numerous sound and visual effects. In addition to party emblems, flags of the United States and many European countries appear for the first time. In Podgorica, a joint meeting of students and professors of the University of Montenegro is held as a token of support for the student protest.

**Dec. 7, 1996**—The Supreme Court of Serbia dismisses the complaint of the City Election Commission of Belgrade against the ruling of the First Municipal Court. The public learns of the arrest of Dejan Bulatović, the demonstrator who, the day before, carried the effigy of Milošević. The president of the American Committee to Protect Journalists, Kati Marton, talks with Milošević, who, according to her, promises that the independent media will not be prevented from operating and that the army and the police will not intervene against the mass protests. During their walk, students plant a "Serbian plum tree" in the Park of Friendship. They say that the tree will bear fruit when democracy comes to Serbia. Students ask to be blessed by the patriarch of the Serbian Orthodox Church or another church dignitary, but the patriarch declines the proposal, saying that the church should not expose itself too much in these difficult times.

**Dec. 8, 1996**—The Belgrade City Election Commission submits to the Federal Court a request to revise the ruling of the Supreme Court of Serbia dismissing the complaints of both the Commission and the *Zajedno* coalition, as well as the requests for the protection of legality addressed to the federal and republic public prosecutors. The mother of the arrested protester, Dejan Bulatović, says that her son was tortured and sustained serious injuries but received no medical attention.

**Dec. 9, 1996**—American Secretary of State Warren Christopher calls upon Slobodan Milošević to honor the election results, start an open dialogue with the opposition and respect media freedom. Failing that, sanctions against Serbia may be re-imposed. Belgrade students walk to the city secretariat of interior to deliver their request for the urgent transfer of Dejan Bulatović to the Emergency Medical Center and demand that the names of people who tortured him be disclosed. Bulatović's sentence says he was arrested and tried for an attempt to regulate the traffic during the demonstrations, in violation of the public order and peace.

**Dec. 10, 1996**—The Federal Court turns down the request of the Belgrade electoral commission for the extraordinary re-examination of decisions of the Supreme Court of Serbia. The *Zajedno* coalition refuses to take part in the proceedings of the Federal Parliament or to verify any of its mandates. In Belgrade, the University of the Karić Brothers joins the student protest. During their walk, students leave a number of copies of the Constitution of Serbia in front of the Supreme Court. The Independent Student Movement, thus far unknown, requests unobstructed classes, the depoliticization of faculties and extra exam terms. As a token of support for the student protest, Belgrade theaters close their doors.

**Dec. 11, 1996**—Bill Clinton sends a message to Milošević that election results and human and civil rights have to be respected. A resolution of the European Parliament insists on the respect of election results and an investigation into election irregularities. Biljana Plavsić, president of Republika Srpska, supports the peaceful demonstrations of citizens and students in Serbia. The *New York Times* describes the student protest as nationalistic.

**Dec. 12, 1996**—Italian Minister for Foreign Affairs Lamberto Dini meets the president of Serbia and leaders of the *Zajedno* coalition. Speaking at a press conference, Dini states that the opposition's demand for the recognition of election results is unrealistic, that sanctions will not be imposed again and that ways and means should be sought to start a dialogue between the authorities and the opposition. On the 23rd day of the protest, a proclamation of the Serbian Actors' Association concerning the arrest and beating of director Branko Baletić is read to the citizens. The actors say that on that day, as a sign of their protest, all performances will be cancelled. Nemanja Djordjević of the Independent Student Movement tries to deliver a speech at the student protest, but the students turn their backs on him.

**Dec. 13, 1996**—In reply to U.S. Secretary of State Warren Christopher's letter of December 12, Milošević states that the Yugoslav public is well aware of the truth concerning the elections and demonstrations, which appeal to the international community to put pressure on Serbia. The letter also says that the government of Serbia has decided to extend an invitation to a prominent OSCE delegation to visit the country and obtain information on all facts relevant to the elections. More than 100 students from Novi Sad University leave for Belgrade (80 km) on foot to provide support to the students of Belgrade. State and pro-government media mount a campaign against carrying the flags of foreign countries.

**Dec. 14, 1996**—Students from Novi Sad arrive in Belgrade, adding to a joyful atmosphere during the protest walk.

**Dec. 15, 1996**—The municipal court in Niš finds that the complaints lodged by the *Zajedno* coalition are justified. The coalition objected to the decisions of the town's commission concerning the election of members to the City Assembly in the second round of voting. The *Zajedno* coalition publishes a list of towns where protests are organized on a daily basis. These include Belgrade, Niš, Pančevo, Pirot, Kragujevac, Kraljevo, Šabac, Valjevo, Smederevska Palanka, Jagodina, Lapovo, Paraćin, Ćuprija, Zaječar, Novi Kneževac, Prokuplje, Kruševac, Negotin, Knjaževac, Bor and Vršac, as well as Užice, Koceljeva, Bajina Bašta, Vranje, Leskovac, Soko Banja, Kuršumlija and Petrovac na Mlavi. During their walk, citizens of Belgrade, for the first time, hear the hymn of the protest, the song "Voice," composed, played and sung by a group of musicians and actors. Seventeen students from Niš set off to "conquer the top of Serbia" and start a march to Belgrade on foot (220 km). Each of the students is carrying a copy of records from one of 17 polling places in Niš which were falsified by the City Election Commission, giving the votes to the SPS candidates. The students demand to be received by President Milošević upon their arrival in Belgrade. For the first time, Belgrade students walk in the evening under the slogan "Let's illuminate Belgrade." After that, they see off their colleagues from Novi Sad.

**Dec. 16, 1996**—The Legislative Committee of the Serbian Parliament turns down a proposal to set up an inquiry board to investigate the machinations during elections. In protest, deputies representing the *Zajedno* coalition decide not to take part in the work of the Parliament. The Scientific Council of the University of Niš supports the students' demands. Belgrade students announce that a group of them intends to walk to meet their colleagues from Niš. Russian Foreign Minister Primakov repeats his view that developments in Serbia are the internal affairs of the country and that the world should not interfere. The International Organization for Assistance to Media declares B-92 the best radio station in the world for its unbiased reporting under the constant pressure of the regime.

**Dec. 17, 1996**—President Milošević receives students from Niš and states that Serbian problems must be solved within Serbian institutions and that Serbia must not be ruled by a foreign hand. After the students give him the falsified records, he promises to instruct the Ministry of Justice to examine the documentation thoroughly and make a detailed report which will subsequently be made public. Flavio Kotti, chairman of the OSCE, informs the leaders of the *Zajedno* coalition that by December 25 an OSCE mission headed by former Spanish Prime Minister Felipe Gonzalez will come to Belgrade. The purpose of the mission is to examine the election documents and, taking into account information of all political forces, institutions and judicial bodies, give appropriate recommendations. The protest meeting of Belgrade students is, today, marked by the arrival of their colleagues from Niš and their joint walk. Students from Kragujevac also start their protest walk to Belgrade (100 km). The first rally of support for President Milošević is held in Majdanpek.

**Dec. 18, 1996**—Rallies of support for Milošević are held in Vranje, Kosovska Mitrovica and Sremska Mitrovica. Bus transportation is provided for the participants. During their protest walk Belgrade students are prevented from reaching Dedinje by a police cordon. Their encounter results in no conflicts. The students leave behind a pyramid with an inscription, "The forbidden city," and say that in their forthcoming walks they are going to mark the boundaries of that city.

**Dec. 19, 1996**—More than 100,000 citizens of Belgrade, organized by the *Zajedno* coalition, celebrate St. Nicholas' Day on Republic Square. The Serbian president refuses to receive students from Kragujevac. Counter-rallies are held in some other places in Serbia. New Democracy, a coalition partner of the SPS and JUL, fearing further aggravation of the situation, does not approve of SPS counter-rallies.

**Dec. 20, 1996**—The OSCE delegation arrives in Belgrade and meets Milošević and leaders of the *Zajedno* coalition. Momir Bulatović, president of Montenegro, in an interview for the French paper *Figaro*, says that Milošević admitted the victory of the opposition in Belgrade and Niš and that the protests of the opposition and students are perfectly justified. The purpose of the student protest today has been to block all three bridges in Belgrade, but they fail to do that faced with strong police forces barring their way. By doing that, the police actually does what the students intended to do.

**Dec. 21, 1996**—In Kragujevac and Pirot, the police intervene to separate the SPS supporters, who march under the slogan "Serbia shall not be ruled by a foreign hand," wishing to express their loyalty to President Milošević, from the citizens who have been protesting for days against the annulment of local elections throughout Serbia. Belgrade students are joined by their colleagues from Subotica who came to Belgrade by bicycle (180 km).

**Dec. 22, 1996**—At the *Zajedno* coalition rally, the official presenter discloses confidential information from a closed meeting of the SPS that a decision was taken to hold a final rally of support for Milošević on Tuesday, December 24. The information also says that 400,000 people are expected to attend the counter-rally (for whom 10,000 buses have been provided) and that the ralliers will, most probably, be addressed by the president himself. All this is scheduled to take place at Republic Square in Belgrade. The Association of Free Cities and Municipalities of Serbia, consisting of all members of city and municipal assemblies legally elected on November 17, holds its first congress.

**Dec. 23, 1996**—More than 100,000 citizens of the capital walk through the streets in its center. Just as on previous days, a jeep heading the column carries an effigy of the President. Citizens of Belgrade are invited to come the next day, when the "Meeting for Serbia" is scheduled in Belgrade, in as large numbers as possible to show the real Belgrade but to avoid possible provocations. Patriarch Pavle appeals to both the ruling party and the opposition to give up parallel demonstrations, saying that, should a conflict occur, he will have to take the side of the people exposed to the use of force. The SPS information service claims this party is not organizing the rally, while almost all its municipal branches receive applications for free transport to Belgrade. "The Serbian Orthodox Church welcomes and blesses your feeling of truth, justice and democratic respect of the freely expressed will of the people, which is both evangelical and human," reads the message from Patriarch Pavle to the students.

**Dec. 24, 1996**—From the early morning hours, preparations are being made for the counter-rally in Terazije Square, and busloads of SPS supporters begin to arrive. Most of them are surprised by the reception they receive from Belgraders, who make it clear that they are not welcome. Mutual provocations grow into incidents and culminate in fistfights. The conflict reaches its height when Ivica Lazović, member of the SPO, is shot by a man from the SPS column. Only then do large police forces come into the streets. They cordon off the counter-demonstrators, thus preventing further conflicts in the city center. About 50,000 students, many professors and public personalities, who have been addressing the students during their protest, take a walk through the town. The meeting of support for Milošević, under the slogan "Serbia will not be ruled by a foreign hand," is attended by the highest state officials and the President's wife, Mirjana Marković. Milošević in his speech stresses that a strong Serbia is not to the liking of many foreign powers, which is why they are trying to destabilize the country together with the fifth column they have established here. The president mentions that this group does not include the young people who seek to set right the injustices related to the local elections and that he is going to fulfill the promise given to the students to establish the whole truth, naturally within the framework of domestic institutions. At the same time, citizens of Belgrade, headed by prominent public personalities and *Zajedno* coalition leaders, walk along the streets of the city and end their protest by converging on Republic Square. According to estimates of national and foreign agencies, the rally "For Serbia" is attended by 40,000 to 100,000 people, while that of the opposition gathers between 200,000 and 300,000. The RTS, in its live broadcast of the rally "For Serbia," estimates its attendance at half a million. Svetozar Marović, president of the Montenegrin Parliament, receives a delegation of the student protest and expresses his support for the students' fight for the truth. The U.S. State Department, in its press release, states that the Serbian authorities have acted irresponsibly by bringing thousands of people to Belgrade, and thus increasing the tensions, instead of solving the crisis by peaceful means.

**Dec. 25, 1996**—According to the Emergency Center, the final toll of yesterday's conflicts is 58 wounded, while the condition of Ivica Lazović is still critical. The Serbian Ministry of the Interior announces that the police will no longer allow arbitrary blocking of the traffic, as it is damaging for other citizens and the economy. Citizens of Belgrade continue their protest. The students, calling themselves "the sixth column," organize the sweeping and cleaning of Terazije Square. Governments of many countries condemn the President of Serbia for causing the conflicts and intensifying the political situation. Milošević refuses to receive Richard Miles, the head of American mission, who intended to convey the concern of the U.S. government caused by indications that the police prepares to block the peaceful opposition demonstrations in Belgrade and other cities.

**Dec. 26, 1996**—Mass police forces block the citizens who, as usual, intended to begin their protest by a walk. For the first time, people hear the news that Predrag Starčević, who was wounded during the attack of SPS supporters, died on December 24. In contrast with citizens, the students are allowed to walk.

**Dec. 27, 1996**—Felipe Gonzalez, head of the OSCE mission, publishes a report saying that, according to what the mission has established, the *Zajedno* coalition had won the elections in Pirot, Kraljevo, Užice, Smederevska Palanka, Vršac, Niš, Soko Banja, Kragujevac, Pančevo, Jagodina, Lapovo, Šabac, Zrenjanin and nine municipalities in Belgrade, including the City Assembly, where the results were subsequently annulled. Cordons of police once again prevent the protest walks. At the rally, the citizens are invited to attend the funeral of the deceased Predrag Starčević the next day instead of coming to their usual gathering. After the end of the rally, citizens who "played with the traffic lights" are beaten by the police, while some "walkers" are clubbed by a group of young men armed with baseball bats. The students, who are now for the first time prevented from making their protest walk, stroll through Knez Mihajlova Street (a pedestrian zone in the city center), their hands on the back of their heads, simulating a prison march.

**Dec. 28, 1996**—The U.S. government invites Milošević to accept the findings and recommendations of the Gonzalez Report, expressing its confidence that urgent implementation of OSCE recommendations is "the best possible way to solve the crisis in Serbia." The European Union reiterates its appeal to Belgrade to refrain from the use of force. New Democracy, the coalition partner of the SPS, supports the conclusions of the OSCE and invites both the authorities and the opposition to accept and implement them. On the 39th day of the protest, the citizens of Belgrade pay homage to Predrag Starčević. At a meeting of representatives of all universities in Serbia, the Initiative Board of the 1996–97 student protest is set up. A petition supporting the students' demands has been signed by 1800 professors and associates of both Belgrade universities.

**Dec. 29, 1996**—A proclamation written by some officers serving in various army units and addressed to the students of Niš, General Perišić, Chief of General Staff, and Milošević is read to the citizens at their rally in Belgrade. The officers say that they stand firmly by their people, that they will not allow the fall of Serbia and will be the first to defend it if necessary. The protesters today again insist on taking a walk in the "prison compound" (area bordered by Čika Ljubina and Knez Mihajlova streets). The police prohibition against walking also applies to students.

**Dec. 30, 1996**—The police block the pedestrian zone so that citizens can walk only through Knez Mihajlova St. Students announce that they will be at the plaza in front of the Faculty of Philosophy for New Year's Eve. The Yugoslav Army General Staff says that the army is carrying out its duties as defined by the Constitution and that it will not depart from its established social and constitutional role.

**Dec. 31, 1996**—The citizens, in an atmosphere thus far unseen in Belgrade, wait for the arrival of the New Year in the streets. According to estimates of national and foreign agencies, between 300,000 and 500,000 citizens gather in the center of Belgrade.

**Jan. 2, 1997**—The Holy Synod of the Serbian Orthodox Church, after a two-day extraordinary session, issues a statement saying that "only respect for democratic principles and rights and the recognition of the November 17 elections may give the Serbian nation and other citizens of Serbia hope for a better future and peaceful life." After a day's break, civil and student protests continue.

**Jan. 3, 1997** —Yugoslav Foreign Minister Milan Milutinović sends a letter to the OSCE acknowledging the victory of the *Zajedno* coalition in Užice, Zrenjanin and Kragujevac. As for other towns referred to in the OSCE report, the victory of the left wing is noted or additional information required. U.S. Secretary of State Christopher sends a message to Milošević requesting the president of Serbia to promptly and in concrete terms inform the United States and the OSCE what he proposes to do about the binding conclusions of the international commission.

**Jan. 5, 1997**—On the 47th day of the civil protest, an action called "blockade of the blockade" is carried out. In this action, upon the invitation of *Zajedno* coalition leaders, citizens use their cars to create a complete gridlock of the city center and thus enable tens of thousands of demonstrators to engage in their walk.

**Jan. 6, 1997**—Between 300,000 and 500,000 citizens and students celebrate Christmas Eve (according to the Orthodox calendar) in front of St. Sava's Church. Representatives of the student protest talk to General Perišić, who promises that the Army will remain neutral in political developments. Nine deans of the University of Belgrade faculties send a letter to the president of Serbia, the prime minister and the president of the Serbian Parliament appealing to the authorities of the Republic of Serbia to recognize the results of the November 17, 1996, elections as established by the OSCE, which is also the main demand of the student protest.

**Jan. 7, 1997**—The citizens are again prevented from walking by strong police forces. Many demonstrators approach police officers to wish them a merry Christmas. Svetozar Marović, president of the Montenegrin Parliament, states that, unless Serbia finds a prompt political solution through dialogue and recognition of electoral results, Montenegro may have to think seriously about its next moves.

**Jan. 8, 1997**—The Serbian government, after fifty days of the protest, concludes that the *Zajedno* coalition has won in Niš and that the responsibility of those who caused irregularities during elections in Niš will be established. The French government again calls on the Yugoslav authorities to recognize the electoral victory of the opposition.

**Jan. 9, 1997**—Fifty-two members of the Serbian Academy of Sciences and Arts address an open letter to the public requesting the recognition of elections of November 17, 1996, and an investigation into the abuses of government, judicial and party officials involved in unlawful actions, along with demands for an independent judiciary, the autonomy of the university and independent media. Special police forces block the center of Belgrade to prevent another "protest drive" of its citizens. Students start an action called the "cordon against cordon" to show that they are going to outlast the police cordon and after that walk freely through the city. After fourteen hours, the police cordon withdraws, and the students noisily celebrate the successful end of their action.

**Jan. 11, 1997**—A delegation of the student protest is received by vice-presidents of the Serbian government, who promise that the government will order the Ministry of Justice to finish establishing the final results of the elections without further delay. After many hours of standing in Kolarčeva Street, the "cordon against cordon" action is once again successfully performed.

**Jan. 13, 1997**—Foreign and national reporters estimate that the celebration of the Orthodox New Year, organized by the student protest in Belgrade, is attended by 500,000 to 1 million citizens. Throughout Serbia, citizens celebrate the New Year in city squares. The Scientific Council of the University of Belgrade (consisting of faculty deans) lends its support to the students' demands.

**Jan. 14, 1997**—Election commissions in Belgrade and Niš recognize the preliminary results of November 17 elections. The Socialist Party of Serbia expels the mayor of Belgrade, Nebojsa Čović, from its membership because of his statements to the media supporting the students' protest. Mile Ilić, until recently the head of the Socialists in Niš, is also expelled from the party membership at the same meeting.

**Jan. 15, 1997**—The Belgrade University Board (consisting of representatives of faculties and the republic's government on par basis), at a seven-hour session, votes for two completely opposed positions. First, the students' demands are supported by an oral vote, but then one of their demands—for the replacement of rector Dragutin Veličković—is rejected by secret ballot.

**Jan. 16, 1997**—Disgusted by the decision of the Belgrade University Board, the students use brooms and a water hose to wash the rectorate building.

**Jan. 20, 1997**—Since the police forces have not withdrawn from the streets, the "cordon against cordon" action continues throughout the day. University professors and many public personalities join the students. Citizens express their solidarity by bringing students hot drinks and food during the night and in the morning. Patriarch Pavle addresses the students in Kolarčeva Street, which remains blocked by the police. He says: "Your feeling of truth and justice, and the democratic respect of the freely expressed will of the people in a peaceful way, is worthy of you and your and our ancestors." At the civil protest, leaders of the *Zajedno* coalition propose to replace students with citizens in front of the police cordon, but the students decline. At the time state TV news is broadcast, citizens organize and walk around local communities. During these walks, a number of serious incidents happen, and some walkers are beaten by the police.

**Jan. 21, 1997**—Continuing their action "cordon against cordon," students introduce six-hour shifts, while the policemen, from the beginning of the action, are replaced every hour and a half. Many public personalities, members of the Actors' Association, attorneys, judges, taxi drivers and journalists lend their support by their presence vis-à-vis the police cordon.

**Jan. 22, 1997**—Standing day and night in front of a police cordon is made easier by music from loudspeakers, dancing and various witty and entertaining games, including a contest for "Mister Policeman," morning exercises and playing football. One of the *Zajedno* coalition leaders, Vesna Pešić, addresses the session of the Socialist Internationale, which adopts her motions to pass a resolution requesting the recognition of local elections in Serbia.

**Jan. 23, 1997**—In Kragujevac, a blockade of the town by cars, similar to that in Belgrade, is attempted, but the participants are violently dispersed by the police. The students refuse an invitation to speak to the rector of the University of Belgrade. The rector, Dragutin Veličković, says that he and the student vice-rector, Vladimir Djurdjević, will resign if the protest ends and the students go back to lectures. An OSCE ministerial troika offers to mediate between the authorities and opposition in Serbia.

**Jan. 24, 1997**—The 100th hour of the students' uninterrupted standing before the police cordon has passed. Leaders of the *Zajedno* coalition, at the civil protest, publicly decline the OSCE offer of mediation.

**Jan. 25, 1997**—The police beat citizens who walk during the broadcast of state TV news and head for Kolarčeva Street to give their support to students.

**Jan. 26, 1997**—After the beating of citizens the previous day, students turn their backs to the police cordon for three minutes every hour and stop fraternizing with them.

**Jan. 27, 1997**—The police cordon withdraws after 180 hours, and the students go for a walk at 4 a.m., crying out "victory," and "wake up." Several hundred thousand citizens of Belgrade take part in a religious procession dedicated to St. Sava and headed by Patriarch Pavle. The U.S. government presents a demarche to the authorities in Belgrade, asking them to recognize the election results and to refrain from the use of force. The French and Danish foreign ministers repeat their please to Milošević to recognize the results of local elections.

**Jan. 28, 1997**—The 70th rally of the *Zajedno* coalition is held in the evening, after the citizens from all parts of the city have walked to Republic Square.

**Jan. 29, 1997**—The students take another protest walk crying out, among other things, "give us the cordon back." Citizens also walk to Republic Square —the venue of the protest rally—unobstructed, but once there, they are prevented from taking organized walks in any direction by strong police forces.

**Jan. 30, 1997**—Deans of University of Belgrade faculties cease all communication with the rector of the university. Protest walks of citizens are headed by *Zajedno* coalition leaders. The Bar of Belgrade calls a general strike due to nonrecognition of the election results of November 17, 1996.

**Feb. 2, 1997**—After the police blocks the column of walkers coming from New Belgrade, the protest rally is held on both sides of Branko's Bridge (the central bridge in Belgrade). Some time before midnight, the police brutally intervene, using water jets, tear gas and clubs to disperse the demonstrators by a synchronized action on both sides of the bridge. On that occasion, Vesna Pešić, one of the *Zajedno* coalition leaders, is beaten along with many citizens and journalists. The police even break into the Faculty of Philosophy (an act unheard of in the history of the University of Belgrade).

**Feb. 3, 1997**—A large number of citizens gather in the center of the city, but their walk is prevented by strong police forces. Several hundred of the most persistent demonstrators remain standing opposite the police cordon even after the protest rally ends. The police intervene again, dispersing and beating the demonstrators, along with many citizens who happen to be in the very center of the city. The American government sends an official protest to the authorities in Belgrade, requesting Milošević to stop any use of force against the demonstrators immediately and to comply with all the requests of the OSCE mission without delay. The Belgrade University Council strongly condemns the brutality of the police and its intrusion into the Faculty of Philosophy. The Serbian Ministry of Interior makes an announcement that the police intervention on February 2 "was intended to prevent the endangerment of traffic." The students walk across Branko's Bridge. The police do not stop them.

**Feb. 4, 1997**—President Milošević sends a letter to Mirko Marjanović, the prime minister of the Republic of Serbia, proposing that a special law be passed for the recognition of results of some local elections, as established by the OSCE mission. The prime minister enthusiastically seconds the initiative of the Serbian president. The EU and the OSCE condemn the brutal behavior of the police. At their protest meeting in Belgrade, leaders of the *Zajedno* coalition inform the people that the protests will last until all assemblies where the coalition has won are constituted, those who have violated the law punished and the media set free. Cinemas and theaters are closed because of the brutal onslaught of the police on demonstrators on February 2.

**Feb. 6, 1997**—Leaders of the *Zajedno* coalition have talks with the president of France, Jacques Chirac, and his foreign minister, Hervé de Charette, in Paris. Addressing the press, they say that if the election results of November 17, 1996, are established "completely and honestly," the demonstrations will stop.

**Feb. 9, 1997**—Milošević, in his first interview since the beginning of the postelection crisis, tells the Greek newspaper *To vima* that the political crisis in Serbia (to which, he says, foreign elements have also contributed) will soon be solved.

**Feb. 10, 1997**—At the citizens' 83rd protest rally, the *Zajedno* coalition announces that its deputies will not take part in the session of the Serbian Parliament which is to vote on the bill on election results. The Committee for the Defense of Democracy of the University of Belgrade organizes the submission of individual requests for the resignation of the rector, Veličković. Such requests have been made by over 2,500 professors and associates of the University of Belgrade.

**Feb. 11, 1997**—The Serbian Parliament passes a special law on local elections pursuant to the report of the OSCE mission. Prime Minister Mirko Marjanović accuses the *Zajedno* coalition of organizing street demonstrations in order to take power by force. Students organize an action aimed to "save and make wiser" during which they leave two life-belts and a huge sculpture of a brain in front of the Serbian Parliament, as the deputies will need them to vote the *lex specialis* (special law) in.

**Feb. 12, 1997**—The Belgrade University Council agrees to begin classes on February 24, provided all students' demands are complied with by that time.

**Feb. 13, 1997**—The City Election Commission applies the special law and confirms the victory of the *Zajedno* coalition in Belgrade. The students express support for the journalists of the state television who are suspended for supporting them.

**Feb. 15, 1997**—After 88 days, the protest of citizens and the *Zajedno* coalition ends. Leaders of the coalition thank citizens for their support and set a deadline of March 9 for ending the suppression of the media, threatening that otherwise the demonstrations will continue.

**Feb. 21, 1997**—The City Assembly of Belgrade is constituted, as are most other assemblies in municipalities and towns where the *Zajedno* coalition has won. Zoran Djindjić, one of the *Zajedno* coalition leaders, becomes the mayor of Belgrade. Hundreds of thousands of Belgraders come to celebrate the establishment of democratic rule and the symbolic dismantling of the five-pointed star from the building of the City Assembly.

**Feb. 23, 1997**—Students once again try to walk to Dedinje but run into a police cordon.

**Feb. 24, 1997**—The Committee for the Defense of Democracy of the University of Belgrade organizes alternative classes for a special class of "graduate democrats" at the plaza in front of the Faculty of Philosophy. Having thus observed the wish of Dragutin Veličković to have the students back in lectures, the Committee asks the rector to make good on his promise and resign.

**Feb. 27, 1997**—The Belgrade University Council elects Professor Dragan Kuburović, vice-rector, acting rector of the University of Belgrade. The students support the election of Kuburović but point out that their protests will end when their demands are fulfilled, i.e., after the dismissal or resignation of Veličković and Djurdjević.

**Feb. 28, 1997**—The Ministry of Education states that the decisions of a group of deans and directors of institutes are totally illegal, as only the rector is entitled to convene the Council. The Ministry also appeals to professors, students and associates to resume their work by March 3 at the latest, so as not to lose the school year.

**Mar. 1, 1997**—During the jubilee 100th walk, students visit all the places where developments important to the protest have occurred.

**Mar. 2, 1997**—The first Assembly of Belgrade University Institutions, attended by about 1,000 professors and associates of the University of Belgrade, welcomes the election of Professor Dragan Kuburović as acting rector and votes for the position taken by the Council that Professor Dragutin Veličković is no longer the rector of the University of Belgrade.

**Mar. 3, 1997**—The Ministry of Education proclaims the assembly illegal. The Scientific Council of the Faculty of Agriculture, where Veličković has been a professor for years, invites him to resign as rector of the University of Belgrade.

**Mar. 4, 1997**—The rector of the University of Belgrade asks the competent authorities to dismiss vice-rector Dragan Kuburović, all directors of the institutes within the University of Belgrade and 13 faculty deans. The Minister of Education Jovo Todorović, in a statement for the state television, points out that the school year will be lost unless classes at faculties start within a week.

**Mar. 5, 1997**—Members of the Belgrade University Council, Main and Initiative Boards of the student protest agree that the students should go back to classes conditionally for a day in order to see whether the rector and student vice-rector intend to keep their promises. Unless they submit their resignations, the protest will continue with expanded demands.

**Mar. 6, 1997**—Students gathered at the plaza in front of the Faculty of Philosophy protest against the decision of the Main Board of the 1996–97 student protest to go back to classes for a day.

**Mar. 7, 1997**—Rector Veličković and student vice-rector Djurdjević submit their resignations as lectures formally take place at some of the faculties. Belgrade University Council calls upon the students to resume classes on March 10. In their protest walk, students celebrate the resignation of the rector and, surrounding the offices of the Serbian Presidency, cry out, "Slobo, you are next."

**Mar. 9, 1997**—The *Zajedno* coalition organizes a rally to mark the sixth anniversary of March 9 (large antiregime demonstrations), where its leaders state that they will invite citizens to gather again unless the authorities initiate a dialogue by March 20.

**Mar. 10, 1997**—The Main Board of the student protest, on the basis of voting by faculties, decides that the protest should continue in an unchanged form until the resignations of Veličković and Djurdjević are accepted by the University Board. The University Council confirms the decision to resume lessons on March 10.

**Mar. 11, 1997**—More than 10,000 students protest for the 110th time by walking the streets of Belgrade.

**Mar. 13, 1997**—Belgrade University Council takes a decision to hold a session of the University Board on March 19. Students continue with daily protest walks.

**Mar. 19, 1997**—The University Board confirms the resignations of Veličković and Djurdjević.

**Mar. 20, 1997**—More than 50,000 students gather at the plaza in front of the Faculty of Philosophy to celebrate the victory and the end of the student protest. In a festive atmosphere, the celebration reaches its climax when, to the beating of the drums, the building of the rectorate is covered by a white cloth with the lettering "To be continued ..."

## Note

1. This chronology of events has been made on the basis of articles published in the following dailies: *Naša borba, Politika, Demokratija, Blic, Borba* and *Dnevni telegraf.*

# Sample Design

## *Slobodan Cvejić*

The sample design for this particular research of the civil protest could not be defined with great precision. The phenomenon we undertook to study is relatively new in this country, and there are hardly any records related to it, which is why the research had to be essentially exploratory. We had only subjective estimates of the size and characteristics of the researched population. The demonstrators were partly in motion and partly standing in front of a rostrum. Some people took part only in walks; others were there merely for the duration of the program, while others remained throughout. Despite the fact that we had an average of seven interviewers working every day, the survey took a few days to complete, given the length of the questionnaire and the average daily duration of the demonstrations of three hours.

For these reasons it was impossible to realize a probability or even a quota sample. The only thing we could do was to try to approach a random, and a simple random sample to the extent possible. We tried to make up for these deficiencies by giving the interviewers precise instructions. Not only were they explained the principle for choosing respondents, but they were also provided a complete insight into the concept of the entire project, so as to develop a feeling for the representativeness of the chosen segment of demonstrators as well as the reliability of the collected information. We believe that, owing to their qualifications, the interviewers managed to reduce subjectivity to the maximum degree possible and thereby also prevent resulting bias.

The procedure for the selection of respondents was linked with a territorial principle which, again, due to the fluctuation of demonstrators, could not be particularly accurate but certainly represented a better solution than a convenience sample. The interviewers were asked to try to identify the lines among demonstrators (rows during walks, bent lines or concentric circles before the rostrum) and then fairly systematically select every n-th demonstrator, mindful to cover the entire territory of the demonstrations in their research (including both the head and tail end of the column, those who stood next to the rostrum and others lingering on the fringes of the group). After a day's work, the experiences of interviewers were summed up to identify solutions required to correct the sample (for instance, on the day before the last day, the interviewers were instructed to focus on those who walked in the front lines or stood next to the rostrum. These demonstrators had been underrepresented during the previous days due to the extremely difficult conditions for interviewing in such spots because of noise, the increased concentration of the demonstrations themselves, a large number of refusals to respond, etc.).

The size of the sample was provisionally set at 500, with the expectation that this number could provide for sufficiently reliable conclusions on the basic population. Relying on our insight and estimates, which are necessarily imprecise, we have assessed this population at an average of 80,000–120,000 people per day, consisting of 20,000–30,000 "listeners" and 60,000–90,000 "walkers" (20–30 people per row, one row per meter in a column about 3 kilometers long). After seven days of interviews and the logical control, we had 483 completed questionnaires as the basis for our analysis of the protest.

# Questionnaire

1. Gender          M         F
2. Age
3. Education        1. Elementary school or less   2. Secondary school
                         3. High school/university     4. Academic degree
4. Job
5. Sector of activity  1. Private      2. Public      3. Mixed
6. Branch of activity
7. Marital status     1. Unmarried   2. Married   3. Divorced/widowed
8. Number of children under 18 years of age
9. Nationality
10. Place of residence 1. City center
                         2. Central areas beyond the city center
                         3. Outskirts of Belgrade
                         4. Outside Belgrade
11. Are you a member or supporter of a political party?
                         No            Yes, member of .............. Party
                                          Yes, supporter of ........... Party
12. Do you think that in his political career Slobodan Milošević has done something useful for Serbia?
                         No         Yes  (state what) .........
13. What do you object to most about the current Serbian president?
                         Nothing in particular
                         Something (state what) ..........

*Could you assign grades (from 1 to 5) for the political activity of the following political personalities:*

| | | | | | |
|---|---|---|---|---|---|
| 14. | Vesna Pešić | 1 | 2 | 3 | 4 | 5 |
| 15. | Danica Drašković | 1 | 2 | 3 | 4 | 5 |
| 16. | Vojislav Koštunica | 1 | 2 | 3 | 4 | 5 |
| 17. | Mirjana Marković | 1 | 2 | 3 | 4 | 5 |
| 18. | Vuk Drašković | 1 | 2 | 3 | 4 | 5 |
| 19. | Zoran Djindjić | 1 | 2 | 3 | 4 | 5 |
| 20. | Slobodan Milošević | 1 | 2 | 3 | 4 | 5 |
| 21. | Vojislav Šešelj | 1 | 2 | 3 | 4 | 5 |

22. Which of the public personalities who, for whatever reason, has not appeared would you like to see at the rostrum?
> No one in particular
> I would like to see (state whom) ..........

23. Which of the many statements of support for the protests particularly pleased you?
> None in particular
> I was particularly pleased with the support of ..........

24. What has, in your view, contributed most to the duration of the protest?
> Pressure from the authorities
> The popular will
> Opposition leaders
> The resoluteness of every individual to persist in his/her demands
> International support
> Biased media
> Student protest
> Something else (state what) ..........

*To what extent do you agree with the following statements*
*(1: I do not agree at all — 5: I completely agree)*

25. The most important thing for the success of any group is to have an energetic and just leader whom everybody would obey.
> 1   2   3   4   5

26. The President must be subjected to Parliament.
> 1   2   3   4   5

27. Without a leader every nation is like a man without a head.
> 1   2   3   4   5

28. A man should not trust foreigners too much.
> 1   2   3   4   5

29. A nation that does not cherish its tradition deserves to perish.
> 1   2   3   4   5

30. The progress of a nation may only rest on private ownership.
> 1   2   3   4   5

31. There can be no justice without material equality.
> 1   2   3   4   5

32. Which of the protest demands do you consider the most important? (State up to three demands)
> ..........      ..........      ..........

33. Do you think that the list of demands should be expanded (now or after the existing ones are met)?
> No
> Yes (state the most important additional demand) ..........

34. What motivated you most to join the protest?
> The desire for justice and free elections
> The overthrow of communism

The support of opposition leaders
The overthrow of the personal rule of Slobodan Milošević
The construction of a new society similar to those in Western
    Europe
Other (state what) ..........

35. Do you think that Serbia should build a system similar to that in Western
Europe?
    Yes             No
36. What do you think would change in Serbia after the downfall of the
existing ruling regime (tick the most important change)?
    The overall social standard would increase.
    I would feel more dignified and free.
    It would enable me to advance in my career or begin a new job.
    I would be sure of my children's future.
    The Serbian nation would win the right to live in a single state.
    Other (state what) ..........
37. Have you participated in a similar protest before?
    No
    Yes (state when) ..........
38. When did you join the protest (state on which day) ..........
39. How many days so far have you participated in the demonstrations? ........
40. How long do you usually stay in the rallies?
    From beginning to end
    Only during walks
    Only during the program
41. Which of the slogans do you prefer to shout?
    None
    I prefer (state the slogan) ..........
41.1.   Which paraphernalia do you use? ..........
42. Do you think that the protest should remain peaceful until the end?
    Yes             No
43. Do you think that the boys who hurled stones were unjustly arrested?
    Yes             No
44. Would you be ready to hurl eggs if you knew that you were being filmed
by a police camera?
    Yes             No
45. Do you expect that the demands expressed in the protest will be met?
    No, not at all.
    Yes, partly.
    Yes, all of them, within the next seven days.
    Yes, all of them, within the next 15 days.
    Yes, all of them, within the next (state the number of days).
46. Are you prepared to actively support the protest until all demands are
met, however long it might take?
    Yes             No

47. Which do you think is the easiest way to force the authorities to honor the protest demands?
> Pressure from abroad.
> Long, drawn-out peaceful protest.
> A general strike by most employees.
> A military coup.
> Something else (state what) ..........

*To what extent are you satisfied with the following elements of the protest organization?*
(1: completely dissatisfied — 5: completely satisfied)

48. The speeches delivered by opposition leaders.
> 1       2       3       4       5
49. The selection of guests.
> 1       2       3       4       5
50. The creativity of activities.
> 1       2       3       4       5
51. The number of demonstrators.
> 1       2       3       4       5
52. The internal security.
> 1       2       3       4       5
53. The behavior of demonstrators.
> 1       2       3       4       5
54. My personal contribution to the protest.
> 1       2       3       4       5
55. What do you think makes these demonstrations different from previous ones? ..........